Philosophy
and the Modern Mind

Philosophy and the Modern Mind

*A Philosophical Critique
of Modern Western Civilization*

by E. M. Adams

The University of North Carolina Press

Chapel Hill

Copyright © 1975 by The University of North Carolina Press
All rights reserved
Manufactured in the United States of America
ISBN 0-8078-1242-0
Library of Congress Catalog Card Number 74-23458
First printing, November 1975
Second printing, July 1976

Library of Congress Cataloging in Publication Data

Adams, Elie Maynard, 1919-
    Philosophy and the modern mind.

    Includes index.
    1. Civilization, Modern—1950-   2. Civilization—
Philosophy.   I. Title.
CB428.A35   910'.03'1812   74-23458
ISBN 0-8078-1242-0

To Steve and Jill

Contents

Preface

This work is addressed to both professional and lay philosophers, for all fully aware people sense that our ordinary ways of approaching problematic situations do not today reveal and come to grips with our real problems. There is a growing awareness that our difficulties are intractable because they penetrate to the depths of our way of life, even to our ways of exercising our powers in our efforts to know and to cope with reality. In this time of loss of confidence and of little hope, people are writhing and turning in search of a new light. Many are "philosophizing," but few turn to or expect much from professional philosophers, for they are widely regarded as an esoteric set who talk only to each other about highly technical but trivial matters.

Contrary to those who believe that philosophy is dead or that it is trivial, the present work attempts to show that it is concerned with the profoundest problems of the human mind and the most significant and far-reaching troubles in our culture. Even the most technical work which only some other philosophers can comprehend, when properly understood, is seen to bear upon issues significant for all. No individual nor the culture at large, it is argued, can ignore philosophy and come to grips with the basic problems of life in our time.

It is a thesis of this work that the intellectual foundations of our institutions and life-sustaining attitudes are eroding and collapsing because of false philosophical assumptions about the knowledge-yielding powers of the human mind that generate a threatening, all-encompassing subjectivism. The pervasive naturalistic assumption that knowledge of the world is obtained only through sensory perception under scientific refinement and thought grounded therein calls into question all other areas of our culture, especially the humanities. Indeed the thrust toward skepticism and subjectivism engendered by naturalism has been so great that the fight to safeguard and to protect even science as an island of objectivity has been a losing battle. Such a loss of a philosophical sense of reality on the part of a culture, it is contended, is a derangement of the cultural mind that infects the lives of all who embrace it.

Philosophy, as a serious intellectual discipline, by exploring the philosophical perplexities our cultural mind generates and working toward a clear and correct philosophical understanding of the constitutional principles and powers of the human mind, the culture, and the world, offers a way of diagnosing and correcting the derangement of our modern Western mind, which is systematically thwarting us in our efforts to know and to cope with reality and to live meaningfully and successfully.

In our detailed philosophical analysis of modern Western civilization, the deranging assumptions of our cultural mind are located and critically examined. The key ones pertain to the humanistic categories of value and meaning. The most important result of our study is, we believe, the validation of an objective, realistic philosophy of the humanities. We conclude that our cultural derangement can be overcome only by the humanities reasserting themselves in terms of their own indigenous categories and regaining their rightful place of leadership in our intellectual and cultural life. Only in this way, it is argued, will we be able to achieve an intellectual vision of man and the world that will support and sustain a great civilization and make a meaningful life possible for man.

Philosophy cannot make its contribution on these vitally important matters if philosophers write only for philosophers. All concerned with the intellectual life of our culture must be engaged in the exploration of and debate on these issues. It is my hope that this work will be read by both professional philosophers and concerned intellectuals in whatever field and will make some contribution to a culture-wide study and debate on these issues. But the writing in this work has been addressed to and shaped by the problems under discussion rather than the intended audience. The problems could not be dealt with adequately otherwise. The book may be thought of as a progressive exploration of a set of problems which require us to go deeper and deeper to get to the bottom of the issues with which we begin. The mode of thought and writing varies according to what is appropriate for the problems at issue at any given point in the investigation. Chapters 1, 2, 3 (in part), and 9 will be more readily available to the nonprofessional reader. With the summary at the beginning of 9, these chapters contain the major theses of the book. The hard work to validate the major philosophical claims comes in chapters 3-8. These I think can be read with understanding and profit by the general reader, but they will be more demanding.

This work has been gestating for a number of years. It was first conceived in something like its present form in response to an essay in *Time* magazine in 1966 entitled "What (If Anything) to Expect from Today's Philosophers?" Some of the ideas here developed have been presented in courses at The University of North Carolina at Chapel Hill, the University of Southern California, and the State University of New York at Albany, as well as in public lectures and conferences at many universities and in a number of published papers. But the working out and embodiment of these ideas into a book manuscript was made possible by a research leave from The University of North Carolina at Chapel Hill in 1972. A substantial part of the book was written during the leave of absence.

I have made use of portions of the following previously published material: "Classical Moral Philosophy and Metaethics," *Ethics* 74, no. 2 (January 1964): 99-110; "Mental Causality," *Mind*, n.s. 75, no. 300 (October 1966): 552-63; "Mind and the Language of Psychology," *Ratio* 9, no. 2 (December 1967): 122-39; "What, If Anything, Can We Expect From Philosophy Today?" *Personalist* 49, no. 1 (Winter 1968): 37-60; "A Changing America: Morale and Morality," *Vital Speeches* 34, no. 19 (15 July 1968): 590-96; "The Academic Revolution," *Modern Age* 13, no. 3 (Summer 1969): 270-76; The Scientific and the Humanistic Images of Man-in-the-World," *Man and World* 4, no. 2 (May 1971): 174-92; "Population Control: A Scientific or a Humanistic Approach," *Journal of Value Inquiry* 6, no. 1 (Winter 1972): 50-56; and "Linguistic Analysis and Epistemic Encounters," *Philosophy and Phenomenological Research* 34, no. 3 (March 1974): 404-14. I am indebted to the editors of these journals and to the editors and publishers who have given permission for me to quote from the writings of others as indicated in the text.

I am grateful to the university for the leave in 1972, for providing secretarial assistance in the preparation of the manuscript, and for a publication subvention through the University Research Council. My colleagues Richard Smyth, Robert Kolb, and Patrick Tarr read the manuscript and made a number of critical and compositional suggestions which led to improvements. Jill Adams and Paul Betz did the basic work on the index. I am also indebted to the Stark sisters, Judy and Ronnie, for expert secretarial service. Malcolm MacDonald, chief editor, Tony Harvey, editor, and the staff of The University of North Carolina Press have been most cooperative and helpful in making this book a reality and with fewer linguistic blemishes.

My intellectual obligations are too numerous and fused to be singled out for special mention, but I do want to acknowledge that the greatest impact on my thinking in recent years has come from my students, both undergraduate and graduate, and most of all from my son and daughter, Steve and Jill, to whom I dedicate this book. The experience of participating in their education, sharing their perceptions and problems, and the long hours of intense discussion and debate in wrestling with their vital questions in trying to come to terms with life and the world from within our cultural perspective have contributed greatly to my own understanding of our cultural condition.

And there are the sustaining love and confidence of Phyllis which have never faltered for thirty-five years. There is no measure for such a power in one's life and work.

Philosophy
and the Modern Mind

Culture, Social Structure, and Reality

Revolution occurs in a society when a gap develops between the culture and the social structure, leaving the institutions exposed and unsupported in the consciousness of the people—unsupported in their feelings, emotions, and aspirations.

The culture of a society, as I am using the term, is that structure of meaning, the spiritual soil and climate, on which people and institutions depend for their nourishment, health, and vitality. We cannot simply create an institution at will without regard for the culture on which it must depend. Regardless of how badly needed, a world government, for example, is not now a possibility, for there is no common worldwide perspective constituted by shared beliefs, attitudes, aspirations, and commitments to give life and spirit to such an institution and to sustain it in its work. Whenever the culture of a society ceases to support and to sustain its existing institutions, either they or the culture must be reformed, for social structures can be maintained by force for only so long. Like all dead things, they disintegrate in time.

Totalitarians recognize, and this is their defining characteristic, that if new social structures are to be created without regard for the existing culture or if old institutions no longer sustained by the contemporary culture are to be maintained, the culture itself must be tailored to the institutions in question by manipulation and control. In our libertarian tradition, we have regarded totalitarian society as pathological in the worst possible way, for it pulls its own nerves, so to speak, so that it cannot discover its own ills and therefore cannot maintain its health.

Some respected intellectuals high in the establishment as well as active revolutionaries are saying that America as a nation is already dead, that life and spirit have gone out of her and that only a corpse remains, for the rationale for our institutions is no longer convincing to a large number of people, especially the younger generation. The cry for law and order as well as the voice of the revolutionary reflects the decay of the foundations of our institutions. Our economic, social, educational, and religious institutions as well as our political system are in trouble. Even the family seems to be giving way. At this point we cannot be sure that the social concepts of man and woman will survive. Indeed the very concept of person is eroding.

Institutions as such, not just our existing ones, are in question. Many agree with a fugitive from the draft residing in Canada who said in the early seventies: "God is dead and so is the state. Everyone is now on his own." The incongruity between our emerging culture and social structure is already so great that in times of crisis we seem to be dangerously close to a violent revolutionary situation.

Our social structures and institutions are under impact from two directions. Man's material mode of existence, thanks to science and technology, has undergone more change in the lifetime of our senior citizens than in all previous recorded history. It is difficult to reform our institutions fast enough to keep them adjusted to these changing conditions. And, too, the rapid change tends to divorce them from the feelings and emotions of people and thereby deprive them of their support. Furthermore, contrary to the view that our culture is simply a reflection of the material conditions of our existence, there are pressures for social change and causes of alienation growing out of internal developments within our culture itself. Indeed it is a thesis of this work that these are the most important of all, for only ideational change occasions profound revolutions.

A liberal is one who feels the tension between the emerging culture and the existing social structures, but, standing firmly within the perspective of the new culture, he locates all the troubles within the social order and seeks to reform it. The conservative remains wedded to the older structure of consciousness and resists efforts to reform the society except for the purpose of adjusting it to changing material conditions. The radical tries to restructure the consciousness of the people. His attack is aimed more directly at the older but still prevailing culture. His methods are not those of rational persuasion and education, for such methods, for the most part, provide movement only within a basic framework of thought. Radicalization is a conversion process. It is not a movement within one's thought but a flip of one's mind that gives birth to a new self and a new world. Shock methods of caricature, ridicule, defiling the symbols of the existing culture, doing and saying the taboo things, hostile confrontations, deeply emotional experiences in the new mode and the growth of new symbols to give expression to and to communicate the new perspective and the experiences and ways it generates—these, not rational dialogue, are the techniques of mass radicalization.

The purpose of this study is to try to transcend the battles of the liberal, the conservative, and the radical to gain a deeper and fuller understanding of what is happening in Western civilization and why—to locate the ultimate source of our difficulties, to gain an understanding of the dynamics of our culture, and hopefully to shed some light on the way to a life-sustaining culture for people and institutions.

In our scientifically oriented culture, we are likely to locate all our troubles within the patterns of observable behavior and the material conditions of our existence, for these are what lend themselves to scientific study. No doubt there are serious problems within the social structure and many social reforms are urgently needed. However, we shall explore the possibility that our worst troubles lie within our culture and thus within the structure of our consciousness. Indeed many of the problems we "see" in the social order may really lie within the culture itself. This may be why social reforms seem increasingly ineffectual.

Nevertheless, as the gap widens and the tensions mount between our culture and the existing social order, it may be necessary to reform the social structures to bring them more in line with the developing culture to prevent the breakdown of society and violent revolution and thereby gain time and preserve the freedom necessary for long-range cultural therapy. We could of course try to close the gap and reduce the explosive tension by controlling the culture to bring it in line with the institutions. This in itself would involve extensive institutional reform within our society and would require considerable coercion and time. Even to try it might provoke the revolution it was undertaken to prevent. But most importantly, it would destroy what it was trying to preserve and foreclose any possibility of solving the real problems. It is better to keep the culture free and, if necessary, adjust the social order to it than to have the social order control the culture or be in violent opposition to it, for in no other way can we keep the self-corrective powers of the human mind and spirit free to work their salvation. Such work must be done in its own way. It is not easy and it takes time. It cannot be controlled; nor can it be coerced. The culture is within us—and it is difficult to overcome our provincialism and gain a critical perspective on it.

Although it may be important to find immediate ways of relieving the dangerous tensions between our emerging culture and our social structures, we must, if I am right in my fundamental thesis, be at work on the problems within our culture, for internal developments within the culture have called into question the relationship of the culture itself to the structure of reality. Here, in my opinion, is where the real gap lies. If our culture were healthy and sound vis-à-vis reality, we would have no unmanageable problem about the social order.

We have said that the culture of a society is a structure of meaning on which people and institutions depend for spiritual nourishment, health, and vitality. This needs some elaboration. For present purposes, let us say that meaning is in a way parallel with existence. We may describe a book, for example, by giving its physical dimensions: weight, color, number of pages, and the like. This is to approach it simply as a structure of existence. On the other hand, we may talk about what is semantically in the book—the people, places, situations, issues, actions, and the like. This is to deal with it as a structure of meaning. The focus is on what is semantically in the book in contrast with what is existentially in it. To ask about whether the book is fiction or history, and, if history, whether it is true, is to ask about whether what is semantically in the book is existentially in the world. Of course we can also describe the book by saying how many words, sentences, paragraphs, and chapters it contains, and by characterizing them; by talking about the concepts, statements, and questions in the book in terms of the properties (including relations) they exemplify; and so forth. Here we are approaching the book existentially but at a higher level where what exists is itself (or includes) a structure of meaning. The concern is with what is existentially present in that structure of meaning as distinct from what is present in it as meant. One may be concerned, for example, with whether a given word *is* transitive or whether it *means* transitive.

The book, of course, is an expression of the mind of the author and a way of communicating to others what was in his mind. So what is in the book was first in the experience, memory, imagination, and thought of the author, and comes to be in the mind of the reader. Thus we may speak of something being semantically in a mind in much the same sense in which we speak of something's being semantically in a book. And we may speak of a mind itself as a structure of meaning. Indeed the psychological, including the behavioral, is, I suggest, that which has a semantic dimension, that which is a structure of meaning, in the primary sense. This is the nature of subjectivity. The so-called "inner world" is not a subjective private realm of existence with peculiar objects in contrast with and yet problematically related to the objects of the public world; but rather it is a realm of meaning in which ordinary things and features of the public world are inexistentially present as meant, much as the things, events, and characteristics semantically in a book are those in (or at least could be in) the objective public world.

A person located at a given time and place has certain things existentially present with him and in a sense the whole existent world may impinge on him causally through them. But we must sharply distinguish between that which is existentially present with him and that which is semantically present to him. Of course that which is existentially present may also be semantically present, but in its semantic presence it may be different from the way it is in its existential presence. But much more may be semantically present in a true or distorted form—past events through present perception (the distant star which has ceased to exist), memory, and historical knowledge; spatially distant contemporary happenings through electronic communications or reliable predictions; the future through prediction and expectation; the possible through imagination and thought; the imperative through desire, feeling, attitude, purpose, and thought; that semantically present in the consciousness of others through perceptual understanding of them; and the whole of reality through general feelings and attitudes and general knowledge. It is what is semantically present to us and the form it has in its semantic presence that enter into and guide our human responses and actions. Of course that which is merely existentially present can affect us existentially and impose limitations on what we can do. But we cannot respond to it or be guided by it unless it is also semantically present. Thus the way and the extent to which the world is semantically present to us and the way in which we can deal with it semantically is the most distinctive and the most important aspect of human existence.

Our earlier remarks about a book as expression of its author's mind, as semantically containing what was semantically in his thought, may be misleading. It suggests that language has only an expressive, communicative function. This is not so. Language is a set of semantic tools which enable us to perform what would otherwise be impossible semantic acts. The author could never have had the thoughts expressed in the book without the instrumentality of language, and the conceptual system and knowledge made possible through the development and refinement of language profoundly influences and shapes our experiences, memory, and imagination. So what is semantically available to us at all is, to a large extent, a function of our language and symbolism.

This is not to deny, however, that man has a natural rudimentary power to relate semantically to himself and to his world without the aid of semantic tools. The situation seems parallel with our power to act physically on our environment. It was because of our natural power to act on and to change things that we were able to make physical tools with which to extend such powers. In like manner, we must have natural powers for rudimentary experience, memory, and imagination, for without such powers how would we have been able to develop and to learn to use semantic tools?

The culture of a society, then, as I am using the term, consists most fundamentally of its ways and means of semantically relating to and appropriating the world and secondarily the world as semantically appropriated in the shared experiences and aspirations of the people and their accumulated knowledge and wisdom. Thus a culture consists of the language, symbols, myths, rituals, pageants, religion, art, skills, ethics, history, science, mathematics, theology, and philosophy a society has developed or learned from others and is prepared to transmit to the new generation.

It is clear that the culture of a society is most intimately related to the structure of the consciousness of the people. It has developed out of the long semantic commerce of the people with reality. It began in the dim past with beings not yet people who became human beings only at a certain stage of cultural development. Indeed one cannot be a human being, in the full sense of the term, merely by being biologically generated by human parents and physically maturing. A rabbit biologically generated and physically nurtured for a short time can go on to become a mature rabbit without ever contacting another rabbit after birth, and he will live the life of a rabbit. But a human being has to be culturally generated and nurtured. Under his own development, if he could physically survive, a man would, no doubt, come to have rudimentary experiences, memory, and imagination, and perhaps in a more advanced form than other animals because of a greater native intelligence. He would perhaps develop some rudimentary semantic tools, but not enough to extend his semantic powers to the point he would have distinctly human modes of consciousness. Without language and symbols to deepen and to structure his subjectivity, without beliefs, myths, and theories to organize his consciousness into a unity and to form an image of the self and the world, one would not be an "I," a person, capable of moral, religious, and artistic experiences and intellectual thought. Man's center of gravity is not in his biological being, but in his selfhood. This is the truth in the claim that man is not an animal among other animals, but a spiritual being. And as a spiritual being he is culturally dependent in much the way Max Gerard wrote of Salvador Dali, the great painter:

> I am the tool! Dali said to me one day.
> And this tool is that of an artisan,
> he who digs to the bottom of his trade,
> he whom centuries of skill have perfected,
>   disciplined, and strengthened;
> the tool of good usage,
> the tool of tradition, for
> All that does not spring from
>   tradition is plagiarism . . .
> I am the tool!
> And there is only one way to take a tool
>   in hand,
> There is the way of the beauty makers,
> the way of the inherited example,
> the manner which gave birth to many
>   masterpieces.

Begin by drawing and painting like
    the old masters;
After that do as you wish,
You will always be respected.[1]

Because we are culturally generated, we think it appropriate, indeed very important, for one to have special feelings toward his country as well as toward his parents. It is very difficult, if not impossible, for one to have a healthy self-respect without a certain natural piety toward his origins. It is not without significance that people most everywhere speak of their "fatherland," and that the Russians speak of "Mother Russia."

The point we are making is that as the culture goes so goes the people. And if there is a widening gap between our emerging culture and our social structures, this can only result in people being alienated from those social structures.

The culture of a society has, of course, a close dynamic relationship with the society's social structures and institutions, which are constituted by functional systems of offices or social positions with their inherent responsibilities, rights and privileges, and their interrelationships. But social structures and institutions are not immediately responsive to the growing edge of cultural change, especially not as responsive as the structure of consciousness of the intellectuals, artists, and the younger generation, in whose minds the logical implications of the culture are worked out and the culture moves forward in its line of development through them. Reversing the famous sociological dictum, there is always a social lag with respect to cultural change. There is a built-in inertia in the social order. There are always vested interests in the status quo and support from the older culture which lingers. So societies in time of rapid cultural change tend to depend more heavily on police power and repressive measures to maintain the social structures and to keep the institutions functioning. But if the emerging culture leaves the social structures and institutions and the powers on which they depend exposed, stripped of legitimacy, they cannot be maintained for long. They or the culture must yield to reform which results in cloaking the social structures and institutions with legitimacy or there will be disintegration or violent revolution.

A culture as a complex structure of meaning may seem to be a very diffused thing, difficult to grasp and to understand in its workings. Different ways of studying it yield quite different findings, for each method of study can find only what it by its nature can locate. An empirical scientific approach in a behavioral mode, which is prominent in the social sciences, would reduce all that I am calling the structure of consciousness to dispositions to behave in publicly observable ways and all that I am calling culture to behavioral dispositions which manifest themselves in social structures and institutions, or, according to this view, observable patterns of behavior. And for the more positivistically inclined who reject contrary-to-fact conditionals, even the dispositions drop out and we have only patterns of behavior. This, I think, fails to delineate the subject matter in its own indigenous categories and, therefore, social science, in this mode, is condemned to systematic misrepresentation and falsification. It tells a lot of little truths from within its perspective in the interest of a big falsehood. This is but an aspect of the difficulty in modern culture which we have already intimated and are to probe more deeply. Only a humanistic approach, the proper approach of the humanities, can grasp a culture in terms of its own structure and thus not be distorting. This is to relate to and to try to understand the contents, structure, and workings of a culture in much the same way as we try to understand a person from within the perspective of a human, a person to person, encounter with him. This involves being open to him, that is, having all our channels open through which we can acquire knowledge of him and gain insight into and understanding of him. Unless we come to understand the world in general and the particular situations of his life as they are semantically present to him, and the presuppositions, assumptions, and aspirations from which he reasons and deliberates, we will have missed him entirely. Much the same can be said in our study of a culture.

As indicated earlier, the most fundamental and the most important aspect of a culture is its accepted ways and means of semantically relating to and appropriating the world. These, whether ever articulated or not, constitute the basic philosophical assumptions of the culture about the semantic and knowledge-yielding powers of the human mind.

In the case of governments, and of organizations in general, we have constitutions. They are sets of normative principles which define the structure, powers, and ways of acting of their respective organizations. In the area of language, we have a normative structure, which may be formulated as grammatical and semantical rules, that determines the structure of sentences and what makes linguistic sense. In a somewhat parallel way, we may speak of the constitutional principles or logical grammar of the human mind by virtue of which we have the powers to experience, to think, to reason, to talk, and to act in the various ways in which we do. We may also speak of them as categorial principles, for philosophers have long spoken of whatever can be known about the objects of knowledge and of the world in general from the constitutional structure of experience and thought as the categorial structure of reality. For example, it seems that we can determine that there are *facts* and something about their structure from the logical grammar of statements, i.e., that some at least involve the exemplification of properties by particulars (e.g., this pencil is blue). These terms ("facts," "particulars," "properties," "exemplification") are taken to be categorial concepts and thus to indicate categorial features of reality. They have quite a different status in our conceptual system than empirical concepts, such as "buildings," "boards," "nails," and "paint."

The assumptions of a culture about these principles of the mind may be spoken of as a cultural mind, for they constitute the perspective of the culture on the world and define the forms and limits of the structure of meaning which they generate. They determine what is possible, impossible, and necessary from within the cultural view, leaving only what is actual among the possible to be determined by encounters with the world in the accepted ways. Of course a cultural mind may be affected in subtle and indirect ways by the people's commerce with the world from within the cultural perspective, but the assumptions which constitute the cultural mind have considerable staying power, for they legislate what the results of such encounters can and cannot be and therefore are not responsible to nor subject to control by such findings, at least not in any direct way.

Consider the existential question, "Are there ghosts?" It looks very much like "Are there tigers in Africa?" or "Are there flying saucers?" If it were like these questions, empirical investigations would be the way to seek an answer. But for two people in disagreement about whether there are ghosts, assuming their disagreement to be typical for believers and disbelievers in such matters, empirical investigations would not lead to agreement. What seemed or appeared to them to be the case in a given situation might be identical. Yet one might say that he saw a ghost, whereas the other would not. Both might agree that their perceptual experiences were such that they were not veridical experiences of a person with a physical body. For the disbeliever, this would mean that their experiences simply were not veridical. The believer, however, might take them to be veridical experiences of a real but nonphysical object. This would not be regarded as a possibility by the disbeliever, for his assumptions about the principles of veridical experience and thus about the marks of real objects of perception would rule it out. Thus if they should try to settle their disagreement in an intelligent, responsible manner, they would not resort to empirical investigations but to a critical examination of their assumptions about the constitutional principles of veridical perceptions and the categorial marks of the real.

Our categorial assumptions show themselves in the way in which we define and attempt to solve problems. Some years ago strange happenings in a house on Long Island attracted national attention. A housewife was disturbed by dishes jumping off tables, bottles unscrewing their caps and jumping off shelves, furniture moving around in the house, and the like. When she first told her husband about some of these occurrences, he thought she needed a vacation. But then some of them happened in his presence. In the end a number of people were involved in investigating the situation. The local police department put a special investigator on the case. Bell Laboratories sent a physicist. The Parapsychology Department of Duke University sent an investigator. The family's priest was involved. The priest entertained the possibility that the house was demon possessed and performed an ancient ceremony of exorcism. The parapsychologist talked seriously about the possibility of a poltergeist. The physicist concluded that the disturbances were caused by high frequency sound waves from subterranean machinery that happened to converge on the house from different directions on certain days because of the depth of the freezing of the earth. No such waves were detected nor their sources located. But this was the only uneliminated possibility open to the physicist. Neither the demon nor the poltergeist hypothesis was a possibility for him.

In this case, we find the investigators operating with different philosophical assumptions about the constitutional principles of the mind and the categorial structure of the world. The physicist, and most of us in the modern world would agree with him, does not simply reject the hypothesis of the priest and the parapsychologist as false or improbable but as superstition. He does not regard them as formulating possibilities for the world as he conceives it. It is not that the "statements" are false but that the "concepts" in terms of which they are formulated have no place in his conceptual system. They are regarded as pseudo or meaningless. That whole way of thinking is rejected as groundless on the basis of certain assumptions or beliefs about the epistemic (knowledge-yielding) powers of the human mind.

A culture with a distorted world view grounded in false assumptions about the constitutional principles of the human mind is deranged. Life lived from within it is like that of a mad man. One cannot through the exercise of his powers, structured by the internalized culture, know and cope with reality. All his efforts from within the culture suffer from the cultural defects, and, therefore, he cannot discover and correct these defects themselves without transcending the distorted world view and its underlying assumptions about the categorial structure of experience and thought.

The situation is much like that of Aristotle's account of the wicked man. Wickedness, the opposite of moral virtue, according to Aristotle, is a state or condition of a person involving his emotions, produced by training and practice, which systematically results in error in one's basic value judgments, in one's ends of conduct. Once in this state, one cannot through the exercise of one's own faculties correct the condition, for the condition is a disease of just these faculties themselves and therefore corrupts all their activities. It is a form of derangement which precludes one from coming to grips with reality in its value dimension.

The Christian doctrine of original sin is interpreted by some in a similar way. Man is said to be corrupted in his decision-making faculties through his self-centeredness, his paranoid anxiety about his value status in reality. We all know how an insecure person, overly anxious and concerned about his social status and how he is regarded by others, feels himself to be at issue in every situation and because of this misjudges the matters on which he has to make decisions. In like manner, everyone's value judgments in his natural state or condition, according to the doctrine of original sin, are systematically distorted by a sense of ontological insecurity or religious anxiety in such a way that no one can work out his own salvation or cure through the exercise of his natural powers. If salvation or therapy is to be had, if man's perverted faculties are to be corrected, the Christian contends, he must be transformed, he must become a new creature, by the grace of God, in much the same way as demonstrated love and concern may redeem the antisocial delinquent.

Philosophy cannot offer divine grace, not even philosophical grace, as a cure for cultural derangement, but it does offer a kind of diagnosis and therapy. There are two symptoms of derangement to which we should be alert, namely (1) a general depression or spiritual malaise of a people whose lives are structured by the culture and (2) the philosophical perplexities the culture generates.

We all know what it is to feel listless and debilitated, to feel bad or not to feel well, or simply to feel sick without any specific pains or other indications of what is wrong with the way one's body is functioning. And we know what it is to feel good, to feel fully alive and healthy. We live with a pervasive sense or awareness of how well we are functioning physiologically. This general sense of the normative state of one's body is not adequate to tell one what is wrong when something is, but only that something is wrong. Detailed and extensive scientific examinations may be required to reveal the specific difficulties.

In a somewhat parallel manner, happiness or unhappiness is one's awareness of the normative state of one's personal (as contrasted with biological) life. It is a matter of life-morale. For comparison, consider job-morale. To have good job-morale is (1) to feel that one's job is an important part of a worthwhile enterprise; (2) to feel that it is worthy of oneself; (3) to feel challenged and engaged by its demands; (4) to feel oneself worthy of the job and competent to handle it; (5) to feel that one is functioning well in the job; and (6) to have confirmation of these things through the recognition and appreciation of others. In a parallel way, high life-morale (or happiness) involves feeling that the human enterprise itself is eminently worthwhile. One may try to run away from this issue, to avoid it, by busying oneself with this or that special enterprise—with being a student, a lawyer, a physician, a traveler, or whatever. But these will be empty and meaningless minor campaigns in an empty and senseless cause if life itself is not felt to be worthwhile. They may provide some temporary excitement and fill up some of the days or even years, but they will add up to nothing in the end. Like Hemingway's fisherman in *The Old Man and the Sea*, he may catch his "fish," but he can bring home only "the bare bones," for the underlying boredom and despair will eat away and destroy everything of worth in it.

To feel that the human enterprise is worthwhile involves, of course, believing that there is a human enterprise, that there is something for one to be or to become as a human being, that to be a human being is to have an office as it were, to have responsibilities to fulfill, to be under an imperative or set of imperatives that defines for him a way of life. We judge men as teachers, lawyers, brickmasons, carpenters, designers, and the like. We judge them on the basis of their competence, skill, and performance in fulfilling the imperatives that define their trade or profession. When we judge men morally we are judging them in terms of their competence, skill, and performance in fulfilling the office of a human being. Every office is defined not only by some set of imperatives or responsibilities but by certain rights and privileges. The rights that pertain to an office consist of the areas of freedom that the officeholder must have in order to fulfill the responsibilities of the office. The privileges of an office are those areas of freedom that can safely be left to the officeholder in the performance of his duties. Human rights and privileges are those that go with the responsibilities of being a human being. This package, the responsibilities of one as a human being together with their correlative rights and privileges, constitutes the human status, station, position. We distinguish between the respect appropriate to one by virtue of his office or position as a human being and the respect he merits by virtue of the way he fulfills the office just as we distinguish between the respect due to the president of the United States by virtue of his office and that due him by virtue of his qualifications for and performance in that office.

One cannot, of course, just be a human being. The office is highly determinable and becomes determinate in a variety of ways. We are male and female and here roles and functions divide. We have different talents and capacities and find ourselves in different places and times. And so the specific imperatives that shape and define our lives in detail vary immensely. Although we all share a common office as human beings and thus at this level are equal, at more concrete levels we occupy positions defined by responsibilities and their correlative rights and privileges that are and must be quite unequal.

Physical space is that in which physical objects exist or have spatial position. We may speak in a parallel manner of social space in which people exist, in which people have social positions or offices, the most basic one being that of a human being. Social space, like physical space, must be three dimensional, for there must be higher and lower social positions as well as those on the same social plane. It must also be correlated with time to provide a four dimensional continuum. People are not only related socially to their contemporaries, but to their ancestors and to future generations. Traditional religions think of social space as extended in such ways as to make possible the existence or position of God and other personal beings in the divine hierarchy.

High life-morale involves an awareness of a social space-time continuum and of oneself as having a position in it. It further involves a sense that one's position is important, that it challenges and engages one's total being, and that one is filling the position well. The ordinary unhappy person is one who feels either that he is not what he ought to be or that he is not functioning well or both. There is an extraordinary or deeper unhappiness that is a feeling that nothing matters, that there isn't anything that one ought to be or to do and therefore no such thing as malfunctioning, unless it is being conventional, that is, acting as though there were something one ought to be and ought to do. And living well, on this view, insofar as this way of talking can have meaning at all from within this perspective, is taken to be a matter of unspoiled, and thus unconventional and unreasoned, response to every situation as it arises. This perhaps is the greatest sickness of spirit of which man is capable, for it is sickness without hope.

The spirit of a culture is the pervasive sense of the normative state of life lived from within the cultural perspective. It may be happy and optimistic or unhappy and despairing. The issue is whether the cultural mind, as a way of structuring the experience, thought, aspirations, and action of the people, makes possible knowledge of reality, competence and strength in coping with reality, and, in general, high life-morale and human well being. A systematic tendency toward general depression and wretchedness of the spirit of a people indicates derangement in the cultural mind that distorts our efforts to know and to cope with reality.

Where the general spirit of a culture, or at least the persistent mood of the people, especially a good spirit and high morale in the face of particular adversities or general depression in the face of particular successes, may indicate something about the normative state of the culture in general, the philosophical perplexities a culture generates may be more specific. They are like localized pains. Examination of the trouble spots they locate may reveal specific perverting philosophical assumptions in the makeup of the cultural mind. But in order to be able to recognize a philosophical perplexity, we must be able to sort out philosophical problems from other kinds.

Problems in general involve something's being wrong, something's not being the way it ought to be. But not merely this. A tree may be deformed or have deficiencies, but it does not have problems. Problems exist only where there is the possibility of their being felt or known and solved by inquiry or action or both. Those that lend themselves to being solved primarily by inquiry are intellectual problems; those that require overt action other than that subsidiary to inquiry are practical problems.

The wrong or deficiency that gives rise to an intellectual problem lies in the subjective conditions of man, in his experience and thought. The most basic mark of trouble in our experiences, thoughts, decisions, and the like is inconsistency or some form of logical incompatibility. The primary basis we have for suspecting the veridicality of any experience, the truth of any thought, or the soundness of any plan is its apparent logical incompatibility with something else in the fabric of experience and thought. And such suspicion is what initiates reflection and inquiry.

Consider several examples: A man who is engaged in a small construction project goes to a builder's supply house to buy an item. Before leaving home, he removes a bag of cement, previously purchased, from the trunk of his car. Yet thirty minutes later at the builder's supply house, when he opens his trunk to put in his new purchase, he sees a bag of cement in the trunk. He is puzzled, for he has a clear memory of removing the only bag of cement in the trunk just thirty minutes before and yet he now has a clear visual experience of a bag of cement there in the trunk before him. There seems to be an inconsistency between the memory and visual experience. He is presented with a problem. He can solve it by discrediting his memory or his present visual experience; or by accepting some explanation that would make possible the veridicality of both the memory and the visual experience, like, for example, an attendant at the supply house having mistakenly placed someone else's bag of cement in his car.

Second, consider the Warren Commission's report on the assassination of President Kennedy. The commission and its investigators collected a mass of reports of what hundreds of people, including those present in Dallas at the scene of the assassination and at related events and those who examined the physical evidence, "saw," "heard," "remembered," and thought. As in any case like this, the reports embodied many inconsistencies. After collecting the reports, the task of the commission was to achieve a coherent account by discrediting some reports and by constructing hypotheses that would show how the truth of the accepted reports was possible. The critics of the commission have had a field day by taking the same corpus of reports and accepting and rejecting in a different pattern to achieve a coherent picture of what happened.

Last, consider the problem that Einstein faced in physics in the early years of the present century. The law of the addition of velocities had long been accepted. For example, if a car traveling at seventy miles an hour passes one going fifty miles an hour, relative to the second car, the first one is traveling twenty miles an hour. If it should run into the rear of the second car, the impact would be that of a car going twenty miles an hour hitting a parked car. If the two cars were traveling in opposite directions and had a headon collision the impact would be that of the collision of a car traveling one hundred and twenty miles an hour with a parked car. Yet the Michelson and Morley experiments with light in 1887 had led to the belief that the velocity of light is constant in relation to all frames of reference, regardless of whether they are stationary, approaching, or receding relative to the source of light. Thus we have what appears to be an inconsistency in the beliefs of physicists. Einstein's theory of space and time was constructed to show how both claims could be true. It concerns how to translate spatial and temporal units of measurement in the observation reports made from one frame of reference into observation reports of the same motions made from another frame of reference that is in motion relative to the first.

Sensitivity to logical incompatibility in experience and thought is as essential to the intellectual enterprise as the capacity for pain is to the task of staying healthy. Any artificial restriction on exposure to experiences and thoughts that might contradict those accepted as true is as dangerous to the intellectual life as permanently anesthetizing parts of the body would be to one's biological life. It restricts one's capacity to discern the troubles and deficiencies that may exist in experience and thought.

Ordinary logical incompatibilities call into question the veridicality of some experience, the legitimacy of some desire, the soundness of some decision, plan, or policy, or the truth of some belief. Matters can be set right by a reassignment of legitimacy or truth values, like, for example, rejecting the veridicality of some experience or the truth of some proposition. Apparent inconsistencies of this kind initiate ordinary inquiries and scientific investigation. Such problems are solved when we achieve a network of experiences, expectations, beliefs, attitudes, plans, and the like that are not only free from inconsistency but are coherent in the sense that they are mutually supporting. To replace any item in a coherent network with its negative would generate a logical incompatibility (which may be weaker than a full-blown inconsistency) within the system. Just as logical incompatibility is our chief symptom of trouble, coherence is our chief mark of correctness and truth.

There are logical difficulties more vicious than ordinary logical incompatibilities. In the area of discourse, such difficulties not only call into question the *truth* of some statement, for example, but whether some apparent statement taken to be true is even a genuine statement at all. In other words, the difficulty calls into question the meaningfulness of some sentence or type of sentence rather than merely its truth-value.

These difficulties often show themselves in brain-teasing paradoxes. One is the so-called liar's paradox. In its ancient form, it was stated this way: Epimenides, the Cretan, said, "All Cretans are liars." It needs more careful formulation. Something like this would be better: Epimenides, the Cretan, said, "All Cretans, including myself, always lie." A stronger version can be presented in the following way. Consider an index card with one side labeled "*A*" and the reverse side "*B*" and with only one sentence written on each side. The sentence on *A* is: "The sentence on *B* is true." And the sentence on *B* is: "The sentence on *A* is false." Now consider the logical relationships between these two sentences. Calling each by the name of the side of the card on which it appears, if *A* is true, since it says that *B* is true, *B* must be true also. But if *B* is true, since it says that *A* is false, *A* must be false. Thus it follows that if *A* is true, then *A* is false, and from this we may conclude that *A* is false, for it is a simple logical truth that if a proposition implies its own negation, its negation is true. But if *A* is false, since it says that *B* is true, *B* must be false also. And if *B* is false, since it says that *A* is false, *A* must be true. Therefore, if *A* is false, as we concluded from our first line of reasoning, then *A* is true. From this, we may conclude that *A* is true. We have now proven from our two innocent looking sentences both that *A* is false and that *A* is true. The trouble here revealed does not call into question merely the truth-value of some statement, but rather the meaningfulness of sentences *A* and *B* or the validity of the principles of logic themselves.

Consider another simple example, the so-called heterological paradox. A homological word is by definition one that is true of itself. For example, "short" is a *short* word, containing only five letters. A heterological word is by definition one that is not homological. "Long," for example, is heterological, for it is not *long*, having only four letters. It seems obvious that every word must be either homological or heterological. But what about the word "heterological"? If it is *homological* (true of itself), then it is heterological, for we are talking about the word "heterological" itself. But also if it is homological, then it is not heterological, for "homological" and "heterological" are by definition negates of each other. Furthermore if "heterological" is *heterological*, then it is homological by virtue of what the statement says. Thus if "heterological" is true of itself, it is both true of itself and not true of itself; and if it is not true of itself, it is both not true of itself and true of itself. This is another logical difficulty that does not simply call into question the truth value of some statement, but the very meaningfulness of what appears to be an innocent sentence.

These examples may seem trivial, for the particular sentences whose meaningfulness is brought into question are of no great moment. But they exemplify an important kind of perplexity, that generated not by ordinary inconsistencies or logical incompatibilities but by paradoxes, antinomies, paralogisms, and other logical oddities and incongruities which are symptoms of trouble in our ways of semantically appropriating reality and relating to the world, trouble in our ways of experiencing and thinking. This locates the difficulty in either the constitutional principles of the human mind as such or in our assumptions and views about them. With respect to important philosophical perplexities, such as we shall consider in the next chapter, either is a serious matter; the first, far more so. We do not make, form, or adopt the constitutional principles of the mind, at least not in any deliberate way. They are simply the natural normative structure of the human mind with respect to which the general functioning of a mind may be judged to be normal or abnormal, sane or insane. Serious trouble here would mean that even if human minds functioned perfectly with respect to their own inherent normative structures, they would be self-defeating and condemned to failure with no correction possible. Such a tragic view of man may not be totally absurd, but it should not be indulged in the face of any plausible alternative.

While acknowledging the widening gap between our emerging culture and the existing social structures and the dangers involved, we have tried to focus attention on the possibility that this gap may be at least in part a product of a more serious gap between our culture and the structure of reality. What this would amount to should now be somewhat clearer. The question is whether the modern Western mind is deranged— whether the distinctively modern Western assumptions about the constitutional principles of the human mind are in error in such a way that they systematically thwart us in our efforts to know and to cope with reality and to live successfully. We shall make a preliminary approach to this problem in the following chapter.

II

Is the Modern Western Mind Deranged?

We have developed the concept of a cultural mind as constituted by a set of philosophical assumptions, whether ever articulated or not, about the constitutional principles of the human mind which shapes the way in which the people of a culture exercise their powers in their efforts to know and to cope with reality and therefore determines the structure of the culture itself. We have also seen how error in these assumptions can systematically thwart a people in their efforts to know and to cope with reality and generate a gap between the culture they develop and the structure of reality. So serious errors at this level would constitute a derangement of the cultural mind and pervert the lives of all whose consciousness was structured by the culture.

The issue we are raising in this chapter is whether the modern Western mind is deranged in this manner. In our first approach to this question, we shall look at our sense of the normative state of life lived from within our cultural perspective as manifested in the spirit of our culture and at some of the characteristic philosophical perplexities our culture generates.

1. The spirit of modern man

It is not always easy to paint the soulscape of a people, but at this point in our history no one can fail to sense the somber, melancholy mood that engulfs us like a cold, damp fog, chilling to the bone. Those who analyze, express, and portray the spirit of our people bear consistent testimony for the most part to the low morale and general depression of life in our time, even though they frequently locate the troubles differently.

It is commonplace for television commentators, editorial writers, and columnists to talk about loss of confidence, crisis of legitimacy, spiritual malaise, and the like. Politicians for a generation have addressed themselves to the problem of the spirit of the people. President Eisenhower talked about the need for spiritual renewal and moral regeneration in the

20

fifties. In the early sixties, John F. Kennedy sought to lift the American spirit and to get the country moving again by a vision of new frontiers. Senator Barry Goldwater said in the 1964 presidential campaign that there exists "a virtual despair amongst the many who look beyond material success to the inner meanings of their lives." In his state of the union message in 1968, President Lyndon Johnson spoke, in a classic understatement, of "a certain restlessness" in the land. President Richard Nixon said in 1971 that "the United States is turning to 'drugs and defeatism' and approaching the decadence that destroyed history's great civilizations." Senator George McGovern said in 1972 that he wanted to be president in order to help America regain her lost spirit of confidence, pride, and hope. There has been so much gloomy, pessimistic talk that Daniel P. Moynihan, among others, complained in 1972 about "this incessant rhetoric of disaster and doom" as a major contributing factor to the crisis of confidence that prevails.[1]

Our low morale as a nation is in part a response to three obvious conditions. (1) The United States felt it to be its responsibility in the wake of the Second World War, because of its great power, to contain the Communist powers. In trying to do so, we became involved in problems all over the world at great cost, sacrifice, and danger to the country. Furthermore, there has been a growing sense that we became perverted and corrupted in the process.

(2) Many have become acutely conscious of the fact that our society has been throughout its history and still is to a large extent a racist society; that is, there is the social position or office of the black man, the white man, the Indian, etc. This permeates our social structure. Many feel that it morally invalidates our society.

(3) Many, especially the younger generation, feel that in our complicated technological society the key social positions are not those of persons, not even the office of white man, but big government, big business corporations, big universities, and the like, and that people as such are no longer considered important and are sacrificed to the efficiency of the technological system. Many of our young people are, as Jacobs and Landau said about the youth movement of the sixties, in "revolt against the postwar 'overdeveloped society,' with its large bureaucracies in government, corporations, trade unions, and universities. To those in the movement," he says, "the new technologies of automation and cybernation, with their computers and memory-bank machines, are instruments of alienation, depersonalizing human relations to a frightening degree" and "all that remains is nineteenth century rhetoric about democracy and freedom, and technology has drained the words of their content."[2]

Yet even popular analysts point out that our troubles go much deeper. Consider a few selected comments. "Economic stagnation is real, but it is also a visible symbol for more spirit-shrinking afflictions. Material well-being is only an instrument for pursuit of more fulfilling, freer lives. Yet wealth has brought not liberation, but increasing confinement. The pleasures of place, neighborhood and street, are eroded by physical decay and psychic evictions; work, the principal object of human vitality, declines from satisfaction to obligation to pain; the organic units which provide one with the acceptance and respect of fellow—family and community and place—crumble under powerful, ill-comprehended forces of dissolution. The individual realizes that he no longer shapes the conditions of his existence, that he has become an instrument, and object, of some uncontrollable social process. Impotence can stimulate defiance; but more often it breeds insecurity, fear, hostility, and even violence. . . . Our present afflictions are fundamental. They are not produced by malfunctions or poor administration, but flow from the operation of a social and economic process unsuited to modern conditions."[3] William V. Shannon, laying the fault at a deeper level, writes in the *New York Times* (7 July 1972): "Ignorance of history and disdain for history are symptomatic of the malaise of today's youth culture and of the larger society which nurtures it. This malaise is the logical outcome of intellectual trends which began with the onset of the modern industrial age. . . . With the coming of industrialism, life became geared to the artificial pace of technology . . . we set out to kill time off . . . we began paring away the time needed to do different things . . . resenting death, we murdered time. Now, time vanquished, we lie exhausted alongside our victims. . . . To evade the limits and significance of time is to empty life of its limits and significance. It is that meaninglessness which pervades this age of instant gratification and instant results and permanent dissatisfaction."

In August 1964, Walter Lippman wrote in his newspaper column: "The modern sickness is the despair James Thompson called 'the insufferable inane.' It is to be found among the rich and the poor, among the grandees and the groundlings, and it has nothing to do with an unbalanced budget, a swollen bureaucracy, with communism or anticommunism, with the New Deal or the New Frontier. Some forty years ago I was writing that the promises of liberalism have not been fulfilled. We are living in the midst of that vast dissolution of ancient habits which the emancipators believed would restore our birthright of happiness. We know now that they did not see very clearly beyond the evils against which they were rebelling. . . . The poignant question not yet answered, is how, with the ancestral order dissolved and with the ancient religious certainties eroded by science, the modern man can find meaning which binds his experiences and engages his faculties and his passions."

Paul Goodman, writing in the *New York Times Magazine* (14 September 1969), says: "Contemporary conditions of life have certainly deprived people, and especially young people, of a meaningful world in which they can act and find themselves. Many writers and the dissenting students have spelled it out. For instance, in both schools and corporations, people cannot pursue their own interests or exercise initiative. . . . worst of all, the authorities who make the decisions are incompetent to cope with modern times: we are in danger of extinction, the biosphere is being destroyed, two-thirds of mankind are starving. . . . There is a lapse of faith in science . . . and rationality itself is discredited. Probably it is more significant than we like to think that intelligent young people dabble in astrology, witchcraft, psychedelic dreams, and whatever else is despised by science. . . ."

Many psychiatrists and psychotherapists are deeply concerned about the prevalence of mental illness in our society and the conditions that contribute to it. Dr. Dana L. Farnsworth, former director of Harvard University Health Services, said in an address before the American Medical Association in 1961: "The great sickness of our age is aimlessness, boredom, and lack of meaning and purpose in living. . . . All persons, with or without mental health, are obliged to suffer in various ways. It is the nature of man to experience frustrations, grief, pain, tension, conflict, jealousy, fear and anxiety. . . . To endure their troubles people need feelings of basic confidence in one's self and basic faith that the whole human situation is worthwhile. Medicine has made enormous strides in alleviating pain and prolonging life. Now an expanded task for doctors is to give meaning to life."

Rollo May, a psychotherapist, says that neurosis springs from the unconscious and "presents an image of man that is as yet present only in those members of the society who, by virtue of their own sensitized consciousness, live on the frontier of their society with one foot in the future."[4] Today, he says, "when practically all our patients are compulsive-obsessional neurotics (or character problems, which is a more general and less intense form of the same thing), we find that the chief block to therapy is the incapacity to feel. These patients, generally intellectuals, can talk from now until doomsday about their problems, but they cannot experience genuine feelings."[5] In his book, Love and Will,[6] Rollo May describes our world as schizoid, a term he defines as meaning "out of touch; avoiding close relationships; the inability to feel." He says "the schizoid man is the natural product of the technological man."[7] Agreeing with Leslie Farber's claim, in his book The Ways of the Will,[8] that this should be called the "age of the disordered will," May says that what underlies this particular pathology of our age is "a state of feelinglessness, the despairing possibility that nothing matters, a condition very close to apathy."[9] "The old myths and symbols by which we oriented ourselves are gone, anxiety is rampant; we cling to each other and try to persuade ourselves that what we feel is love; we do not will because we are afraid that if we choose one thing or one person we'll lose the other and we are too insecure to take that chance. The bottom then drops out of the conjunctive emotions and processes—of which love and will are the two foremost examples. The individual is forced to turn inward; he becomes obsessed with the new form of the problem of identity, namely, Even-if-I-know-who-I-am, I-have-no-significance. I am unable to influence others. The next step is apathy. And the step following that is violence."[10]

Erich Fromm, a psychoanalyst, in the conclusion of his book, *The Sane Society*,[11] which was written and first published in the mid-fifties, says that the automatization and alienation developing in both capitalism and communism lead "to an ever-increasing insanity." "Both systems," he says, "are developing into managerial societies, their inhabitants well fed, well clad, having their wishes satisfied, and not having wishes which cannot be satisfied; automatons, who follow without force, who are guided without leaders—; men, whose reason deteriorates while their intelligence rises . . . ," a situation in which "[l]ife has no meaning, there is no joy, no faith, no reality. Everybody is 'happy'—except that he does not feel, does not reason, does not love."[12] "But given man's nature," he says, "robots cannot live and remain sane, they become 'Golems,' they will destroy their world and themselves because they cannot stand any longer the boredom of a meaningless life."[13]

The best place to explore the spirit of a people is in their art, especially literature, for creative artists are sensitive to the implications of the culture for life. Their works are expressions of the cultural psyche, often in deep, dark symbols which they themselves may not comprehend, like the night dreams of the individual. And their characters are fleshed out life-hypotheses, exhibiting their implications in lived experience. Artists, in a developing, moving culture, are like television sets with their antennas turned to the future, for what is present in the cultural mind only by implication in one generation will become part of lived experience in a later period. The characters of the great novels of one age move on to the streets in the next.

Thomas Hardy, writing at the peak of Victorian confidence and optimism, painted for us in some of the most descriptive passages in English literature a picture in Egdon Heath (in *The Return of the Native*) of the twentieth-century wasteland in which people endure meaningless lives, a world without a structure of value and meaning, which Hardy saw, in the wake of Darwin, as a consequence of our developing intellectual life. We find portrayed in Clym Yeobright the plight of twentieth-century man. Hardy describes him thus: "In Clym Yeobright's face could be dimly seen the typical countenance of the future. Should there be a classic period to art hereafter, its Pheidias may produce such faces. The view of life as a thing to be put up with, replacing that zest for existence which was so intense in early civilizations, must enter so thoroughly into the constitution of the advanced races that its facial expression will become accepted as a new artistic departure. People already feel that a man who lives without disturbing a curve of feature, or setting a mark of mental concern anywhere upon himself, is too far removed from modern perceptiveness to be a modern type. Physically beautiful men—the glory of the race when it was young—are almost an anachronism now; and we may wonder whether, at some time or other, physically beautiful women may not be an anachronism likewise."

We have the new classic period in art and Picasso is its Pheidias. In 1959 the New York Museum of Modern Art had an exhibition entitled "New Images of Man." The well-known art critic, Aline B. Saarinen, said of it: "The new images of man that will confront the spectator in this exhibition are disturbing, disquieting, even unhinging. Here are human figures with bodies distorted, misshapen, mutilated. Sometimes their flesh is decayed and corrupt, sometimes corroded or charred. Here are faceless figures—or figures that seem to have death's heads—looming, leering out of nightmarish nothingness. Here are giant effigies and huge heads . . . some of them savagely present, others existing enigmatically in life and death. Here are figures possessed by animal and erotic frenzies. Here are figures that seem imprisoned in cage-like spaces and others incarcerated in spaces 'measureless to man.' If the exhibition had a sound track, it would be a cacophonous medley of anguished cries and screeches and the quiet sighs and sobs of loneliness and longing."[14]

The modern novel is for the most part a study in the plight of selfhood in the modern world. A somewhat common form of the spirit of man is found in the greatest literary works our culture has produced, the writings of such men as Dostoyevsky, Kafka, Faulkner, Joyce, Eliot, Gide, Mann, Camus. There are no national boundaries here. Nothing less than the experience and life of man in modern Western civilization is being expressed. Some would simply say that it is the life of man as such, but this betrays a provincialism, an unawareness of the existence and power of the cultural mind. The condition presented in these works is that of a distorted, thwarted, anguished self, thrashing about in an impoverished world, stripped of life-supporting, life-sustaining resources like a fish removed from the water or a man thrust into a vacuum. "If . . . there is in literary modernism a dominant preoccupation . . . , it is," Irving Howe writes, "the specter of nihilism," which involves, he says, "an all-embracing rebellion against traditional authority," "a consciously affirmed and accepted loss of belief in transcendent imperatives and secular values as guides to moral conduct, together with the feeling that there is no meaning resident—or, at least, further resident in human existence," and "a loss of tacit impulsions toward an active and striving existence that we do not even know to be at work in our consciousness until we have become aware of their decline." "Fundamentally," Howe concludes, "nihilism comes to simply a loss of connection with sources of life, so that both in experience and literature it is always related to, while analytically distinguishable from the blight of boredom."[15] Nathan A. Scott, Jr., a perceptive student of modern literature, and of the human soul, entitles a collection of his studies of the modern novel "Craters of the Spirit."[16] Pearl K. Bell, in commenting on the contemporary literary scene, says: "Surely there has been a suffocating excess in the last few years of novels about young men of no will, good or bad, caught in a vice of indecision and disdain, shambling their way through a dreary succession of erotic episodes. . . ."[17]

But even nineteenth-century romantic writers, expecially the continental ones like Chateaubriand, Lamartine, Holderlin, Leopardi, Vigny, Baudelaire, Rimbaud, and Lautreamont deeply felt the metaphysical isolation and estrangement of man in the wake of the eighteenth-century enlightenment and knew well the modern existentialist angst.

Thus we find in the art and literature of the modern age, in the words of Nathan Scott, paraphrasing Yeats's famous line (from "The Second Coming"), "the very flavor and sensation that life takes on when things have fallen apart, when the center no longer holds, and 'mere anarchy is loosed upon the world.' "[18] "Alienation," "aloneness," "anguish," "dread," "nothingness," "meaninglessness," "anomie," "absurdity," and the like are the key terms that have emerged for the description of life lived from within the modern perspective.

Existentialism, as Paul Henle has remarked,[19] elevates these features of consciousness from symptoms to philosophical categories. The claim of the existentialist is that a human being cannot achieve an authentic existence, cannot become fully lucid and self-conscious, confronting himself as a being-in-the-world, with all illusions and self-deceptions stripped away, except through these categories. Maurice Natanson says that to suggest that these categories (his list includes fear, dread, anguish, suffering, aloneness, choice, authenticity, and death) "are generated out of the awareness of man's being in reality is to claim that what is new and commanding in existentialism is its very procedure in exploring man's being *through* categories which are independent of common sense experience and scientific method and which take as their object not particular features of human existence, but existence itself."[20]

Perhaps the worst form and the most advanced stage of cultural derangement is reached when the marks of disease, perversity, disorder, and insanity become converted into criteria of health, normality, sanity, and wisdom. Of course it is no easy matter to determine when this has happened, for by what can we judge without begging the question? No straightforward answer can be given, but this is true, as we shall see, of all philosophical issues. This does not mean, however, that we are paralyzed, defeated, or driven to an utter relativism in which anything goes. There is a way of exploring philosophical problems, as we shall try to show later, which can lead to responsible, defensible conclusions. In the meantime, let us proceed on the assumption that there is a prima facie case for regarding the systematic tendency for life in the modern Western world toward alienation, depression, boredom, sense of futility, and the like to be negative modes of affective consciousness, a form of pain, indicating that something fundamental is wrong in our way of life.

Perhaps alienation is the key phenomenon in this syndrome. It is a matter of disaffection, inability to relate emotionally in a positive way to others, to the conditions of one's life, to one's culture and social institutions, or to the world itself. In its more total form it results in a feeling of aloneness, isolation, futility, meaninglessness, boredom, lack of will, and despair. Hegel was the first philosopher to give an extended treatment of the subject. He thought of alienation primarily as an individual's loss of identity with what he calls the social substance, the objectification of spirit—the social, political, and cultural institutions of his society. The alienated individual feels that the social substance is external and opposed to him. The spirit that animates him is different from and in opposition to that embodied in the social reality. In terms of our earlier discussion, such alienation occurs when there is a gap between the emerging culture and the lives structured and animated by it and the existing social structure. This means self-alienation, according to Hegel, for the individual's true self is the world spirit objectified in the social substance.

Marx, in his early writings, attempts to reduce Hegel's social substance to the political economy of a society. It is the productive process, he maintains, by which spirit or personality is objectified and individuals find self-actualization. Thus wage labor in a capitalistic society is said to be alienated labor. The worker does not objectify his will and his personality in the products of his labor; nor can he dispose of his products as he pleases. He is simply a tool of the will of another. This, according to Marx, is self-alienating and dehumanizing. The laborer is estranged from his essential nature. Furthermore, living in civil society, organized to promote the accumulation of private property through exploitation, develops a society of egoists, Marx claims, and alienates people from one another. This was the moral motivation for his assaults on capitalism. Unlike Hegel, he faulted the social system rather than the alienated individual. Communism was conceived as a way of achieving meaningful labor and social solidarity in an industrial society and thereby overcome the spiritual blight of alienation.

Sociologists and psychologists have produced an extensive literature on alienation.[21] Various forms have been described and a number of theories developed. But there is general agreement that alienation is a widespread and rapidly increasing phenomenon in modern society and that it, in all of its various forms, if extended, is a malady and tends to be destructive both to individuals and institutions. Durkheim linked it with suicide. Camus, who has made one of the greatest literary studies of alienation, said that the only philosophical problem of our time is suicide.

There are those who say that alienation is in no way peculiar to life within our modern Western culture, for it is a distinctively human phenomenon and has always been with us.[22] This is, of course, true to a considerable extent. Adolescence is a period of alienation in the developmental pattern of the life of the individual. It is a time of identity crisis and rebellion for most. The problem is the matter of coming to relate emotionally and volitionally to the realities of adult life. But even this is more acute in modern society because of the long years of limbo between childhood and entry into a fully adult role. And there has always been the alienation and despair that comes in the declining, decadent years of a civilization like fourteenth- and early fifteenth-century Europe, the end of the Roman empire, and the Hellenistic period in Greece. But in a more profound sense reason and knowledge have always presented man with a world that complicated his emotional relationships. This is the truth in the story of the apple of the tree of knowledge of good and evil and the fall of man. Christianity conceived of sin as a way of life that alienates man from God and salvation as a way of overcoming the estrangement and achieving in one's feelings, emotions, and will the right relationship with reality. Martin Luther voiced the anguish of an alienated spirit in his cry: "God has turned his face away, things have no meaning, I am estranged in the world."

Yet there is something new in the alienation of modern man. In addition to that endemic to the human condition and that of a decadent civilization, we have that peculiar to our complex technocratic society of big corporations, big universities, and big government. But not only this. We have a new dimension of alienation generated by the distinctive form our intellectual life has taken in the modern era. We have generated a view of man and the world which poses entirely new problems for man's emotional and rational life and compounds all of the old ones inherent in human existence. It is not only that life in our time seems to have lost its flavor and everything seems flat and meaningless; all our seasoning has lost its savor. The materialistic values of our culture prove to be fool's gold. Our higher moral and spiritual values have eroded. Erotic episodes, drugs, compulsive relating, temporary causes, false primitivism, and make-believe cults provide no real seasoning of life. The form of our intellectual grasp of things squeezes out all the life-supporting juices of value and meaning, leaving everything, including man himself, trivialized. Thus the desperate concern of the young, schooled in the best we offer, is expressed in the black humor of the question, Is there life before death?

The new form of alienation is to common varieties as philosophical skepticism is to ordinary doubt.[23] Philosophical skepticism is generated by assumptions or views about what it is to know or about particular modes of experience and thought which, if true, render knowledge impossible. One caught in the grips of such assumptions may be seriously perplexed and impaired in his efforts to know an external, independent world in general or certain apparent dimensions of reality. Philosophical alienation is a form of skepticism, but one which not only perplexes and thwarts us in our efforts to know but also in our efforts to live, in our efforts to exercise our powers in knowing, relating emotionally to, and coping with reality.

Thus we may conclude from our brief examination of the spirit of life lived from within the perspective of the modern Western cultural mind, especially where the vestiges of classical Hebraic, Greek, and Christian cultures have been most thoroughly expunged, that there are striking symptoms that indicate that we are being systematically thwarted in our efforts to know and to cope with reality and to live successfully and that the modern Western mind is deranged.

2. Philosophical problems in our culture

The philosophical perplexities our modern Western culture generates are perhaps even more compelling grounds for the suspicion that the modern mind is suffering from serious derangement. They are like localized pains. Examination of the specific trouble spots they indicate may reveal just what is wrong. Let us consider three such problems that are widely felt and that are of such a nature that they can be brought to self-consciousness fairly easily even for those who have never been consciously bothered by them.

First, let us consider the ways in which people of our culture talk about *why* things happen the way they do, particularly things important to us. In the Bible, which is still read as part of living literature by many in our own time, disasters like the destruction of Sodom and Gomorrah are explained as punitive acts of God for the wickedness of the people. Spectacular escapes from or victories over their enemies are explained by Israel as divine acts of deliverance. The great smallpox epidemic in New England in the eighteenth century was interpreted by the Puritans as divine punishment for the sins of the people. When a doctor in Boston, who had heard that in England a smallpox epidemic had been arrested by a serum that gave people a mild case of cowpox, proposed to vaccinate the people, they threatened to run him out of town, for they could no more think of resisting the administration of divine justice than good citizens could bring themselves to free a legally condemned man from the officers of the law preparing to hang him. They could not in good conscience forcibly resist respected authority. Furthermore, they reasoned that the punishment so far had not been anything compared to what they would receive if they lifted their hand against God and thus defied his authority and provoked his wrath. Even in our own time, there are communities where prayer meetings are held to pray for rain in time of drought, for the healing of the desperately sick, and for many other desired things that seem beyond the reach of human powers.

Many today who would not think of explaining an earthquake in Alaska that destroyed a town or a landslide in Italy that buried a village as an act of God to punish the people, nor think of explaining the stunning and spectacular victory of little Israel over the Arab nations in 1967 as the deliverance of the "chosen people" by a miraculous act of God, still ask *why* certain crucial events in their lives happen the way they do with a sense that demands an answer that would make each such event intelligible by placing it in a value structure in which things happen in fulfillment of what ought to be and therefore would show that it was good for the particular event to have occurred regardless of how disturbing it might seem. If an anguished widow asks in her grief why her husband, a man in his prime, had to die so young when he had so much to live for and so much to offer the world, her "why?" asks for quite a different kind of answer than the "why?" of the medical examiner. The autopsy report that describes the conditions of his heart and the coronary arteries and explains scientifically why the fatal heart attack occurred is irrelevant to her question. It leaves the untimely death unintelligible, senseless, and absurd from within the framework of ideas that she experiences the death of her husband and asks her question.

Not many in our culture today would attempt to answer her question with any confidence. Most people would not take it to be a genuine question at all but a rhetorical way of expressing grief. Some, however, would take the question seriously and at face value but contend that there was no reason for the happening; that it was simply senseless, unintelligible, absurd, and that this is true of all history, including human existence itself. The *Book of Job*, MacLeish's *J.B.*, Camus's *Myth of Sisyphus*, and Agee's *A Death in the Family* are classic studies of this problem.

Many who would not feel this kind of problem nor ask this kind of question about any "natural" event (any occurrence that is independent of or uncaused by human action) speak of some happenings in a behavioral situation as senseless or absurd in just this way. The death of a nineteen-year-old college student in a silly fraternity initiation seems senseless and absurd. Many Americans feel that the deaths in the Vietnam war were senseless. On the other hand not many Americans, however much they grieved the loss of a relative or friend in World War II, felt the death to be senseless. The difference lies in the fact that most Americans understood and thought about our involvement in World War II in such a way that the risks and losses were seen to be worthwhile and necessary. In any behavioral situation in which the values at issue are trivial but the risks and losses are great, the losses are felt to be senseless and absurd. The mother of the fraternity pledge killed in the trivial initiation ceremony cannot be consoled, for the death is meaningless, it does not make sense, it cannot be rendered intelligible by being placed in a value structure that would show it to be worthwhile in any way. Mrs. Jacqueline Kennedy's lament, upon learning that President Kennedy's assassin was a lone, alienated, would-be-Communist misfit, "It had to be a dirty little Communist. He didn't even have the satisfaction of dying for civil rights," expresses poignantly the demand for intelligibility in terms of values.

Some have contended that intelligibility per se consists of explanation in terms of values. Socrates says: "When I was young . . . I had a prodigious desire . . . to know the causes of things . . . I heard someone reading, as he said, from a book of Anaxagoras, that mind was the disposer and cause of all, and I was delighted at this notion, . . . and I said to myself: If mind is the disposer, mind will dispose all for the best, and put each particular in the best place; and I argued that if anyone desired to find out the cause of the generation or destruction or existence of anything, he must find out what state of being or doing or suffering was best for that thing . . . and I rejoiced to think that I had found in Anaxagoras a teacher of the causes of existence such as I desired, and I imagined that he would tell me first whether the earth is flat or round; and whichever was true, he would proceed to explain the cause and the necessity of this being so, that this was best; and if he said the earth was in the centre, he would explain further that this position was the best, and I should be satisfied with the explanation given and not want any other sort of cause."[24] W. M. Urban, an American philosopher, wrote in 1929: "The ultimate inseparability of value and reality is . . . almost axiomatic; to attempt to divorce them can issue only in unintelligibility. . . . Traditional metaphysics is . . . a value-charged scheme of thought. . . . It represents the 'natural metaphysic of the human mind,' a natural bent of the intellect which it is impossible to unbend."[25] Yet, as previously remarked, modern science seeks a value-free framework of thought in terms of which to describe and to explain whatever happens whether an earthquake that destroys a city, a smallpox epidemic, a historical event, a social movement, or even the order of the observable world.

A value-free conceptual system was first achieved in the physical sciences. The medieval physicist, like the Greek scientist before him, explained natural events in terms of value judgments. Consider, for example, his explanation of how the suction pump works. It was said that nature abhors a vacuum; that is, there ought not to be a vacuum, or, what amounts to the same thing, there ought to be a plenitude of being. This ought, this normative requirement, is regarded as the explanatory reason for the water's rising in the pipe when the pump removes the air, creating a vacuum. The fact that water could be lifted only about thirty-four feet at sea level and even less on a mountain with a suction pump was neatly explained as a "compromise" between conflicting oughts. Everything, it was said, has its natural place, that is, a place where it ought to be. Earthy things ought to be at the bottom, and then water, air, and fire and their like in that order. Therefore, the ought pertaining to the place of water, it was said, is in conflict with the requirement for a plenitude of being in the case of the suction pump. At sea level the compromise point is higher than on the mountain and this is why water cannot be lifted as high on a mountain with a suction pump as at sea level. The modern scientific explanation, of course, is that a column of air sits on the surface of the water and that its weight pushes the water up in the pipe when a vacuum is created, so that the height of the column of water in the pipe is a measure of the weight of the column of air. But what is weight? We say it is a function of gravity. But what is gravity? The medievalist would have said that it is the pull or constraint of an ought with regard to place. The modern physicist would not see this as a possibility. His methodology precludes it.

The biological sciences were much later than the physical sciences in becoming value-free in their descriptive-explanatory account of their subject-matter. This was the central issue in the controversy over the Darwinian theory of biological evolution. Darwin proposed what seemed to some to be a satisfactory account of why organisms are structured the way they are without the use of any value concepts. He operated entirely within the naturalistic concepts of change and causality which had been developed within the physical sciences. Many theologically minded people saw in this, as indeed they had in a value-free physics, a serious challenge to a theistic world view and all modes of normative thought.

Behavioristic psychology extends the value-free scientific mode of thought to human behavior itself and the social sciences apply it to social change.

In our culture we have come, for the most part, to regard the empirical scientific method as the only way to get at truth about reality. "Superstition" is defined in some school textbooks as any belief which cannot be scientifically verified. Our whole educational system tends to reinforce this naturalistic view of experience, thought, and reality.

Thus our culture, taken as a whole, teaches us to ask two "whys?" They seek intelligibility of the same things in terms of two teams of concepts that seem incompatible with one another. Some have tried to resolve the conflict by saying that science doesn't ask "why?" only "how?" Those who accept this solution to the apparent conflict obviously take "why?" to ask for an explanation that would involve a value as an explanatory reason. They interpret science as giving only a partial account of things to be supplemented by theology or philosophy. But our culture increasingly regards science to be in search of the full account of why things are the way they are and firmly believes that only an empirical scientific account can be intellectually respectable. In fact, the scientific "why?" has gained such a grip upon the modern mind that it has all but crowded out the traditional "why?" in most areas of thought. Thus philosophical perplexity generated by the conflict is not so intense nor widespread as it was in earlier generations.

But the matter is not a dead issue in our own times and certainly not in the lives of many individuals. The "death of God" controversy was news in the public press and elicited serious discussion and debate in the sixties. Nietzsche's madman proclaimed in the nineteenth century "whither is God . . . I will tell you. We have killed him—you and I. All of us are his murderers. But how did we do this? How were we able to drink up the sea? Who gave us the sponge to wipe away the entire horizon? What were we doing when we unchained this earth from its sun? Whither is it moving now? Whither are we moving? Away from all suns? Are we not plunging continually? Backward, sideward, forward, in all directions? Is there any up or down? Are we not straying as through an infinite nothing? Do we not feel the breath of empty space? Has it not become colder? Is not night continually closing in on us? . . . God is dead. God remains dead. And we have killed him."[26]

How did we kill God? One answer is that we switched "why"s. Those for whom God is not dead have not switched, and many of them would rather fight than switch. But the revolution takes place imperceptibly in the foundations of one's thought and it may take time for the superstructure to collapse. What Nietzsche's madman said of the culture may be true of the individual: "I have come too early, . . . My time is not yet. This tremendous event is still on its way . . . ; it has not yet reached the ears of men. Lightning and thunder require time, the light of the stars requires time, deeds, though done, still require time to be seen and heard. This deed is still more distant from them than the most distant stars—and yet *they have done it themselves.*"[27]

But our inquest should go further. First of all, what does a belief in God amount to philosophically? I venture to say that minimally it involves believing that there is an objective value structure in the world and that values are involved in what things are and why things are the way they are; that change is value oriented; that the natural forces of the

world work toward the realization of what is good; that causality is teleological; that the dynamic forces of reality are normative requirements,
the constraints and pulls of what ought to be in the process of becoming.
There are other categorial issues involved, but these are essential to any
theistic view of the world. It is almost universally agreed that value language cannot be funded with meaning, cannot be semantically grounded
to items and features of the world, through sensory perception. Therefore, the denial of a descriptive-explanatory role for value language in
modern science by its commitment to sensory perceptions as the sole data-
gathering or knowledge-yielding mode of experience and thus the only
experiential ground for semantic ties between language and the world
eliminated God-talk from the realm of science. And as the scientific
pattern of thought comes to dominate the intellectual life of the culture
and the thought of everyone, which is increasingly the case because of the
success of our educational programs, value language is denied any
descriptive-explanatory role and the meaning of God-talk gradually
drains out, leaving only a swamp of superstition and the apparel of disgust
and invective.

Thus involved in the conflict of the two "why"s are two conceptual
systems grounded in two incompatible assumptions or views about the
constitutional principles of the mind and its knowledge-yielding powers.
Those whose consciousness is structured by both teams of concepts, and
this has been true of most people in the modern era, to the extent that they
become self-aware, experience the conflict in the form of philosophical
perplexity, a kind of intellectual cramp. But, as previously remarked, for
the most part this is not as acute for our contemporaries as it was for
earlier generations, for the logical development of the modern mind has
largely uprooted the theistic conceptual system from our consciousness.

This has not been accomplished without consequences, however. It
was something like an emotional lobotomy. It severed man's affective and
conative life and the value dimension of culture from their ontological
foundations, and set them loose in subjectivity without ontological support or a unifying theory. No one has seen this clearer than Sartre. He
writes: "And when we speak of 'abandonment'—a favorite word of
Heidegger—we only mean to say that God does not exist, and that it is
necessary to draw the consequences of his absence right to the end. The
existentialist is strongly opposed to a certain type of secular moralism
which seeks to suppress God at the least possible expense. . . . The existentialist . . . finds it extremely embarrassing that God does not exist.
. . . Dostoyevsky once wrote 'If God did not exist, everything would be
permitted;' and that, for existentialism, is the starting point. Everything is
indeed permitted if God does not exist, and man is in consequence forlorn,
for he cannot find anything to depend upon either within or outside him-

self. He discovers forthwith, that he is without excuse . . . [O]ne will never be able to explain one's action by reference to a given and specific human nature. . . . Nor, on the other hand, . . . are we provided with any values or commands that could legitimize our behavior. Thus we have neither behind us, nor before us a luminous realm of values, any means of justification or excuse. We are left alone, without excuse. That is what I mean when I say that man is condemned to be free. . . ."[28]

This brings us to the second philosophical perplexity I would like to point out. It is closely related to the first. All human enterprise, including scientific inquiry and theory construction, involves and is indeed based on value judgments. They tie in with the springs of action and both move and guide us in what we do. We also use them in appraising action. Error in value judgments misleads us in our undertakings. Sound judgment on important matters is a virtue of great price. We call it wisdom. There seems to be a clearly recognizable difference between a wise man and a fool. And we argue about moral judgments, claiming that some are valid and some not. Yet the acceptance of the modern scientific method has not only denied value language a descriptive-explanatory role in our intellectual life; it seems to rule out the possibility of value knowledge of any kind and to call into question the cognitive meaningfulness and semantic objectivity of all value language. This has given rise to a widespread skepticism, not merely about the validity of the existing value structure of our contemporary society, but about the possibility of a *valid* value system of any kind. All value judgments are, for the most part, taken to be subjective and private and therefore value disagreements are increasingly regarded as not subject to rational resolution except insofar as they may result from factual disagreements.

In the area of religion, politics, morals, aesthetics, and on all other basic value issues, we tend to feel that everyone is not only entitled to his opinion, but that anyone's opinion is just as good as anyone else's, which is to admit that no one's is worth anything as far as truth is concerned. Where we hold that there is truth we do not believe that everyone is entitled to his opinion. We do not believe, for example, that one is entitled to his opinion that five times six is thirty-six or that the capitol of the United States is in North Carolina. Many of us take great pride in our tolerance. We count it a virtue to be able to grant to others their moral judgments which are contrary to our own without feeling any disturbance whatever. In areas where we think truth is possible, contrary opinions on the part of others disturb us, unless we are prepared simply to reject theirs as false by some general way of discrediting the people concerned.

We hold that one's factual beliefs can be shaped either by conditioning or by instruction. In general, we tend to oppose efforts to instill beliefs in people by causal influence. We call it propaganda, indoctrination, or brainwashing. In the field of education, at least, we insist on instruction—on appeal to experience, reason, and insight.

The contrast between the techniques of propaganda, advertising, and indoctrination on the one hand and instruction on the other is well known. Briefly the difference is this. The goal of propaganda or indoctrination is to produce a certain frame of mind or set of beliefs and the means are chosen on the basis of their effectiveness in achieving this end. Passive, docile minds are preferred. An environment free from opposing influences is better. Only one side of issues is allowed to be voiced if possible. Everything unfavorable to the desired end is avoided. People are exposed over and over again under the most favorable conditions to expressions of the desired beliefs and attitudes. The aim of instruction, on the other hand, is to help those being taught to arrive at the truth, or at least the most probable beliefs, about the subject matter through the exercise of their own powers. Alert, active, critical minds are necessary for success. The student is taught to free himself through self-criticism of any perverting bias or prejudice. He is encouraged to examine all sides of the issues involved and to weigh carefully all relevant considerations. In education, more emphasis is put on developing the skills for success in such inquiries than in getting a student to accept a particular body of alleged truths.

While we hold, in our culture, that instruction is desirable in factual and logical matters, we tend to believe that only one approach is possible in the area of value judgments, namely, the way of conditioning, causal influence, propaganda, and indoctrination. If a political scientist in a course in American government, for example, goes beyond the facts and makes value judgments, he will be opposed by this faction or that. If he makes so-called "liberal" value judgments, he will be attacked by conservatives for injecting his own bias, for expressing his own personal and private opinions. If he makes conservative value judgments, he will be accused of being prejudiced. Whenever a person makes value judgments, he is regarded as being subjective, as merely expressing his own feelings and sentiments.

There has been a flurry of interest in recent years in developing methods for teaching values in public schools. One manual for teachers on the subject cautions the teacher to keep in mind that with regard to value questions there are no right answers. The method advocated is a process for the student to follow in arriving at his own answer to the value questions about his actions. In a given action-situation, the individual is to ask himself whether what he is doing, or considering doing, will really further what he wants. If he is fully informed about the facts of his situation and the likely effects of his action and he can still accept it as promoting what he wants, then there is nothing further for him to consider. All his value judgments are to be derived from his wants and knowledge of the facts. There is no such thing as educating his wants and feelings and emotions except for them to be enlightened by factual knowledge.

If a student learns this lesson well, how is he to react to the requirements of the curriculum and the regulations of the school when they conflict with his wants as they are actively present to him and the facts of the situation as he comprehends them? Can he be expected to see these requirements as anything more than what the teacher and the administration want and thus totally irrelevant to his wants except insofar as they have the power to impose their will on him? Consider the testimony of two young people. A seventeen-year-old girl from Madison, Wisconsin, wrote: "I don't know why my parents are such puritans. . . . Maybe they always wanted to have control over me . . . that's the way it turned out, at least for awhile. The first couple of times I did anything with boys I felt really uptight. My parents' teaching sort of haunted me. Fortunately, I'm now able to ignore them, and I can do whatever I want."[29] An eighteen-year-old boy from Greensboro, North Carolina, wrote: "All the institutions you come in contact with . . . families, schools, and the government put you into categories and packages. They don't let you be yourself. By the time you reach five years old you can't show natural emotions. You're so manipulated that an honest relationship with yourself is impossible. . . . We have to smash a system that controls peoples' lives. We should be able to enjoy life."[30] Dr. Seymour L. Halleck, formerly professor of psychiatry and director of student health psychiatry at the University of Wisconsin and now at Chapel Hill, says: "In my more recent work with students I have come to realize that their perceptions of the world are growing more and more like those of prisoners. . . . Many feel that they are trapped in a world that cannot or will not satisfy their needs."[31]

It was this subjectivistic view of value judgments that gave rise to the ideological theory of culture, which holds that the normative aspects of a culture, including social, economic, and political thought, morals, law, art, and religion, are simply instruments of the power structure of the society by which it imposes its will upon the society and cloaks its naked power with "legitimacy" and "respectability." "In the prevailing popular culture," Walter Lippmann says, "all philosophies are the instruments of some man's purpose, all truths are self-centered and self-regarding, all principles are the rationalizations of some special interest."[32]

Lippmann charges, in *The Public Philosophy*, that because of the popular assumption that value judgments are subjective and private and that value disagreements do not lend themselves to rational debate and resolution, our Western liberal democracies are deranged in their political institutions and incapable of responsible government. Our heads of state, he maintains, are puppets of an irrational, stupid, capricious, demanding sovereign, and can only try to manipulate, placate, and soothe him. This sovereign is public opinion. Our governments, he says, do not ask "What is right?" but only "What will be popular?"

There is little wonder that a crisis of authority exists. It is felt in the home, the school, the city, and the nation. This is true not only in America but in varying degrees throughout the Western world. No doubt society is more complex and more demanding as well as more difficult to comprehend, but can anyone believe that by any objective measure it is less just and more morally repressive than in earlier days? The structure of authority is crumbling largely from the erosion of its intellectual foundations. The philosophical assumptions on which authority as such, not just the authority of our existing institutions, is founded are being rapidly rejected in our culture, especially by the more self-aware and better educated of the younger generation, because of the apparent inconsistency of these assumptions with other deep and firm commitments of the modern Western mind.

To have moral authority, as distinct from epistemic authority (the authority of a specialist in an area of knowledge), is to have an office or position constituted by certain responsibilities and rights that involve making decisions that obligate certain others, at least prima facie, to accept and to comply with them, regardless of what their personal decision about the matter otherwise would have been. In the very nature of the case, the voice of authority is at least prima facie overriding for those subject to or obligated by the authority. Furthermore, the authority, or some other agency whose function it is, has the right and indeed the responsibility to enforce compliance. Such is the case with the parent, the teacher, the foreman, the judge, the legislative body, the head of state, etc. How can one be obligated by the decision of another in this way?

No one simply as a human being has authority over another. It is always with respect to some special office or position that one holds. The authority of a parent with respect to a minor child, for example, is not simply grounded in a biological fact but in an office defined by certain responsibilities and rights, an office that one may, under some conditions, voluntarily relinquish, and one from which one can be dismissed. Competence to fulfill the responsibilities and to exercise the rights of the office is assumed. The parent has the right and the responsibility to decide for the child and the child is subject to and is obligated to obey the parent in those areas in which the child is incompetent to decide for himself. As the child matures and becomes more and more capable of responsible self-direction, the responsibility and authority of the parent diminish accordingly until the office becomes purely honorary.

It is clear that one important factor in the authority of the parent in relation to his child and in the obligation of the child to accept the decision of his parent and to act on it, even though his own decision, if left unto himself, would have been quite different, is that the parent is in a better position to know what ought to be done and is more likely to make the right decision. Therefore, from the child's point of view, the rational thing for him to do in most cases, even without taking into account penalties for disobedience, is to accept and to act on the decision of the parent. Much the same is true for the whole structure of authority. If the offices that exercise authority are wisely constituted and if the general competence of officeholders is maintained, then those subject to the authority of a particular office have good reasons to comply with the authority in question quite apart from whatever penalties there may be for disobedience. And there are reasons for not disobeying the authority even when it is reasonably clear that the authority may be in error, for more than the merits of the particular case is at issue, namely, the structure of authority as such and its significance for the society.

But on the assumption that there is no value knowledge and that value judgments are subjective and private, all so-called "authority" collapses into a pure power structure. All institutionalized living, all conventional morality, all law enforcement become repressive. The individual feels himself smothered and destroyed by society and he is likely to strike out against it in whatever ways he can.

Paul Goodman tells[33] of his experience in a course on professionalism at the New School for Social Research in New York in the late sixties. He says that he developed the concept of a professional as one who acknowledges responsibility to only the nature of things, the judgments of his peers, and the interests of his client and the public. He brought to the class paradigm professionals from a number of fields to talk about their professions and professionalism. But the class of graduate students from several fields resisted the very concept of professionalism and denied the possibility of professionals. Goodman says that it took him some time to realize that the basis of their resistance was the rejection of the assumption that there is a nature of things for one to be responsible to in one's judgments. Without this assumption of course they couldn't acknowledge any reason for one to be responsible to the judgment of one's so-called "peers." And if there is no way to check one's judgments against the nature of things and no reason to check them against the judgments of others, then there is no rationale for any law, custom, or structure of authority. Social institutions are at best arbitrary but usually embodiments of special interests and always repressive and enslaving.

The subjectivistic view of moral experience and thought, however, does not mean the end of moral concern, but rather a transformation of it. Morality is a matter of what is fitting or unfitting for one to do as a human being; what is in accord with, fulfills, or does violence to our image of a person. When we come to believe, as we have for the most part in our culture, that there is no objective nature of a person for our moral judgments to be responsible to, and that all public moral judgments are expressions of what the power structure, for self-serving reasons, wants human beings to be, then anyone who accepts any form of public morality is seen as permitting the wants and decisions of others to constitute his own life rather than his being self-constituting and self-directing through his own decisions. Paradoxically it is said, as the existentialists do, that the self, in one sense devoid of any objective nature to which moral judgments could be responsible, is nevertheless free in the sense that it has no inherent normative structure and thus should be self-constituting and self-directing and that therefore the imposition of or acquiescence in someone else's or society's moral judgments would do violence to one's "nature" as a free human being. Thus from the traditional point of view morality becomes converted into anti-morality and heroes into anti-heroes. When this revolution occurs others must follow. The moral idealism and crusading of youth become to a large extent an attack on traditional values and established institutions. Many students today believe that individuals left unto themselves do no wrong; that it is only society that is morally evil and only the agents of society are capable of morally wrong deeds. Faced with this inverted morality, traditionalists are bewildered, for they cannot understand how all their cherished values and the wisdom of the ages can be assaulted by those who claim the moral heights for themselves.

The revolutionaries of recent years cry out for freedom and individualism as did our forefathers, but the concept of liberty has undergone a radical transformation along with the concept of morality. Individualism and freedom from within a subjectivistic point of view are radically different from individualism and freedom from within a perspective that acknowledges a normative structure in the nature of things which one can gain knowledge of through the critical use of his own epistemic powers. In the latter case, individual liberty is compatible with a rational social order; in the former case, a rational social order is not a possibility and individual freedom and institutionalized ways of doing things are antithetical.

According to Sartre, the free man is one who recognizes or feels no restraints or obligations from any source other than his own will, which is subject to nothing. There are no objective requirements or guidelines. Everything is permitted. "The existentialist," Sartre says, ". . . thinks that every man, without any support or help whatever, is condemned at every instant to invent man."[34]

Claiming that the end of all modern literature is "freedom from society itself," Lionel Trilling says, "I venture to say that the idea . . . of escaping wholly from societal bonds, is an 'element' somewhere in the mind of every modern person who dares to think of . . . 'the fullness of spiritual perfection.' "[35] This is the form of what Charles Reich, in *The Greening of America*,[36] calls consciousness III, the consciousness of the youth movement in contrast with the consciousness of traditionalists and conservatism (I) on the one hand and the old liberalism (II) on the other. "The foundation of Consciousness III is liberation," Reich says. "The meaning of liberation," he continues, "is that the individual is free to build his own philosophy and values, his own life-style, and his own culture from a new beginning."[37] The beginning for each is with himself, for as Reich says, "Consciousness III . . . declares that the individual self is the only true reality";[38] "its intent is to start from life";[39] "Because there are no governing standards, no one is rejected."[40] "Older people," Reich says, "are inclined to think of work, injustice and war, and of the bitter frustrations of life, as the human condition. Their capacity for outrage is consequently dulled. But to those who have glimpsed the real possibilities of life, who have tasted liberation and love, who have seen the promised land . . . ," Reich continues, "the most basic limitations of life—the job, the working day, the part one can play in life, the limits of sex, love and relationships, the limits of knowledge and experience—all vanish, leaving open a life that can be lived without the guideposts of the past."[41]

A young person, a graduate student, came to see me some time ago to talk about a personal problem. She had had a close, intimate love affair with a young man for several years. They both agreed, she said, that "freedom" is one of the beautiful words and so they wanted each other to be free. They agreed that neither was to make any demands on the other. And in their freedom both of them had had several affairs with others. But she found herself feeling that his relationship with her imposed some requirements and limitations on him and that she wanted to make demands on him. Yet she felt guilty because she wanted to make demands on him and was afraid that she was coming to hate him. Her problem was why couldn't she live with their freedom without these emotional complications. She, in her understanding of things, faulted only her emotional experiences, not her conception of freedom and the life-style it implied.

One might think it would be wonderful to be free in this sense—to recognize no rules, no requirements, no prohibitions. But the existentialist sees, even if Reich does not, that such a free man is forlorn and anguished. Marjorie Greene significantly entitled her book on the subject "Dreadful Freedom."[42] Even though freedom in this sense is possible only through aloneness, dread, and anguish, man, Sartre contends, is condemned to be free.

Although belief in the subjectivity of value judgments gives rise to resistance to the established ways of society and to the establishment on the part of individuals in search of their personal identity, it naturally leads to efforts on the part of the power structure of society to control the attitudes and value thought of the people. Where there is no conviction that free inquiring minds will move toward agreement by discovering an objective truth, it is felt that propaganda, indoctrination, censorship and the like must be employed to safeguard and to protect cherished institutions and ways of living, indeed to assure that consensus in attitudes necessary for society to function. These are not really contradictory results. The one is simply the reaction of the individual and the other the response of the society to the loss of faith in the possibility of value knowledge.

But there is a contradictory result. Value subjectivism arises from a theory of knowledge based on science as a paradigm. Yet value subjectivism undermines even the structure of scientific knowledge. This is so because the concept of knowledge embodies an essential value component. To claim to know even some scientific or mathematical proposition is not only to claim that it is true, but that one has *good* grounds or *justifying* reasons for the truth-claim, indeed that his reasons are so *good* that he does not need any *better* ones and that therefore for him the issue is settled. Furthermore, he claims that his "good reasons" are such that reasonable, informed people will acknowledge that his reasons are good and adequate and that his truth-claim is an expression of knowledge. Anyone who makes knowledge-claims of any kind or even engages in the pursuit of knowledge must acknowledge that some propositions are *unworthy* of acceptance, that whatever counts as evidence for any proposition makes it more *worthy* of belief, that two propositions which contradict one another are not both *worthy* of assent. Intellectual integrity, compliance with the ethics of thought, is an indispensible condition for science, mathematics, or any quest for knowledge. The ethics of thought as well as other modes of value-thought lose even the possibility of objective validity within a general value subjectivism. This undermines the possibility of knowledge in general. "Science," as Polanyi says, "can then no longer hope to survive on an island of positive facts, around which the rest of man's intellectual heritage sinks to the status of subjective emotionalism."[43]

Thus, in the sense in which the logical difficulty involved in our first philosophical problem forced elimination of value concepts from our descriptive-explanatory conceptual system and thereby gave rise to the death of God, the difficulty in our second perplexity has driven the modern mind toward general value subjectivism, thereby undermining the structure of authority, social institutions, and, if carried to its logical conclusions, even knowledge in general.

Our third philosophical perplexity focuses on man himself. It concerns the ways in which we talk about human beings and their behavior. In ordinary discourse, we appraise human behavior as rational or irrational, responsible or irresponsible, justified or unjustified, praise-worthy or blameworthy, excusable or inexcusable, defensible or indefensible, correct or in error, and the like. We so appraise, at least in part, our sensory experiences, feelings, emotions, attitudes, desires, longings, ambitions, purposes, intentions, decisions, plans, policies, promises, projects, beliefs, thoughts, assumptions, memories, statements, and actions of whatever kind. We could not be agents engaged in knowing, doing, and undertaking things without being subject to such appraisals.

Rational appraisal use of value language involves semantic and logical concepts as well, for anything which does not embody a structure of meaning in some mode or which is unresponsive to that which is semantically present and to the matrix of logical relationships within the structure of meaning is not rational in the sense of being the kind of thing that can be shaped and moved by reasons and therefore is subject to mistakes and errors as well as to getting things right.

We are also deeply committed in our culture to bringing human behavior, including our experiences, thoughts, and overt acts, under the blanket of science. We ask the modern scientific "why?" of behavioral events and demand a scientific description and explanation of them as events among other events, as subject to the same kind of change and causality as physical and biological happenings. We are largely committed, or so it seems, to the development of psychology and the social sciences after the model of the natural sciences. We look to them for the kind of knowledge of behavior, society, and social change that will be power for the manipulation and control of behavior in a process of human and social engineering. Yet the language of science tends to crowd out or to render inapplicable the rational appraisal use of value concepts just as much as it does the descriptive and explanatory uses.

Let us consider several cases. Suppose a man gets up one morning with a radical change in his personality. All his life he has been a quiet, even-tempered, cautious, considerate, and thoroughly responsible person in word and deed. Yet on a particular morning and thereafter he behaves in quite a contrary manner. He is loud, abusive, aggressive, quick to anger, wild, inconsiderate, unpredictable, and undependable. Let us suppose further that a medical examination reveals that he suffered a mild stroke during the night before the change. In so far as his family and associates accepted the medical report as the explanation for his unusual behavior, they would not feel that he was subject to rational appraisal. He would not be taken at face value as a person, to be confronted on equal terms with oneself and to be reasoned with, rationally appraised, and held responsible for what he says and does. They would treat him more as a thing to be explained, manipulated, causally controlled, and changed.

Look at our response to the riots of blacks in our cities in the sixties.

On the one hand the police, the courts, the lawmakers, and the public at large rationally appraised the rioters for their destruction, brutality, and lawlessness. Some were arrested, convicted, and sent to prison. Yet we give sociological and psychological explanations of why the riots occurred. In so far as we think of the conditions cited in these explanations as causes of the riots, in the usual scientific sense of causation, we tend to become bothered about rational appraisal of the persons involved in much the same manner as we do with the man who has suffered the stroke.

As we extend and more widely accept the scientific study of criminal behavior in general, we become more uneasy with rational appraisal of criminals. We tend to think that criminals need treatment, being changed through the manipulation of the causes of their behavior, rather than punishment, which is increasingly regarded as primitive and unenlightened. Those who used to be called wicked are now almost universally regarded as sick. This represents a basic category shift.

But science does not restrict itself to the study of erratic and criminal behavior. It seeks to give a scientific description and explanation of the ordinary as well as of the extraordinary. This means that all behavior, including the experience and thought of scientists, is brought under the observational language of science and the categories of scientific explanation. When this happens, rational appraisal language seems to be crowded out completely. It is left no territory at all.

Yet rational appraisal language and all that it presupposes and implies would appear to be absolutely indispensable. The psychologist and the social scientist, at the very least, must appraise their own scientific activity, if not the behavior of their subjects, in rational appraisal terms. But they cannot claim a privileged position for themselves. To the extent they acknowledge the meaningful application of this team of concepts to their own behavior they must on pain of inconsistency acknowledge that they are applicable also to the behavior of their subjects. Thus to regard the mental or, in the broadest terms, the behavioral as an empirical detail in the world of objects, subject to scientific observation, description, and explanation in the manner of natural events, is to be doomed to paradox, antinomy, and philosophical perplexity.

This is the old problem of freedom versus determinism. Rational appraisal language defines the area of freedom and indicates what it is to be free. The language of scientific description and explanation defines the area of naturalistic determinism and wherein it is deterministic.

The result of the clash between these two teams of concepts has not been simply philosophical perplexity. Efforts to bring different modes of experience under the categories of scientific thought tend to crowd out the meaningful application of semantic, logical, and epistemic categories, leaving a subjective, private realm of occurrences and states of affairs as the objects of knowledge. This way of thinking about experience has driven the modern mind toward skepticism about the powers of the human mind for knowledge of and meaningful talk about an external reality, impoverishing our world, even thrusting us toward total subjectivism and solipsism. David Hume maintained that only carelessness and inattention in thought could save us from this end. "Subjectivity," Irving Howe says, in writing about modernism in literature, "becomes the typical condition of the modernist outlook. . . . Modernism . . . keeps approaching—sometimes even penetrating—the limits of solipsism, the view expressed by the poet Gottfried Benn when he writes that 'there is no outer reality, there is only human consciousness, constantly building, modifying, rebuilding new worlds out of its own creativity.' "[44] Men do not fare very well with the life-style of an Augustinian god. They need the objections of an external, independent reality to cope with in order to be themselves. In commenting on the youth of today, Paul Goodman remarks that "they do not have enough world to have much character."[45] Subjectivism not only diminishes man by diminishing or eliminating his world; it destroys society and its institutions by diminishing or destroying the public world.

But more directly, to bring man under the blanket of empirical scientific categories threatens his very identity. Man, speaking from our ordinary, commonsense perspective, is uniquely and essentially that being who encounters himself as a being-in-the-world. He is indeed a *human* being only by virtue of the specific way in which he categorially delineates himself and the world in his self-encounter and the image of man-in-the-world thereby formed. We may appropriately speak of this as the humanistic image of man-in-the-world.

It is not simply a descriptive account grounded in observation of an independent subject-matter and therefore subject to error in a simple, straightforward way. In a significant sense, it is an "analytic" image in that it is or can be both true of and constitutive of man. Like a human act, which can be correctly described only in terms of its internal conceptual structure as found in the intention and self-knowledge of the agent, man can be correctly conceived only in terms of the internal conceptual structure that constitutes him in his self-knowledge as an agent experientially and actively involved in the world. Man is what he is because he knows himself in terms of this image. Moral concern, for example, is awareness of what is required of one and what one is entitled to *as a human being* in the various situations of life. Without the humanistic self-image one would not be capable of moral consciousness and therefore would not be the moral, social, and political being that he is; one could not seek self-expression and understanding of the human condition in art and literature; one could not have religious concern about the meaning and worth of human existence; indeed one could not have any of our distinctively human needs, aspirations, and achievements. In short, without the image of man-in-the-world indigenous in man's self-encounter, he would not be a man at all, but some other kind of being. Anything that threatens or perverts this image threatens or perverts man himself.

Existentialists have seen that man is constituted by his conception of himself. However, they are in error, I believe, in taking man's self-image to be a product of his arbitrary or unguided decision. It is the conceptual delineation inherent in man's self-encounter as a being-in-the-world. The encounter is a happening that has the character of both discovery and creation. In an important sense to be and to have self-knowledge are indistinguishable for persons. They happen and emerge together. One is what one encounters oneself as. If one has a perverted self-image one is a perverted self. But the very fact that we make sense out of talk about perversion of both the image and the self indicates that there is something to which both are responsible and with which we cannot play fast and loose. It is that *to be actualized* in self-existence and in self-knowledge and therefore is normative. Furthermore, the categorial aspect of the conceptual structure inherent in normal self-knowledge seems to be universal.

But science, in its study of man, begins with behavioristic data as available to sensory observation, granted epistemic status for the time being, and pushes on to neurophysiological processes, biochemical connections, and finally to theoretical entities and theoretical structures. Man, from within this perspective, is seen as a purely physical system, devoid of any structure of meaning, logical relationships, and value structures, with all occurrences naturalistically caused. Thus the humanistic image of man-in-the-world, and even man himself, since, as previously remarked, he is what he is by virtue of his humanistic image of himself, seem to be threatened. A psychologist friend of mine remarked that a typical symptom of psychosis is thinking of oneself and others as things, and yet, he says, most of his colleagues think of people in just this way.

We all seem to be in the plight of the black man on trial for murder. His attorney, according to the story, pleads before the court that the defendant had grown up in the squalor of a black ghetto in the inner city, he had lived as a child in a rat-infested two-room apartment with the other eight members of his family, he had had to fight and to steal to stay alive, his world had always been hostile and threatening, and so forth. He argued that there are sociological and psychological explanations of his client's behavior in terms of his environment and its effects on him, and that therefore, he is neither responsible nor blameworthy for his action, and that society should change the conditions that gave rise to his behavior rather than punish him. Whereupon the defendant stands up in court and repudiates his attorney, saying: "The court may find me guilty of the charge and execute me, but, if my attorney is correct, I am blotted out entirely; I never was."

B. F. Skinner, perhaps the most influential of contemporary psychologists, in his book, *Beyond Freedom and Dignity*,[46] announces the post-human era. Man has been absorbed into the empirical subject-matter of science, and is regarded as fully describable and explainable in scientific categories. This means, when taken to its logical conclusions, that personalitistic and humanistic concepts have no place in the language of knowledge and that, ontologically speaking, there are no persons, neither divine nor human.

"Unable to understand how or why the person we see behaves as he does," Skinner says, "we attribute his behavior to a person we cannot see, whose behavior we cannot explain either, but about whom we are not inclined to ask questions. . . . Explanation stops with him. He is not a mediator between past history and current behavior; he is a *center* from which behavior emanates. He initiates, originates and creates, and in doing so, he remains, as he was for the Greeks, divine. We say that he is autonomous—and so far as the science of behavior is concerned, that means miraculous. . . . Autonomous man serves to explain only the things we are not yet able to explain in other ways. Autonomous man's existence depends upon our ignorance and he naturally loses status as we come to know more about behavior."[47]

There is little room for doubt that the spiritual blight in our culture is at least partly a result of our impoverished view of the world and of our confused and troubled sense of identity as human beings. Floyd Matson says: "The tragic history of the breaking of the human image parallels the disintegration of the inner sense of identity, the flight from autonomous conduct to automaton behavior, in the modern world."[48] Rollo May says that the sin of modern psychology is that it has reduced man from a Dantean tragic figure to a trivial being.[49] Hobart Mowrer, a clinical psychologist, writes: "The same pre-suppositions and intellectual operations that have given us such unprecedented power over nature when extended to ourselves produces a pervasive feeling of helplessness, confusion, resignation, desperation. . . . By the very principles and premises that have led to the conquest of the outer world, we ourselves lose our autonomy, dignity, self-mastery, responsibility, indeed our very identity. Little wonder, then," he continues, "that we feel weak, lost, fearful, 'beat.' Being part of nature, we, too, apparently obey strict cause-and-effect principles. And if this be true, . . . the whole notion of purpose, responsibility, meaning seems to vanish."[50]

This is a sad tale. It is not only that God is dead, that the intellectual foundations of our structures of authority and social institutions are being washed away, and that knowledge and the external world are threatened by skepticism and subjectivism, but even man himself seems about to vanish into nothingness. We have firm intellectual commitments that appear to be driving us relentlessly toward the abyss like lemmings being driven to the sea. Little wonder there is a general spiritual depression and impotence of the heart. For those who feel the full impact of all of this, with a sense of no contact with reality and loss of selfhood and personal identity, life is a Kafkaesque dream-like trip. Conrad Aiken put well the condition of modern man in these words:

> We need a theme? Then let that be our theme:
> that we, poor grovellers between faith and doubt,
> the sun and north star lost, and compass out,
> the heart's weak engine all but stopped, the time
> timeless in this chaos of our wills—
> that we must ask a theme, something to think,
> something to say, between dawn and dark,
> something to hold to, something to love.[51]

3. The great revolution in Western civilization

The classical Greek, Hebraic, and Christian cultures were generated by man standing in the world asking primarily "What does reality require of me? How can I fulfill these requirements? How can I become what I ought to be and do what I ought to do?" There were all the other concerns of man, of course, but they exerted less influence on the culture. This dominant orientation toward the world quite naturally developed a culture fitted to these objectives. Knowledge was conceived and developed in such a way that it would be useful in the human enterprise thus directed. The intellectual dimension of the culture was shaped largely by religious, moral, social, and political concerns and by those engaged in serving them. Enterprises given to meeting the material needs of man, although they involved great skill and practical knowledge, did not, for the most part, engage nor attract the attention of those caught up in intellectual pursuits. Medicine, art, architecture, warfare, and navigation were areas which tended to thrust practical concerns into the sphere of the intellectual, but these did not come to dominate the intellectual life until modern times.

The humanistic view of knowledge generated by the classical orientation of man toward the world presented semantically a rich, multidimensional world which engaged man in all areas of experience and thought and provided ontological grounding for the various sectors of culture and support for the existing social structures. The world thus delineated embraced physical space, social space, logical space, time and eternity; physical particulars, organic beings, persons, social entities, and universals; structures of fact, value, meaning, and necessity; and a complex structure of change and causality involving value, meaning, and necessity as well as fact. This categorial structure, the ground plan of the world, lent itself to being fleshed out in rich detail in the culture and the consciousness of the people in a way that would activate and develop all of man's powers, and perhaps this was more or less achieved at times for some. But the material conditions of the lives of most made for both material and spiritual poverty.

The culture-generating stance of Western man shifted between the thirteenth and the seventeenth centuries to that of man standing before the world asking, "How can I get what I want? How can I impose my will upon the world? How can I manipulate, control, and exploit it for my own purposes?" This shift wrought the great revolution in Western civilization, which is only now approaching its climax.

The new situation gave rise to fresh ways of looking at things and to a kind of knowledge that is power, that is know-how, in the manipulation and control of things. It was thus that modern science was born. It was no accident that the new science served technology. The scientific method and the scientific mentality were forged from within a technological orientation. This is not to deny that there is pure science distinct from technology. Most scientists, no doubt, are concerned with and motivated by purely intellectual problems. They want only to know and to understand their subject matter. But what I am saying is that the scientific methodology, conception of knowledge and of explanation, and indeed the whole conceptual system within which the modern pure scientist operates have been shaped from within and by this modern attitude toward the world.

Within the scientific approach, we count as relevant and genuine only such knowledge as would at least in principle be useful in making, manipulating, and controlling things. The correlative of this is that we count as real only that which we would have to take account of and deal with in controlling and manipulating changes in our world. As the dominant concern of Western man became that of imposing his will upon his world, the modern scientific conception of knowledge became dominant in the culture.

Since we can manipulate and change by physical action only the factual structures of things and since we obtain knowledge of factual structures only through sensory perception, we come to regard sensory perception as our only data-gathering, knowledge-yielding faculty. Therefore it is taken as providing us with all the semantic ties between language and the world and thus as the foundation of our descriptive and explanatory concepts. Furthermore, sensory perception is said to provide us with all the evidence on which the house of knowledge is built. It follows, of course, that in our philosophical view of the world we must take reality to be categorially the way it is delineated in the conceptual system of empirical science. This is modern naturalism. The rich, multidimensional classical world shrinks in its categorial structure to the physical space-time continuum occupied by physical particulars with a factual structure and an appropriately simplified form of change and causality. And even this is threatened by the apparent truth that such a view of the world renders the knowledge on which it is based impossible.

Once we accept the naturalistic view of knowledge and the world, traditional Western culture is disturbed in its very foundations. It constitutes the most radical revolution that has ever occurred in any society. It has given rise to intense intellectual cramps and philosophical perplexities, restructured the culture and the consciousness of the people, and transformed our social structures and institutions. But the fundamental problems throughout this revolution have been and still are philosophical. Never has philosophy had such an opportunity and never has it worked with greater vigor and ingenuity. This is true not only for professional philosophers. Every man has had to be his own philosopher at some level in coming to terms with the tensions in his own consciousness as he tried to digest the internalized ambivalent culture with its new and inherited commitments. The revolution taking place in the foundations of Western civilization surfaced in the reflective consciousness of philosophers in the seventeenth century and philosophers have been preoccupied with these problems until this day. Philosophy and the modern mind have struggled and moved together to adjust to and to work out the conceptual incongruities occasioned in our way of life by the great revolution. It has all but achieved, according to the beliefs of many, a coherent system of categorial beliefs and a world view on naturalistic terms. Here philosophy and the modern mind for the most part have kept in step. Scientific method and its categories have been widely assimilated. All that is inconsistent with the basic attitude of modern man and the naturalistic view of knowledge and reality tends to get crowded out. Whatever is incompatible with naturalism yields in one way or another, even though it may take centuries for it to be completely uprooted. Much of the legacy of the Greek-Hebraic-Christian civilization is still with us in the twentieth century, but it is being eliminated at a more rapid rate than ever before. This is due to the success of our educational system with ever wider sections of the population, especially at the college and university levels. The more knowledgeable and self-aware the people become the more they feel the ambivalences and logical incongruencies within our culture and as they struggle toward consistency, the more purely naturalistic they become, with the consequences we have already indicated. Those wedded to the classical elements in our culture have long feared the effects of modern education.

Lionel Trilling, in writing about how his students respond to his course on modern literature at Columbia University, says: "One response . . . —the readiness of the students to engage in the process that we might call the socialization of the anti-social, or the acculturation of the anticultural, or the legitimization of the subversive. When the term-essays come in, it is plain to one that almost none of the students have been taken aback by what they have read. . . . The chief exceptions are the few who simply do not comprehend, although they may be awed by, the categories of our discourse. In their papers, like poor hunted creatures in a Kafka story, they take refuge first in misunderstood large phrases, then in bad grammar, then in general incoherence. After my pedagogical exasperation has run its course, I find that I am sometimes moved to give them a queer respect, as if they had stood up and said what in fact they don't have the wit to stand up and say: 'Why do you harry us? Leave us alone. We are not Modern Man. We are the Old People. Ours is the Old Faith. We serve the little Old Gods, the gods of the copybook maxims, the small dark, somewhat powerful deities of lawyers, doctors, engineers, accountants. With them is neither sensibility nor *angst*. With them is no disgust—it is they indeed, who make ready the way for "the good and the beautiful" about which low-minded doubts have been raised in this course, that "good and beautiful" which we do not possess and don't want to possess but, which we know justifies our lives. Leave us alone and let us worship our gods in the way they approve, in peace and unawareness.' Crass," Trilling says, "but . . . authentic. The rest, the minds that give me the A papers and the B papers and even the C+ papers, move through the terrors and mysteries of modern literature like so many Parsifals, asking no questions at the behest of wonder and fear. Or like so many seminarists who have been systematically instructed in the constitution of Hell and the ways to damnation. . . . I asked them to look into the abyss, and, both dutifully and gladly, they have looked into the abyss. . . ."[52]

In our effort to get what we want and to impose our will upon the world, we made a Faustian bargain in the early modern period. At the dawn of the modern awareness in the age of Enlightenment, the new age was greeted with great joy, for it was seen that the new science would not only give us power to get what we want and to impose our will on the world, but that general acceptance of the scientific patterns of thought in our intellectual life would liberate the emotions and will of man from all of his deep, dark fears and inner restraints. Preserved Smith says: "The noxious germ of superstition can no more flourish in a world flooded with the light of science than can the germ of tuberculosis flourish in the beams of the sun, even though a few germs linger on and develop sporadically. The greatest triumphs of science," he continues, "have been not its material achievements, wonderful as these are, but the diffusion of the bright light of knowledge and the consequent banishment of ghosts and bugaboos created by man's fears of the dark."[53]

We are all acutely aware at last that in our conquest of nature through science and technology we are endangering man himself. The waste from our production and consumption threatens the life-supporting powers of our environment. But the "liberation" of man's inner life through scientific enlightenment may prove to be even more damaging by undermining and destroying the life-supporting and life-sustaining dimensions of culture. We have not only banished the ghosts and bugaboos which fed our fears but also the gods that nourished our loves and hopes and sustained our higher emotions and life-morale.

When a culture's intellectual vision of man and his world is so impoverished that it perverts man, impairs his world, and dries up the life-supporting dimensions of his culture, the spirit of man will in time no doubt reassert itself, but most likely in the form of a revolutionary consciousness which repudiates rationality and intellectualism in favor of experience, passion, and will. But these, freed from the guidance and support of intellectual structures and the critical assessment of reason, tend to become demonic. The human tragedy seems to be that man is condemned to fluctuate between deranged intellect and its offspring, demonic passion. Euripides in the Bacchae masterfully portrays the ruthless vengeance of Dionysus, the god of emotion and passion, on those who refuse to recognize him. Aeschylus, in the Oresteia trilogy, presents the conflict between Apollo, the young god of reason, and the Furies, the primitive goddesses of woman and Earth, the sources of life.

This drama has been played out in modern history in struggles between mass cultural movements. The medieval Christian synthesis, grounded in man's total experiential and active involvement with his world but with a primary emphasis on moral and religious concerns, embodied an intellectual structure which acknowledged a multidimensional world with a fourfold structure of fact, value, meaning, and necessity, all interlaced with one another. It was a culture oriented towards man's higher emotions and spiritual needs. It sought to define what reality requires of man and to provide him with the inner resources and cultural supports for becoming what he ought to be and doing what he ought to do. But it became one-sided, overextended, too rigid and immuned from the corrective powers of the human mind and spirit. Its virtues became perverted into vices, as is the way with all civilizations in their decline. So the Christian synthesis began to unravel in the early modern period and man gradually changed his stance in the world and began to reorder his priorities in favor of his wants and desires rather than his higher emotions and spiritual needs. This amounted to a new conception of the good life. Renaissance rationality, although humanistic, became, under the influence of the new priorities, primarily a matter of right reason and virtuous action in the affairs of men in pursuit of the new values. This provoked the counter-Renaissance, the Protestant Reformation. Sensing the erosion of the intellectual foundations of Christianity and perversion of its institutionalized form, the Protestants attacked the Renaissance exaltation of reason and reaffirmed primitive Christianity from within a general framework of irrationalism and anti-intellectualism, repudiating reason, in the words of Luther, as "The harlot of the devil."

The impact on the intellectual life of the West of the scientific reformation of this era and its promise through technology and industrialization, as we have previously observed, generated the second phase of the Renaissance, the so-called Age of Enlightenment, which blossomed in the eighteenth century and is still much alive. It is largely what motivates public support for education and research today.

But there has been a continuing revolt. The second upsurge of irrationalism, the first being the Protestant Reformation, was the Romantic movement which swept across Europe and America in the nineteenth century. The romantics challenged the belief that the advancement of knowledge, as it was by then widely conceived, made for greater happiness. Rationalism (in contrast with irrationalism, not empiricism) was attacked, as H. G. Schenk says, "not on the grounds that the intellectual results yielded by it were false, but rather on the grounds that they were inadequate or in other words that an essential part of human nature was being starved."[54] The romantics had a nostalgia for the past, often for the Middle Ages, a craving for the primitive, and a foreboding for the future. Whenever man's intellectual, institutional, and social structures become, for whatever reasons, divorced from his feelings, emotions, and vital concerns, he develops cravings for and tends to return to simple, elemental experiences for renewal and support. The present emphasis among our youth on personal relationships, community, the ways of the primitive, folk-culture, handicrafts, the earth, nature, and the like, which is a continuation of the romantic revolt, manifests cultural deficiencies and profound cravings of the human spirit.

But in much of romanticism, existentialism, and the life-styles of the "liberated" youth of today we have Dionysus, with ignorance of Apollo. Passion, emotion, and will without limits. No bounds. No requirements. The story of the *Bacchae* is being reenacted. Dionysus denied again by the derangement of reason turns demonic.

4. Diagnosis of our present cultural condition

Is man indeed a tragic being, condemned to shifting between a deranged intellectual life and a reacting demonic spirit? Is there an inherent flaw in the constitution of man, what Christians have called original sin, so that he is incapable of achieving a healthy functioning mind and spirit through the exercise of his own powers? Or is Aeschylus right in the *Eumenides*? Is it possible to resolve the conflict between Apollo and the Furies, as he does, with the transformation of the Furies into Eumenides? This was a conversion of evil spirits into goddesses of good will through their acknowledgment and acceptance of rationality. But are the constitutional principles of the mind such that reason can acknowledge feeling and emotion and the full spectrum of human experience and give them their rightful place so that they can accept rationality?

We seem to face three and only three possibilities. (1) The philosophical assumptions which constitute the modern mind are correct formulations of the constitutional principles of the human mind and the categorial structure of the world. (2) The constitutional principles of the human mind are themselves deranged so that we cannot through the exercise of the natural powers of the human mind in accordance with its own inherent normative structure know and cope with reality and live successfully. And (3) the modern Western mind is deranged by virtue of false philosophical assumptions about the constitutional principles and powers of the human mind so that we are systematically thwarted in our efforts to know and to cope with reality. If we were to accept (1) with all of its implications, life would seem to be absurd and we would have no choice but to grit our teeth and to bear its consequences or take flight from reason and reality through cultural illusions or drugs. On the basis of (2), as we remarked earlier, man is indeed a tragic being. He is condemned by a flaw within his own nature over which he could not possibly gain control. The only hope conceivable would be some form of redemption or transformation by external forces, divine or evolutionary. But if (3) is true, then the impoverishment of our culture and the spiritual malaise of modern man are functions of correctable error within our cultural mind, giving rise to a gap between our emerging subjectivistic culture and the structure of reality. This is the most likely and the most hopeful hypothesis. Certainly neither of the others should be accepted until this one has been thoroughly investigated and discredited.

There are two ways in which a deranged cultural mind may be changed or corrected. In the historical process, forces may work to alter man's basic culture-generating attitude toward the world. Christian culture, for example, was generated by a primary concern with man's higher emotions and the values to which they were related; whereas our modern culture is a product of our preoccupation with our materialistic desires and their values. Thus the role of reason and knowledge shifted from the service of morality and religion to the service of materialistic values. It was then that the spokesmen for morality and religion began to attack reason and to sing the praises of irrationalism. It is possible that historical forces are already at work reordering our priorities in favor of the higher emotions once again. But, as we have already indicated, the dialectical unfolding of the historical process seems to swing from one imbalance to another and not to be really corrective. This, perhaps, is what gives rise to the tragic view of life—to the view that the flaw lies within the constitution of the mind as such.

The second way, philosophical therapy, is most difficult and may further pervert the culture, but it can be corrective, especially in an age when historical forces are already at work changing our culture-generating attitude toward life and the world as the present gives some indications of being. We are being shaken in our cultural provincialism in much the same way as Newtonian physics was disturbed in its foundations at the end of the last century. Leading scientists then became profoundly concerned with the philosophy of science in their efforts to understand and to gain a mastery of what was happening in their own discipline. In the current period of cultural upheaval we should be seriously concerned with the philosophical foundations of our culture and vigorously explore the constitutional principles of the human mind for the possibility of an expanded and enriched intellectual perspective grounded in the full spectrum of experience which would support and nourish the human spirit as well as our technology and again transform the Furies into Eumenides.

III

Philosophy and
Cultural Therapy

Our analysis of the modern Western mind presents us with deep, vast, and overwhelming problems. They concern, as I have tried to point out, our cultural ways of semantically relating to and appropriating the world and therefore affect every facet of our lives. Error at this level systematically perverts our efforts to know and to cope with reality. In addition to a general undefined feeling that something is wrong with our way of life, such errors, as we have already seen, generate intellectual cramps which drive us to philosophical examinaton of the trouble spots in our culture. So we have a right to ask what, in this time of cultural crisis, can we expect from philosophy?

In an article in *Time* some years ago[1] with a similar question for its title, the answer given was "nothing," or at most "nothing important." Philosophers were said to be "relatively obscure academic technicians." "When reason is overturned, blind passions are rampant, and urgent questions mount," the essayist said, "men turn for guidance to scientists, psychiatrists, sociologists, ideologues, politicians, journalists, almost anyone except their traditional guide, the philosopher." "Many feel," the writer continues, "that philosophy has played out its role in the history of human culture." William O'Neill expressed a frequent complaint when he said that in our time there has been an "increasing alienation of philosophy from life" by its gradual transformation "into a more or less narrow and self-conscious sort of detached intellectual game," and that it is "committing suicide through a process of progressive trivialization."[2] Lewis S. Feuer says American philosophy is dead. "The intellectual history of contemporary America could be written today," he contends, "virtually without mention of its . . . professional philosophers."[3] Richard Schlatter, General Editor of *The Princeton Studies in Humanistic Scholarship in America,* said in the foreword of the volume on philosophy, "the present essays leave me with the impression that we have had in recent years no giants who are philosophers pure and simple rather than scholars and historians. Not many of the names mentioned in these pages are recognizable as those of great intellectual leaders and many are unknown even to an old academic hand like myself who has a fair speaking acquaintance with the various humanistic disciplines in America."[4]

It cannot be denied that, although our modern culture has generated more than its share of philosophical problems and a number of philosophical giants, the direction of our cultural development has progressively called into question philosophy as an intellectual discipline, undermined public confidence in it, especially in the intellectual community, and occasioned self-doubt, timidity, and caution on the part of philosophers themselves. We see this already in John Locke in the latter part of the seventeenth century. In "The Epistle to the Reader" of his major work, *An Essay Concerning Human Understanding,* Locke wrote: "I shall always have the satisfaction to have aimed sincerely at truth and usefulness, *though in one of the meanest ways* [Italics added]. The commonwealth of learning is not at this time without master builders, whose mighty designs, in advancing the sciences, will leave lasting monuments to the admiration of posterity; but everyone must not hope to be a Boyle or a Syndenham: and in an age that produces such masters as the great Huygenius and the incomparable Mr. Newton, with some others of that strain, it is ambition enough to be employed as an under-labourer in clearing the ground a little, and removing some of the rubbish that lies in the way to knowledge. . . . " He goes on to indicate that the rubbish to be cleared away by the philosopher consists of "uncouth, affected, or unintelligible terms," "vague and insignificant forms of speech and abuse of language," and "hard and misapplied words, with little or no meaning." Wittgenstein of our own century and his disciples, while fighting skepticism in general, the bogy of modern philosophy, by trying to show that it is a product of bewitchment of the mind by language, operates with an empiricistic conception of knowledge that generates skepticism about philosophy as an intellectual discipline and denial that there is such a thing as philosophical knowledge. The objective of philosophy is seen as relief from philosophical perplexity by liberation from the bewitchment of language so that we can get on with the proper uses of language in ordinary life situations and the legitimate disciplines.

This is a far cry from the grand conception of philosophy as the highest form of intellectual life, the queen of the sciences, the spectator of all time and eternity, and the guide of life. Philosophy itself has been something of a casuality of the derangement of the modern mind. The shift that has taken place in the philosophical assumptions constitutive of our cultural mind has worked a transformation in the way we view the world and understand the different sectors of culture. The empirical sciences and their tool, mathematics, have been elevated to a position of dominance. Religion, theology, and the whole normative dimension of culture have been reduced to superstition at worst and to ideology at best. And philosophy is conceived as the task of underlaborers clarifying the language of science or liberating people from the bewitchment of words. This is not so much a change in the subject matter of philosophy as a shift in the way its subject matter is understood, a transformation occasioned by the great revolution in Western civilization.

Although the impact of the modern mind on philosophy as a discipline has generated a demeaning and often perverting self-understanding and impaired its standing within the intellectual community and its ability to cope with the philosophical problems of our culture, it is, nevertheless, in my judgment, concerned with the profoundest problems of the human mind and the most significant troubles in our culture. Philosophy, quite apart from any perversion in its self-conception, has had to become highly technical to cope with its problems and in doing so even those engaged in it often become preoccupied with the trees and lose sight of the forest. Outsiders seldom know what the problems are; nor are they able to follow the details and see the significance of them. But important work is being done, often by philosophers who are themselves too timid within the prevailing intellectual climate to claim much for it. Nevertheless philosophy does not offer ordinary wisdom for solving ordinary problems. It never did. At best it offers philosophical wisdom concerning the constitutional principles of experience, thought, and action. Philosophers are constitutional lawyers, so to speak; not ordinary lawyers concerned with run-of-the-mill "legal" problems. No individual nor the culture at large can ignore philosophy and hope to come to grips with the basic problems of life in our time.

The philosopher is, to be sure, liable to being victimized along with everyone else by the cultural derangement. He shares the general cultural commitments. If he did not, he would never suffer from philosophical perplexity and thus would never be aroused to philosophical reflection and inquiry. But how can we turn to philosophical thought to free us from the derangement if it is itself subject to being corrupted by the madness? Of course there is no guarantee that philosophy will cure us. It may very well, and often does, make the malady worse. If taken seriously, it can be a dangerous thing. We observed earlier how existentialism interprets what we have regarded as a sickness of spirit and cultural malaise as the normal, healthy state of human consciousness. We see all around us today a form of liberation embraced as a cultural ideal which leaves the individual a formless nothing cut off from all life-supporting relationships. Analytic philosophy also, in my judgment, is largely victimized by the prevailing categorial assumptions in our culture in such a way that it seldom transcends the current cultural perspective sufficiently to consider seriously other possibilities. It is, of course, difficult for philosophy to transcend the categorial assumptions of the age. Philosophy in medieval Europe was said to be the handmaiden of theology. It is equally true that philosophy in the modern age has been the handmaiden of science. In each case philosophy, at least that which gained a hearing in the culture, tended to justify the prevailing categorial assumptions. But the judgment of the philosopher need not simply endorse the culture. The philosopher, through exploring the categorial incompatibilities in the way his culture functions, can gain a perspective which makes possible a responsible judgment on it, whether it be negative or affirmative. His court of ultimate appeal, as Kant realized, is the constitutional principles of the human mind, the categorial structure of experience and thought. Whatever in our assumptions, beliefs, and cultural ways that is incompatible with these is in error and needs correction. Only philosophical reflection and inquiry can locate and expose such errors and work deliberately and intelligently for their correction.

There are two dominant methods of philosophy practiced in the Western world today, namely, phenomenology and linguistic analysis. Phenomenology attempts to get at the essential structure of experience and thought and their objects by direct intuitive inspection. It is not argumentative in character, but purports to be presuppositionless, empirical in an introspective sense, and descriptive. Linguistic analysis, as I interpret it, spurred by philosophical perplexities, attempts, through a systematic analysis of language and exploration of what it makes sense to say about that which is semantically located through language, to get at and to give a coherent account of the categorial structure of experience and thought and of the world as it is available to our epistemic powers. When practiced by one who has a broad philosophical perspective and a feel for philosophical problems, linguistic analysis can, I believe, be a more subtle, disciplined, responsible, and fruitful method than phenomenological intuition.

Critics and even practitioners of the discipline sometimes think of philosophical linguistic analysis simply as a straightforward study of word usage and grammatical forms in a way that confuses philosophy with lexicography and ordinary grammatical studies. For some this may reduce philosophy to a form that is intellectually respectable under prevailing views and assumptions, but separation of questions concerning the meaning and form of language from philosophical problems about knowledge and reality takes them out of the philosophical arena. This happens sometimes, perhaps, but more often than not the epistemological and metaphysical issues are simply kept out of sight while assumptions and prejudices about them shape the efforts at "clarification" of bits and pieces of language. I shall attempt to bring the epistemological issues to the surface and show how they are involved in philosophical clarification of language and the resulting resolution of metaphysical issues.

Philosophical perplexity and reflection, as we observed in the first chapter, are generated by felt inconsistencies, conceptual incongruities, and logical oddities in the ways we experience and think about things. These difficulties, unlike the inconsistencies that give rise to ordinary thought and scientific inquiry, do not simply call into question the veridicality of some experience or the truth of some belief. They indicate trouble not simply in what we experience and think but in our ways of experiencing and thinking about things which distorts and perverts our findings. If we are to come to grips with these problems, we must focus our critical attention upon the constitutional principles of experience and thought and our assumptions about them. But we cannot do this in a straightforward, direct way.

Johnstone[5] contends that philosophy proceeds not by argumentum ad rem, that is, not by an appeal to the objects of experience and thought, but by argumentum ad hominem, by appealing dialectically to a person to show him either that he cannot on pain of inconsistency say a certain thing by virtue of certain commitments he has or that consistency demands that he acknowledge a certain philosophical statement because of some commitment of his that is pointed out. Thus he contends that philosophical statements are not to be interpreted in terms of what they seem to say about their apparent objects and that they are not true or false vis à vis their objects. Rather they are to be understood, he says, in terms of the ad hominem arguments to which they are subject. Such arguments, he contends, do not have universal appeal, but have force and validity only for those who share the commitments to which they appeal. He does admit in the end that some philosophical arguments appeal to commitments inherent in selfhood and that obviously these are universal.

There is, I believe, validity in the distinction between ad rem and ad hominem arguments as Johnstone conceives them and that philosophical argumentation is of the latter kind. Furthermore, some philosophical problems are, as we have argued, generated by philosophical assumptions or views that are not universally shared. But such assumptions and views are not simply volitional commitments without truth values, for they embody claims about the constitutional principles of the mind and the categorial structure of the world. The ultimate appeal in such argumentation is, I contend, to the constitutional principles of the mind themselves. These constitute a normative structure inherent in the nature of the mind and as such are universally shared. But they cannot be gotten at by a simple, straightforward ad rem appeal in the manner of the phenomenologists, even though they are part of the nature of things. To do so we would have to be able to investigate them in a nonquestion-begging way. We would have to have an approach or methodology with respect to which they were neutral. Yet the constitutional principles of the mind are operative within and influence the results of all inquiry. So they cannot be neutral subject matter for our investigation. All of our claims about the constitutional principles of the mind have to be tested with the operating principles of the mind by dialectical ad hominem arguments.

To gain a starting point, I shall assume that knowing that P^* involves (1) thinking that P, (2) being correct in thinking that P, and (3) being responsible in thinking that P.

"Thinking," as here used, is a semitechnical term. Although the use singled out exists in ordinary discourse, it is here isolated and refined. It is, I contend, a component in the ordinary use of "knowing that." Although the term has a dispositional use, and it is in this sense that it is entailed by "knowing that," the disposition indicated is actualized in episodic thinking. It is the episodic use that needs clarification. We must differentiate between thinking which is pondering, reasoning, inferring, etc., and that which is simply thinking that P, which may or may not be the terminus of a process of pondering or reasoning. Neither can we identify thinking that P with having a thought, for simply having a thought need not involve any commitment, the making of any claim, nor the taking of any stand, whereas thinking that P, in the sense under discussion, does. I want to say that thinking that P is a semantic act like saying that P. Indeed saying that P, in the strict sense that presupposes sincerity and veracity, is a form of thinking that P. We do not in most cases think that P and express the thought orally. We do this of course when we rehearse our thoughts before speaking, but most of the time when we talk only one act is involved, namely, thinking out loud or in public. Thus insights into saying that P may illuminate the notion of thinking that P.

To say that P, in the simplest case where "P" has the form "X is F," is to assert a fact. "Fact" here is an ontological category. A fact as the object of an assertion is a proposition just as a married woman is a wife. There is of course an important difference in the two cases: a woman has to exist in order to be married, but a fact does not have to "exist" or obtain in the world in order for it to be asserted. Otherwise there could be no false propositions. This indicates no peculiarity about facts but about assertion.

An assertion is a semantic act which takes as its object a fact and claims that it obtains in the world. The object here is a semantic or intentional object. It is something meant. It does not entail existence. We may speak of something's being *in* one's mind, *in* one's thought, *in* one's memory, *in* one's experience, *in* a book, etc. This is the semantic use of "in" and is to be contrasted with the existential use. Thus we may speak of

---

*"P" in these locutions is to be understood as an arbitrary sentence which semantically locates a fact. Thus what is known when one knows that P is the fact located by "P," not a proposition as such.

something's being semantically and existentially present. In an assertion, a fact is semantically present in the speaker's mind and it is taken (or claimed) to be existentially present in the world. A fact may of course be semantically present to the speaker and semantically presented to his audience without the claim that it obtains in the world. This is done in ordinary discourse by "that"-clauses, participial phrases, and component parts of certain kinds of compound sentences; e.g., "Consider the possibility *that John was at the scene of the crime*," "*John's being there* is unthinkable," "*If John was at the scene of the crime*, then Mary was lying," etc. Of course all apparent existential claims can be canceled by labeling the universe of discourse "fiction" or "story." Then what is said cannot be false in any straightforward sense. "True" and "false" are applicable to sayings or assertions only by virtue of the distinction between the semantic and the existential presence of facts.

The concept we are after is "asserting" and "stating" stripped of their public characteristics, which are tied up with their role in communication, namely, the physical features that make perceptual understanding possible, such as noises, ink marks, and the like. Thinking need not involve these features, but it does no doubt require some physical base. I would hazard that minimally there are involved some perhaps imperceptible neurophysiological processes that function semantically. These may well be truncated versions of the physiological processes involved in talking. This may account for the puzzle about whether one's silent thinking is in English, German, etc. In the strict sense, the answer would seem to be in the negative, but there would be no radical change, only fuller development, for at least some of one's silent thinking to become fully verbalized thinking in English, or some conventional language.

We have already indicated that thinking that *P* may occur in more complex forms such as asserting or saying that *P*. I would also argue, but I will not here, that it may occur in various experiential and memory forms as well. To see an airplane, to hear a car coming at a high speed, to recognize visually Tom Jones, to remember something that happened on a given occasion and the like, all I contend, involve thinking-that. Simply thinking-that may take the form not only of incipient saying-that but incipient remembering (incipient "rerun" experiences), or incipient imagining (incipient "feigned" perception).

"Knowing that," in ordinary language, seems to have only a dispositional use. The disposition indicated is in many cases generated by an episodic thinking-that in a perceptual form and it is actualized and manifested in episodes of thinking-that in some mode or other. It seems to be merely a contingent fact about ordinary language that there is no episodic use of "know" to cover these acts. Such a use would in no way be incongruent with it as an achievement word. Thus for theoretical purposes the word might be given an episodic use. But rather than tamper with ordinary usage, I shall use a technical term and speak of "epistemic episodes."

The second element in our analysis of "knowing that P," namely, being correct, is simply a matter of thinking what is the case, which, in simple empirical cases at least, is a matter of the meant fact's obtaining in the world. Being correct in such areas as theoretical, mathematical, and philosophical thought is more complex, but we need not go into these complications for present purposes. Being responsible in thinking that P, the third factor in our analysis, is a matter of one's having justifying grounds or reasons for thinking that P and those grounds or reasons being responsible for and providing a satisfactory explanation of his getting it right.

But what is it to have and how is it that we have good reasons or grounds for thinking that P? Some seem to think that a case of thinking that P, in whatever mode it may occur, if not grounded in and supported by the rules of language, can be simply supported by and grounded in the facts that obtain. And in a sense this is true, but it doesn't help us with our problem. No fact can be for one a good reason for thinking that P unless it is known to him. And then our problem reappears with respect to the knowledge of it and an infinite regress seems to be in the making. Many have concluded that all cases of thinking-that, if grounded or backed at all, have to be grounded ultimately in some epistemic act that is qualitatively different from thinking-that, some form of intuition (nonmediated grasp of fact) such as rational insight, sensory apprehension of data, or self-knowledge of subjective states. These acts are said to be infallible and to yield certainty in such a way that they are self-grounding and self-validating and therefore neither need nor admit of any ground or validation beyond themselves. Unless something is known with certainty in this manner, nothing, it is argued, can be known with probability. This has been one of the basic theses of the subjectivistic empiricist tradition.

Furthermore, it has been common in traditional empiricism to argue that the meaningfulness of our language must be grounded in such infallible epistemic acts. This is the point of the empirical verifiability theory of meaning, a doctrine much maligned through misunderstanding. Critics have maintained that any linguistic expression is meaningful if it has an intelligible linguistic use. Classical empiricists, concerned with knowledge and reality, were interested in language only insofar as it has or seems to have a semantic use in making knowledge-claims. Thus they were concerned with how it is possible for language to have semantic ties to items and features in the world.

That which is semantically present in one linguistic act may be semantically present in another that uses different linguistic expressions. Therefore, if a linguistic act is not understood by someone, it may be clarified and made intelligible to him by translation, that is, by saying the same thing in different language. If the linguistic act is a knowledge-claim, the two expressions are semantically synonymous: they have the same semantic content. But we can go only so far in clarification by substitution of synonymous expressions. At some point, if understanding is to be achieved, we have to break out of language, so to speak, through experiences that are "synonymous" with (that have the same semantic content as) certain linguistic expressions. In other words, we have to locate the semantic content of some linguistic acts among the semantic contents (or intentional objects) of experience, if it is to have any semantic ties to reality. For example, suppose an English-speaking person should master Russian perfectly in the sense that he could paraphrase in Russian anything said in Russian and yet know no "synonymous" experiences for any Russian expression. In the most important sense, such a person would not know what any Russian expression meant. The language for him would be free floating without any semantic ties to the world.

The classical empiricists were fundamentally right in maintaining that only data-gathering, knowledge-yielding modes of experience provide a way of establishing semantic ties between language and items and features of the world. All semantically meaningful language must be grounded to the world directly through synonymous data-gathering experiences or logically constructed from items of language so grounded. Thus the philosophical questions, "What do you mean?" and "How do you know?" converge on the same point. The kind of experience that provides through its semantic content (or intentional objects) verifying data (evidence) for a truth-claim about the world also provides the experiential ground for semantic ties between the language used in the linguistic act in question and the world.

I see no alternative to the view that thinking, in the special sense in which I am using the term, can be supported only by thinking itself. Our thoughts and takings may hang together in a pattern of mutual support; that is, they may be such within a given set that to replace any one with its negative would give rise to some incompatibility. But such coherence, although necessary for confirmation, is not sufficient. Thoughts and takings provide mutual support by leaning upon each other in a coherent pattern only insofar as some among them at least have some inherent weight of their own. Furthermore, rational resolution of inconsistency requires an order of priorities to guide us in the reassignment of truth-values. Some instances of thinking-that, if there is to be any confirmation at all, must enjoy a privileged position so that in the face of inconsistency they are least suspect and therefore tend to discredit their rivals. I suggest that there are those that have by virtue of their mode of being an inherent justification. They are at least partially self-warranting in that the occurrence of the act of thinking that P in such cases invests the thought with some probability. In other words, a fact's being semantically present in a certain way in one's mind is itself evidence that the fact in question is existentially present in the world.

Here I introduce the concept of an *epistemic encounter*. As the term indicates, an epistemic encounter involves in some way a knowledge-yielding, data-gathering confrontation with reality. As a first approximation, we may say that an epistemic encounter involves (1) thinking that P; (2) being correct in thinking that P; (3) being responsible in thinking that P; and furthermore, (4) the act of thinking that P being at least partially self-warranting.

But more is involved. Any case of thinking that P could be partially self-warranting. Thoughts do not occur in a vacuum but in a logico-semantic field of perceptions, memories, beliefs, assumptions, expectations, and the like. Normally what one thinks is the case in a given situation is what his semantic field (his mind) normatively requires. Suppose a person goes to an experienced and successful diagnostician and, after hearing the patient's complaints and a cursory examination, the doctor thinks that the trouble is cirrhosis of the liver. The fact that under these conditions he thinks that it is cirrhosis of the liver supports what he thinks. The occurrence of the thought invests the thought with some probability. It is partially self-warranting. The doctor's logico-semantic field is such that the thought it requires and produces about the patient's condition is likely to be true, or certainly more likely to be true than the thought about the matter produced by the mind of a layman. But the important point is that the occurrence of a thought in a certain way may invest it with some probability. This seems to be true of sincere thinking-that, especially on the part of an informed and experienced person, in contrast with reverie and "free association." Therefore, our formulation is not sufficient to differentiate some ordinary cases of thinking-that from epistemic encounters.

As the term indicates, in an epistemic *encounter* the working out of the normative requirements in the logico-semantic field of the person involved cannot be the sole determinant in the production of the thinking-that in question. Somehow the existential presence of the fact thought to be the case is a factor. The most obvious way in which this occurs is in sensory perception where there is a physical interaction between the existential situation and the perceiver's body, with the bodily effect being a determinant somehow in the production of the perception. We are tempted to insist that such a causal interaction is involved in every epistemic encounter. No doubt there is some kind of dependency of the occurrence of the thought on the existential presence of what is thought. But we should not prematurely restrict the form this dependency might take by confining our attention to a paradigm, even a good one.

I shall later explore whether our emotive experiences, broadly conceived to include our affective and conative experiences, are knowledge-yielding and may provide us with epistemic encounters. One peculiarity of such experiences is that for the most part they seem to be supervenient upon an otherwise *comprehended* factual situation. I say "for the most part" because it is not clear that this is the case for somatic value experiences like aches, pains, and feeling bad, nor for simple somatic desires like hunger and thirst. But we have value experiences of external situations only insofar as they are semantically present to us in some mode. Any mode will do, experiential or otherwise. So, if value experiences are knowledge-yielding, we can experientially discern values in situations described to us, even hypothetical and ficticious ones. Thought experiments appear to work in this realm. To think of an actual or possible situation, to pay attention to the details of it, will suffice for us to have an emotive response to it and to make a value judgment about it. Further thought experiments seem sufficient to corroborate or to refute the initial emotive response and judgment.

If we should acknowledge this possibility in the case of value experiences, would we be driven to admit that there are also supervenient facts that can be discerned on the basis of a description of the situation on which they depend so that thought experiments would suffice for their "perception" or discernment? Are there properties, say F and G, which are such that we can perceive by attending to the matter in thought that nothing can be F without being G? Or are all such apparent discernments of supervenient facts actually discernments of logical truths grounded in meaning or the rules of language? "If one is an uncle, then he is a male" is obviously a logical truth. "If something is red, then it is colored" is perhaps also logical. "If something is colored, then it is extended" has seemed more questionable to some. What about geometrical truths like "If something is a cube, then it has twelve edges"?

If one sets out to prove that all such truths are analytic, he can no doubt convince himself that they are, especially if his epistemological assumptions render them unintelligible otherwise. C. I. Lewis, for example, does just this, but it is interesting to notice how he proceeds. He holds that the way to determine what a sentence like "X is F" means is to discover what *must* be the case, what facts *must* obtain, in order for the sentence to be true. Then he turns around and contends that all "must"-truths are grounded in meaning. He can make out his latter claim, it seems, only because he has embraced all that must be the case for a given sentence to be true in the meaning of the sentence.

There is little doubt that we can so enrich the meaning of language that all necessary truths about apparent supervenient facts become logical truths within the enriched language. But our question concerns whether the human mind has the capacity to discern such truths from within an impoverished language in which these would not be logical truths. Even if the mathematician's constructed language is sufficient to yield geometrical truths as analytic, it is not clear that Meno's slave boy's language was adequate for this purpose.* Yet upon attending to certain facts pointed out to him, he had new thoughts that seem to have been perceptions. This, of course, is the heart of the rationalist's claim, namely, that some cases of thinking that P, where P is some objective, nonlogical necessity and the thinking is abstract, are epistemic encounters.

And in the case of structures of meaning, we seem to be able to perceive their logical relationships regardless of the mode of their presence to us. Of course one can "see" the logical relationships of anyone's statements regardless of whether he hears them made or reads them or has a report of them. The same is true of actions in general. One can "see" the implications of another's action in a given situation regardless of whether he personally perceives the act and the situation or they are only reported to him.

In these cases, the experience of values, and the discernment of supervenient facts and the logical relationships of structures of meaning, if there are such, the realities on which the values and necessities supervene or depend have to be only semantically present to the person concerned. Therefore there cannot be the *kind* of causal dependency of the perception, if there is perception in such cases, on what is perceived as in the case of sensory experience. Nevertheless the occurrence of the emotive perception or the discernment of natural or logical necessity, if they are indeed epistemic encounters, must in some way be dependent on the structures of value or of necessity in the semantically presented situations. A mark of such dependency would be some genuine semantic input provided by the "thinking" in question. I think we can get the results we want, without going into the kind of causation involved, by adding the following condition to our definition of "epistemic encounter." (5) An epistemic encounter, or rather a mode of epistemic encounter, must be a source of new ideas, either empirical or categorial. It must have, or be capable of providing, an original, indigenous semantic content. It must fund, or be capable of funding, some segment of language with meaning by providing a ground for semantic ties between language and contingent or categorial features of the world.

Although the distinction between empirical (or contingent) and categorial items and features of the world was intimated in chapter 1 and will be dealt with more fully later, perhaps some clarification is needed here. By way of illustration, physical particulars with properties in spatial, temporal, and causal relationships are part of the categorial structure of

*In Plato's dialogue *Meno*, Socrates has Meno's slave boy, who has never been instructed in mathematics, prove a geometrical truth by asking him leading questions.

the world, but blue pens on my desk at the time of this writing are part of the empirical and contingent makeup of the world. The concept of a physical particular is a categorial concept; the concept of a pen is an empirical concept. The concept of property is categorial; the concept of blue is empirical. We form empirical concepts by experientially discriminating details of the objective world and building linguistic constructions thereon; whereas categorial concepts function in and render possible experience of and thought about items and features in the world. They are tied up with and structure our ways of semantically relating to and appropriating the world—what we have called the constitutional principles of the mind. For this reason, they are sometimes spoken of as a priori concepts in contrast with empirical concepts. They have even been called innate ideas; not so much in the sense that we are born with them, but that they are given birth from within the mind rather than acquired from our experience of the world. Nevertheless, categorial concepts apply to the world as well, to the objects of experience and thought.

Here is a problem of the first magnitude. Do the categorial concepts apply to the world and its contents only in their semantic presence, only to them as they are experienced, imagined, thought, talked about, etc.? Or do they apply to them in their purely existential status as well? Aristotle said "yes" to the latter question; Kant said "no." The issue turns on how it is possible for us to have a priori knowledge of categorial structures if they pertain to the realm of existence as such. For Kant and many moderns, with their view of the epistemic powers of the mind, a priori knowledge of categorial structures is possible only insofar as they pertain to things in their semantic presence to us. This is a matter we will have to go into later. But whether the overall issue is resolved in favor of Kant or Aristotle or some other way, there are compelling reasons for the thesis that there is a categorial structure to the world in its semantic presence to us and we have knowledge of that structure and categorial concepts apply to it.

Therefore, we are justified, I think, in our claim that, if a given mode of experience is a source of either empirical or categorial concepts, along with the other conditions specified, it is a mode of epistemic encounter; it is a primary and original way of semantically relating to and appropriating the world.

It will be noted that an epistemic encounter is still a case of thinking-that. Its peculiarity lies in the fact that it is partially self-warranting and the fact that it provides a ground for semantic ties between language and the world. Thus epistemic encounters provide the basic inputs for a mind and the foundation for our semantic outreach to an objective world.

Perhaps the most important question in philosophy concerns what areas of experience and thought provide us with epistemic encounters. The answer we give or assume to this question determines what areas of discourse appear philosophically opaque and how we seek philosophical clarity. One may conclude that by virtue of the epistemic-encounter powers of the human mind some saying and others of its kind cannot mean what they seem to mean and that they really mean something else. For example, the phenomenalist's analysis of physical-object language. He concludes in effect that sensing is our only mode of epistemic encounter and that its object is existentially just the way it is in its semantic presentation. In other words, error in sensing is not possible. But this is accomplished by obliterating the distinction between the semantic and the existential presence of the object. Thus Berkeley's esse est percipi. The objects of acts of sensing, then, have no independence of the acts of sensing and therefore are private. Physical-object language seems to be both grounded in sensory experience and about objective, public independent objects. But if the epistemic encounters involved in sensory experience are acts of sensing with subjective, private, dependent objects, how can physical-object language mean what it seems to mean? How can it have semantic ties to the external, independent, public items and features in the world? The phenomenalist concludes that it cannot; that the meaning of physical-object language is not and cannot be what it seems to be, for the human mind, in his view, simply does not have the power to fund language with such meaning. He proceeds to try to show what it really means by translating or giving a recipe for the translation of physical-object sentences into sets of sentences which are semantically related to only subjective, private objects of acts of sensing. He claims that physical-object sentences can be in principle translated into a set of phenomenalistic sentences without loss in sayable content, even though it would take an infinite number of such sentences to express the meaning of each physical-object sentence.

In some cases one may conclude that sayings rendered suspect by one's views or assumptions about the epistemic-encounter powers of the mind make sense in that the language used has a use but does not semantically mean anything. The emotive theory of value language is a case in point. It maintains, in its purest form, that value utterances as such say nothing, have no semantic dimension, but are used to evince or to show the feelings or attitudes of the speaker or writer and to elicit or to incite like feelings or attitudes in one's audience. Indeed there may be a problem about how any expression can have a semantic outreach to something in the world; and one may conclude that none does, that language has only a directional function for action as the pragmatists claim, that it is to be understood not in terms of "synonymous" experiences that establish semantic ties with the world, but in terms of forms of life. In other words, this whole array of problems concerns whether it is possible or how it is possible to mean what we seem to mean by certain expressions or modes of discourse. If it is not possible to mean what we seem to mean when we say certain things, what do we mean, if anything? If we do not *mean* anything, what sense or use, if any, do the expressions in question have? If they have no linguistic use, what explanation can be given for the appearance to the contrary? These latter questions are of interest and have to be answered in a convincing way in order to defend the conclusion that the expressions do not *mean* anything in a semantic sense.

How can we determine whether a given mode of experience has epistemic-encounter capability? We cannot look to empirical psychology for an answer, for it is not an empirical issue. We want to know about the categorial nature of the mode of experience in question. This is to be gotten at, I suggest, by a kind of linguistic analysis of it. Once something is semantically located by the use of an expression, the grammar of the expression indicates something about the categorial nature of the object. For example, as we pointed out earlier, the fact that something is semantically located by a predicate indicates that it has the categorial status of a property. The fact that something is semantically located by a declarative sentence, a "that"-clause, or a participial phrase indicates that it has the categorial form of a fact. But such prima facie indications must not be accepted uncritically. They may be incomplete or misleading. We have to explore the full range of what it makes sense to say about the object. Earlier in this chapter I attempted a philosophical clarification of "thinking that" and "epistemic encounter." We were not attempting to formulate rules of language in the manner of a dictionarymaker. Rather we used the expression "thinking that," for example, to locate a kind of personal act and then proceeded to explore what it makes sense to say and does not make sense to say about that act. In this way we discover not contingencies but what must be true and what cannot be true of it. But we must not conclude that all such findings follow from any simple definition of the word concerned nor from any existing network of conventional linguistic rules alone. Often assumptions about our epistemic-encounter powers are involved. For example, we know that numbers cannot be blue and that robin eggs cannot have square roots because we know that our ways of encountering such things cannot provide any grounds for such predications. In like manner, some have argued that G. E. Moore's analysis of good as a nonnatural quality cannot be correct because our epistemic-encounter powers are such that we could not establish a semantic tie between "good" and a quality with such a categorial status. However we analyze it and explain it, and this itself is at least partially determined by our views or assumptions about the epistemic-encounter powers of the mind, our sense of what it makes sense to say and what it does not make sense to say is what philosophy appeals to in the last analysis. Nevertheless any conclusion about the categorial nature of something based on consideration of the grammar of the expression used to locate it semantically and what it makes sense to say about it must be further tested by exploring how it, with all of the implications involved, fits in with our total philosophical account of things and how readily and satisfactorily the total range of experience, thought, and culture can be interpreted and rendered intelligible in terms of our comprehensive philosophical theory. Philosophy is a systematic discipline in the sense that a stand on one issue has implications for others and may be overturned by the position we may be forced to take on them. This is not so much a matter of our findings about particular areas of experience and thought being at the mercy of systematic theory as systematic theory being at the mercy of our detailed findings about all the areas of experience and thought and having to render them all intelligible in a coherent and systematic way.

The only way we can determine whether a given mode of experience has epistemic-encounter power, then, is to explore its categorial nature and structure by considering the grammar of the language used to report and to describe such experiences and what it makes sense and does not make sense to say about the experiences themselves, especially with regard to semantic, logical, and epistemic concepts; and how our conclusions thus arrived at can be squared with the relevant sectors of culture grounded in the area of experience in question and our total philosophical view of things. Does the reporting language for a given mode of experience, for example, involve multiverbed sentences such as "He felt that it would be unkind to press the point further"? Does it make sense to speak of expressing the experience in language as distinct from reporting or describing it? Does it make sense to speak of the experience as logically inconsistent with other experiences or beliefs? Does it make sense to speak of the experience as in error, veridical, corrigible, rational, or irrational, etc.? Is any sector of language grounded in the area of experience in question? Does this area of experience provide the opportunity to break out of language, so to speak, and to locate among its objects the semantic content of some linguistic expressions used to make truth-claims about the public world? If one should lack such a mode of experience, how would his ability to master our language be impaired? On the assumption that the mode of experience in question does not have epistemic-encounter capabilities, how could the area of language and culture grounded in it, if there are such, be rendered philosophically intelligible? What are the implications of the conclusions reached on these grounds for one's overall philosophy? Exploration of these and similar questions may reveal whether the mode of experience in question has the categorial form that makes possible epistemic encounters with reality.

In light of the dimensions of experience, the structure of language, the divisions of culture, and the history of philosophy, the primary candidates for epistemic-encounter power seem to be somatic sensations, sensory perceptions, affective and conative experiences, self-awareness, perceptual understanding of structures of meaning (including people and their behavior), and rational insight or intuition. The conclusions that one reaches or the assumptions that one operates with about the epistemic-encounter character of these or any other candidates will affect the kinds of philosophical problems he encounters in the various sectors of discourse and determine the range of his philosophical skepticism and the extent realistic interpretations of the various sectors of culture (science, mathematics, ethics, religion, art, philosophy, etc.) are open to him. And philosophical clarification of language against the background of these assumptions and views about the epistemic-encounter powers of the mind and the problems they generate will yield a philosophy of culture and an account of the categorial nature and structure of the world from within the human perspective. Clarification of language divorced from such epistemological concerns cannot yield metaphysical conclusions, but it would seem arbitrary to call it philosophical.

Here we are going against the grain of a persistent skepticism of the modern era. We have already noted that Wittgenstein's epistemological assumptions generated a complete skepticism about the possibility of philosophical knowledge. Most philosophers have not gone that far, but skepticism about metaphysics, in name at least, has been widespread. Many who believe in the possibility of epistemology and philosophy of culture reject the possibility of metaphysics. The empiricistic penchant of the modern mind makes it most difficult for one to acknowledge the possibility of nonempirical knowledge of the world. Many who have claimed to reject metaphysics, however, have done so under a certain interpretation, usually under a conception that goes with and requires a rationalistic epistemology, while actually developing a "metaphysics" of their own appropriate to their own theory of knowledge. A prime example of this is A. J. Ayer in *Language, Truth, and Logic*. The first chapter is entitled "The Elimination of Metaphysics." And yet the book goes on to develop a worldview according to which there are neither physical objects nor mental substances, but only sense-data; there are no universals, objective essences, necessary connections, negative facts, or values, but only facts and contingent connections. Thus he developed a metaphysics but failed to produce a philosophy of metaphysics consistent with his epistemology. Consequently he thought that in rejecting the rationalistic philosophy of metaphysics he was rejecting metaphysics.

Empiricists throughout the modern period have focused their attention on the subject side of the subject-object, knowledge-world chasm. At an earlier time the emphasis was on sensations and ideas. In more recent times the focus of attention has been on language. Some no doubt have thought of philosophy as a study of the structure of consciousness or of language with these conceived as details within the world, but the more sophisticated have always thought of philosophy as, or taken it to be, a study of what we have called the constitutional principles of experience and thought (or what amounts to the same thing, the logical grammar of language) in semantically relating to and appropriating the world. This kind of study of experience, thought, and language has always provided insights into and produced claims about the structure of the object-world. Indeed experience, thought, and language are such that we cannot give an adequate philosophical account of them without at the same time giving a philosophical account of their objects. As we observed earlier, we cannot get beyond the apparent logical grammar of an expression to its real structure without determining whether it has a semantic object and, if so, what it makes sense to say and does not make sense to say about the object. Any philosophical map of the structure of consciousness or language may also be read as a philosophical map of the world. It tells us what would be true of all possible empirical worlds and what would not be true of any possible empirical world; or, what amounts to the same thing, what is necessarily true and what is necessarily false of our world.

But in all of this we are concerned with the world as the correlate of experience and thought or of language. In other words, we are talking about the world as it is semantically appropriated by us and what must be and cannot be true of it in its semantic presence. Through knowledge of the constitutional principles of the mind and thus of our semantic powers and acts we know something about the form of everything that can be caught in our semantic nets. Even Kant who denied in name the possibility of metaphysical knowledge admitted in fact metaphysical knowledge of this kind. But the categorial structure of the world as known, on this view, is mind- or language-dependent. In other words, this is a subjectivistic interpretation of metaphysics. Kant called it transcendental idealism.

The categorial structure of experience and thought presents a special problem, for experience and thought are both part of the world of existence and semantically of and about the world. And, if we cannot at least get at the categorial structure of experience and thought in their own existential status, how can we know that any mode of experience has an epistemic-encounter capability and that we can establish any semantic ties to items and features of the world? It would seem that even metaphysics as knowledge of the world in its semantic presence would not be possible. And if we can get at the categorial structure of experience and thought in their existential status, then why can we not do the same for other areas of reality?

I have argued that we discover the categorial structure of a mode of experience by examining, in light of all relevant philosophical problems and an overall philosophical position, the language we use to report and to describe instances of the experience in question and what it makes sense to say and does not make sense to say about them. This is exactly the procedure we would use in exploring the categorial structure of the objects of any mode of experience or thought. If there are compelling reasons, as indicated above, for concluding that this method will yield knowledge of the categorial structure of experience in its existential status, then it would seem to be plausible to believe that it would yield like results elsewhere.

The view toward which I am driven cannot be told without assuming a whole philosophical position, which has not yet been presented, and will not be convincing or perhaps not even plausible to those who do not share or will not seriously consider the overall position. This kind of anticipation and presupposition is necessary, however, since philosophy is a systematic discipline and everything cannot be said at once. One basic thesis is that there is an objective normative structure in the nature of things. There is, for example, or so I shall contend, a function inherent in what the heart is and it is structured the way it is so that when it performs normally, that is, according to its own normative structure, it fulfills its function. In like manner, what I have called the constitutional principles of the mind constitute the mind's inherent normative structure for semantically relating to and appropriating the world and acting rationally for the achievement of values which could not otherwise be realized. It seems reasonable to assume that when the epistemic powers of the mind are exercised in accordance with their own inherent normative structure, they succeed in their function of knowing the world as it is in its own structure. In other words, it seems reasonable to believe from within the overall philosophical position I am developing that the categorial structure of the mind is the way it is in order to make possible knowledge of the structure of the world as it is. Otherwise the success of rational action shaped and guided by the semantic presence of the environment would be unintelligible.

The position I am suggesting, then, is that we can have a priori knowledge of the categorial structure of the world as it is in its semantic presence to us through knowledge of the constitutional principles of the mind or the logical grammar of language; and that it is reasonable to believe that the categorial structure of the world in its semantic presence to us is at least part of the structure of the world in its existential status, for, according to our view, the mind is structured the way it is to make possible knowledge of the structure of the world. To maintain, for example, that there are no physical particulars involving spatial, temporal, and causal relationships in the realm of existence per se but only in the world's semantic presence to us puts too much of a burden on the philosophical assumptions which drive us to this absurdity.

This realistic interpretation of the categorial structure of both experience and thought on one hand and of the objects of experience and thought on the other does not enable us to escape the human perspective on the world. Even if it is true, and I suggest it is, that the categorial structure of the world in its semantic presence to us also pertains to the realm of existence as such, it does not follow that whatever structures there are in the realm of existence per se are knowable to us. It may be that we simply do not have the kind of epistemic powers that make it possible for us to relate semantically to and to appropriate all the dimensions there are to the realm of existence per se. But we cannot talk meaningfully about what we lack the power to know except indirectly in terms of some vaguely possible but indescribable epistemic powers which we lack but some beings might have. We are for better or for worse locked into the human perspective on the world and cannot escape it, even though we can entertain the possibility that our perspective has its limitations although we cannot know in any specific way what they might be, for to do so would be to transcend them. Even divine revelation would be restricted to what we in terms of our own powers could understand, think, or meaningfully say and therefore would provide no escape from our human perspective.

However the problem with which we are primarily concerned is whether we are through false assumptions and views about the semantic and epistemic powers of the human mind unduly restricting the human perspective on the world and thereby distorting and perverting the culture and losing our grip on reality as we are driven toward an ever expanding subjectivism. We have already found compelling reasons to support the claim that this is so, but the final verdict must be rendered after carefully testing our philosophical assumptions about the constitutional principles of the human mind by a detailed philosophical analysis of the categorial structure of experience and thought and of the whole range of language and culture. When successful, such an analysis yields a coherent philosophy which solves our philosophical perplexities and achieves philosophical intelligibility for the full spectrum of experience and all sectors of our culture. In addition to philosophical understanding, which is perhaps the highest form of intellectual achievement, philosophical work is our most fundamental and important form of cultural therapy. It is the only way in which we can intelligently explore whether there is a gap between our culture and reality and, if so, take corrective steps to reform our culture and bring it in line with the structure of reality. Cultural therapy is the practical side of pure philosophy. It is to philosophy what technology is to science. It is what philosophy, apart from its intrinsic intellectual value, is good for.

What, if anything, may we expect from philosophy today? My answer is twofold. First, we may expect philosophy to provide some measure of philosophical understanding and enlightenment for those who study it and develop responsible, disciplined methods of philosophical thinking. No one who has ever achieved such understanding and enlightenment will deny that they are among the intrinsic values of the human spirit. They elevate one to a new level of knowledge and understanding and thereby open up a new dimension of freedom. They give depth to one's being. Without philosophical understanding of the culture within which we operate and a critical philosophical view of the world as knowable through it, we are enslaved by our culture and our uncritical assumptions about it and the world. And to that extent we are provincial in mind and spirit. Philosophical self-criticism and the enlightenment and understanding thereby obtained are essential for a genuine liberal education.

Second, in addition to the intrinsic value of philosophical understanding and its importance for a deepened and enriched selfhood, philosophy has, as I have argued, an important therapeutic function. An individual or a culture with serious philosophical difficulties in his or its categorial assumptions or views suffers from a derangement that thwarts his or the people of the culture's efforts. Philosophy, in its work to expose and to clear up such difficulties, is concerned with wisdom: philosophical wisdom, not moral wisdom or other common varieties that provide guidance for solving our ordinary problems, but wisdom about the constitutional principles of the mind that guide us in the exercise of our powers in our efforts to know and to cope with reality and to live successfully.

Philosophical therapeutic work often seems, and no doubt often is, ineffectual. The society may simply not be concerned nor receptive to what philosophy has to say. If so, this may be more a judgment on the society than on philosophy. But cultural changes at the depth we are talking about may take centuries. They should not be hurried or coerced. Efforts to do so are likely to be premature and destructive. The Communist movement, which seeks to impose, by governmental indoctrination and thought control, radical changes in the categorial views of a culture, is perhaps the most notable and most destructive instance of this in history. Where cultural changes of this kind are uncoerced, it is difficult to know what is effectual and what is not. One thing I am sure of, however, is that a culture that comes to critical and creative self-consciousness in philosophical perplexity and thought in many sensitive minds with professional skills is a higher and more sophisticated culture than one that proceeds blindly with regard to categorial issues.

Furthermore, individuals do not have to wait for pervasive cultural renewal in order to work changes in the foundations of their own lives. What is ineffectual, or makes only a slight impact on the culture at large, may have dramatic results in the lives of some individuals. In fact, this is the testing ground for the culture itself. The philosopher must, first of all, cure himself. He is indeed fortunate if his work proves helpful for others in their efforts to rid themselves of their culture-bred derangements. But this is a job each must do for himself, with whatever help available, until the culture itself is transformed through individual successes.

Value Subjectivism

The great revolution in Western civilization occasioned by a shift in man's culture-generating orientation toward the world gave rise, as we have already observed, to many philosophical problems; but none has been more important for the life and spirit of man, as our discussion in chapter 2 has already indicated, than those pertaining to value, meaning, and subjectivity. We shall explore the problem of value in the present and the next chapter and that of meaning and subjectivity in the following three, and then consider some of the implications of our conclusions for our cultural crisis in the final chapter.

All three of the philosophical perplexities presented in chapter 2 concerned value language. The first involved the descriptive-explanatory use of value language, the second concerned the evaluative and practical or action-guiding use, and the third, the rational appraisal use. These are not all distinct without overlap, but they do mark differences that are important. At stake in these problems and those pertaining to meaning and subjectivity, as we saw in chapter 2, are belief in God, the viability of authority, the legitimacy of institutions, the house of knowledge, the external world, the rationality of action, and man's humanistic self-image and very existence as a human being. So let no one say that philosophers' preoccupation with language trivializes their subject.

1. Value language and value experience

First of all, we need to be clear about what counts as value language. This is not something readily achieved and cannot be done entirely in a theory-neutral way. We cannot even point out a few unmistakable value words that would elicit universal agreement. The most likely candidate, no doubt, is "good." But what of its use in the sentence, "The good scissors are in the sewing box." Those who distinguish sharply between the descriptive and evaluative functions of language and who identify value language with that which has an evaluative use would say that in the sentence in question "good" is not used as a value word. I have had philosophers tell me that "He is sick" is not a value sentence because it is empirically testable by medical science. So it is very hard to hold theories of value language responsible to an independently identifiable subject matter, for the theory once formed dictates what is to count as its subject matter. This is what suggests that such theories legislate or recommend usage rather than make truth-claims. But this is too easy and superficial. There is something that such a theory is of and about and to which it is responsible. Like all theories, it must be able to distinguish between appearance and reality and account for the appearances and show how and why they might mislead us. And so when a value theory claims that some apparent value word is not really one, it may not be simply legislating or recommending. Indeed the charge that it does simply legislate is a severe indictment. There is a subject matter to be examined and rendered intelligible. In this case, the value sector of language or discourse. What we are responsible to is the philosophically relevant structure of language or discourse and our ways of mapping it which have already been built into our language. To speak of the value sector of discourse indicates, or at least seems to, recognition of a categorial distinction, one that is grounded in a unique constitutional power of the mind. So the important thing for us to try to get clear about is the categorial distinction which appears to have been recognized and conceptualized in our talk about value words, value judgments, and the value sector of language. We may be aided in our effort by looking at and examining what we commonly call value words, value judgments, and the like, while recognizing that all our talk of this kind may not be faithful to the categorial insight reflected in it. One who objects to identifying "good" as a value word in the sentence, "The good scissors are in the sewing box," must read the categorial distinction marked by the concept of value words as different from that marked by the concept of descriptions. And the one who objects to classifying "He is sick" as a value sentence on the grounds that it is medically verifiable takes the categorial distinction to point to some power of the mind other than our empirical cognitive powers utilized in science. It may be that these philosophers fail to grasp the categorial distinction recognized in our talk about value words, value sentences, etc. It may also be the case that there is a very dim and confused recognition of a categorial distinction in our talk about the value sector of language. In any case there is something for us to be responsible to in our philosophical work, namely, the categorial structure of language or of discourse itself. We must begin looking for the categorial distinction indicated by our talk about value words, value sentences, and the whole value sector of discourse, and other categorial distinctions indicated by our talk about other sectors. We may conclude that there is no value categorial distinction, or that the distinction is such that some uses of even such paradigmatic value words as "good," "bad," "right," "wrong," "ought," and the like are not value uses.

So how shall we begin? I suggest that we will be on firmer ground if we

look first to the value dimension of experience and then use it to help identify value language. This is not to reject the possibility that at some points
we may recognize a mode of experience as belonging in the value sector by
its relationship to value language. This is not as odd as it may seem. At
places we may be clearer about the one and again about the other. We
should accept illumination from whatever source. What I am suggesting is
that we can better locate the value sectors of experience and language
taken together than we can either in isolation.

There will be little quarrel with the identification of the whole range
of affective and conative experience as the value sector: pleasure and pain,
enjoyment and suffering, joy and depression, liking and disliking,
favoring and disfavoring, approving and disapproving, wanting, desir-
ing, aversion, feeling compelled, feeling constrained, and the like—all of
our feelings, emotions, passions, impulses, strivings, responses, and
attitudes as distinct from our experiences which in and of themselves are
marked by indifference. Here we have to be careful. We must distinguish
between an indifferent experience of X and an experience of X as
indifferent. We must also mark a distinction between an indifferent experience of X and an experience of X which actually makes no difference.
Indeed an experience of X as indifferent is not itself an indifferent experience. One may have an indifferent experience of X and also be terribly
excited about X as well. Of course it may be difficult to isolate the indifferent experience of X and keep it uninfluenced by the excitement X elicits.
But the distinction can be made. Seeing X is in itself an indifferent mode of
experiencing X even though the X present in visual experience may also be
enjoyed. But to enjoy X, unlike seeing X, is not an indifferent mode of
experience. The mark of indifference in a mode of experience is whether it
makes sense to say of one that he experiences X in a given mode and that he
is indifferent to X, that he has no pro or con feeling or attitude toward X, or
that he has either one of these responses toward X without imputing any
conflict to him. We can say of one, for example, that he sees X and that he
is indifferent to X, that he sees X and that he is frightened by X, and that he
sees X and that he likes X. All of these are meaningful and none of them
imputes any conflict to the subject. But if we should say of one that he
enjoyed X and that he was indifferent to it, we would not make sense, at
least not in any straightforward way. If the statement said something that
could be true of him, it would be something very complex and would
need explanation. If we should say of one that he enjoyed X and that he
was frightened by it, we would impute to him conflicting experiences,
which are indeed quite common. But if we should say of one that he enjoyed X and that he liked it, we would in most cases simply be redundant.
However, we can make sense out of "He enjoyed X but he didn't like it." In
such a case, "He didn't like it" would report a higher level valuation than

"He enjoyed it." A literary critic, for example, might say "I enjoyed the book, but I didn't like it."

It is not only that we have to be careful to differentiate an indifferent experience of X from nonindifferent experiences we may have of the presented X, but we have to discriminate between an indifferent experience of X and nonindifferent experiences, concerns, and attitudes that may shape our capacity for a given kind of indifferent experience of an object or even occasion a particular nonindifferent experience of an object. It seems plausible to believe that we have the sensory powers that we do because the kinds of data they make available to us are of interest to us. It is also true that our operative concerns at a given time at least partially determine what we have indifferent experiences of. On several occasions I have stopped at an intersection and looked for oncoming cars and failed to see at first an approaching motorcycle. This is like working at one's desk and not hearing all kinds of things going on while hearing the things one deems important to oneself. The visual experience of a motorcycle in and of itself is an indifferent experience of an object, but at the intersection I am certainly not indifferent to the seen approaching motorcycle and my seeing or not seeing the approaching motorcycle is at least partially occasioned by nonindifferent states or acts of mind. We need to keep all these matters distinct in thought even if they are not separable in fact when we talk about indifferent and nonindifferent modes of experiencing or semantically relating to objects.

Value language is, I suggest, uniquely related to or grounded in value experience. This much will be almost universally acknowledged. The important and controversial question concerns the nature of the relationship. One who would object to calling "The good scissors are in the sewing basket" and "He is sick" value sentences would do so because "good" in the first sentence is used to make an identifying reference, which is presumed to be an indifferent mental act, and both sentences are taken to be confirmable or falsifiable by indifferent experiences and thought about the data thereby obtained. In other words, the objections in both cases are grounded in the assumption that there must be a very close and intimate relationship between the use of a value word on a particular occasion and some nonindifferent experiences or mental acts. Such a belief is no doubt a function of assumptions or beliefs about the categorial nature of value experience which limit the ways in which language can be related to or grounded in it.

If we believe, as we do for the most part in our culture, that nonindifferent experiences are simple events, occurrences, or states of affairs, whether phenomenalistically or behavioristically conceived, without any semantic dimension, subject to being reported, described, and explained in ordinary episodic and factual language, then value language can be related to or grounded in value experience in only two basically distinct ways, although these can be compounded with varying degrees of complexity. Value utterances may be of or about such experiences and the things they are related to causally; or they may be symptoms of or ways of venting or arousing value experiences.

2. Classical naturalistic theories of value language

The first position, the view that value language is of or about value experiences and their causal conditions, generated the classical naturalistic theories of value language.* Bentham maintained, for example, to state his basic theses and assumptions simply, that to say of any x that it is good is to say that it is either desired for its own sake (or, what is taken to amount to the same thing, the occurrence or thought of it arouses desire) or that it is a means to something desired for its own sake or a means to the elimination of something avoided for its own sake; and, furthermore, that one desires for its own sake only one's own pleasure and that one avoids for its own sake only one's own pain. Ralph Barton Perry held that to say of anything that it is good is to say that it is the object of some positive interest, no matter whose; and to say of something that it is bad is to say that it is the object of some negative interest, no matter whose. He defined "interest" in a broad way so that it embraces the whole range of affective and conative experience. For an x to be the object of an interest, according to Perry's theory, is for the interest, a behavioral state or condition, to be an effect of a cognition of x.

A variety of such naturalistic theories have been worked out with great complexity and ingenuity. They all hold that value language is not categorially different from empirical descriptive language. They attempt to make this out by giving a definition of what is taken to be the basic value concept in terms of empirical psychological concepts and thereby provide a recipe for the translation of value discourse into empirical psychological discourse. Such theories are usually taken to hold that value judgments are both cognitive and objective and that value knowledge is possible. However, it should be pointed out that they are really subjectivistic in the most important sense. They maintain that value experiences are states or conditions of the experiencing subject (whether conceived phenomenalistically or behavioristically) related causally, if at all, to the external world, either directly or through the mediation of the semantic dimension of another mode of experience or thought. It is, in other words, an objectivistic theory of value language and of value judgments but a subjectivistic theory of value experiences. There is no semantic outreach through value experience to items and features in the

*For a detailed discussion of the literature in value theory, see my *Ethical Naturalism and the Modern World-View* (Chapel Hill: University of North Carolina Press, 1960; reprint., Westport, Conn.: Greenwood Press, 1973).

objective realm. Value experience is not a window onto the world. It has the opacity of pure existence and brute factuality. Like Hume's sense impressions, value experiences are conceived as original existences with no semantic qualities about them.

This way of conceiving sense experiences denied Hume and his fellow phenomenalists epistemic and semantic access to an external, independent world and saddled them with a total subjectivism, even though they could maintain that physical-object statements are of and about sense experiences and can be verified or falsified. Much the same is true of the classical naturalist in value theory except that he is concerned with only nonindifferent experiences and therefore may have room in his view of things, unlike Hume with his sense impressions, to relate them to external causal conditions.

Most of the criticism of classical naturalistic value theories, however, has focused on their denial that there is a basic categorial difference between value language and factual language. That there is such a categorial distinction which invalidates any reductionistic translation procedure was the point of G. E. Moore's naturalistic fallacy argument. He maintained that we cannot define "good," which he took to be the basic value concept in terms of which all other value concepts could be defined, in terms of any descriptive concept "F," for it would make sense to say of something that it was F but not good. Moore was attempting to reveal through our sense of what it makes sense to say that value judgments just are not factual statements, that the logical grammar of "good" is not that of an ordinary descriptive predicate. He says that to say of something that it is good is not to describe it at all; or at least not in any usual sense. Moore, within the options open to him, concluded that "good" is semantically tied to a feature in the world but that it is a peculiar feature, what he called a nonnatural property. The fundamental point of his claim seems to be that for something to have this nonnatural property does not constitute a fact, that for something to possess the property is not for it to exemplify it. The property is not part of the constitution of the thing. To ascribe the property to something is not to describe it. Moore did not make clear how it is possible for the human mind to establish a semantic tie between value language and such nonnatural properities in the world nor how we can have knowledge of such nonfactual value structures. He seems merely to posit the necessary power without giving any independent identifying marks. Moore, however, succeeded in convincing most value theorists and moral philosophers that there is a basic categorial difference between value and factual language which cannot be ignored, but he met with little success in convincing them of his nonnatural properties or values there in the world. To admit this would be to go against the whole thrust of the modern mind and to acknowledge an essential limitation of empirical science in getting at reality.

Hume recognized something of the same point as Moore in his claim that we cannot logically derive "ought"-judgments from "is"-statements; the two being, he says, "entirely different," with the former of or about none of the relations "that are the objects of science" nor "any *matter of fact*, which can be discovered by the understanding."[1] But predicative value judgments like "X is good" and "X is right" seem to entail "ought"-judgments in some form—"X ought to be," "X ought to continue to be," "X ought to be pursued," "X ought to be done" or whatever is appropriate. Therefore, it was concluded, the so-called predicative value judgment must be systematically misleading in form. It cannot be, it was said, a factual or "is" statement, not even one that ascribes a nonnatural property to whatever is located by the subject-term.

3. The emotive naturalistic theory of value language

Some twentieth-century empiricists (Carnap, Ayer, Stevenson, and others) noted, as Hume had done before them, that value utterances relate to feelings, emotions, desires, and attitudes differently than factual statements. They emphasized that value sentences show the speaker's feelings toward what the utterance is of or about and tend to incite and indeed are used to incite or to arouse feelings and attitudes in the audience. In other words, it was claimed that a value utterance is nonindifferent in much the way in which we said earlier that value experiences are nonindifferent; that there is some kind of inconsistency or linguistic absurdity in saying such a thing as "X is good, but I don't favor it at all" or "X is good, but whatever you do, be completely against it." In short, the function of value sentences is not to make statements, not to report facts, not to describe things or situations, but to evaluate things and to get others to share our evaluations, with this understood as a matter of relating to things and situations emotively, in ways that affect action. Those who subscribe to this general view agree with Moore's claim that value judgments as value judgments do not describe; but where he took them to ascribe a non-characterizing and nonconstitutive property to their subject, the emotivist looks to the subjective side and sees the primary and defining role of value language to be to shape, to extend, and to organize our emotive and active responses to what is semantically presented to us in other modes of experience and thought.

Those who subscribe to this theory of value language obviously cannot countenance as part of value discourse such sentences as "The good scissors are in the sewing box" (where "the good scissors" is taken to make an identifying reference) and "He is sick" (where this is taken to be a claim verifiable by medical science) or any sentence whose linguistic function is other than that of shaping, extending, or organizing our emotive and active responses to things otherwise semantically present to us. But they will count any utterance which functions in the specified way as part of value discourse, regardless of what words it contains or what form it has. In other words, most any utterance can have a value function, and none by its form must be a value sentence.

With the emotivist sharing the classical naturalist's view that affective and conative experiences, categorially speaking, are natural occurrences, states, or conditions, with only a factual structure of the kind indicated by descriptive statements, a problem emerges about how value language can be their instrument. Obviously this way of speaking suggests an analogy with modes of experience and thought taken to have a semantic dimension which makes possible the semantic-tool view of language, but this is denied the kind of emotivist under discussion. Only a causal view of the relationship between affective and conative experience and value language seems to be open to him. Ayer, Stevenson, and others attempted to develop just such a position. A value utterance was said by some to "express" or to evince or to vent the feeling or attitude of the speaker in much the same way as the tone of one's voice might show one's annoyance or displeasure. It was assumed that in the latter case the quality of the voice is an effect of the emotive state and functions for the hearer as a natural sign of its cause in the manner in which smoke means fire and red spots on one's body may mean measles. The analogy cannot be pushed all the way. Value utterances cannot be regarded simply as natural effects of emotive states, but as institutionalized or socially conditioned ways of evincing or venting the emotive states of the speaker or writer and of arousing similar states in the audience, much like exclamation marks and inflections of the voice that show feeling and attitude.

On this view of the nature of value experience and its relationship to value discourse, it is not only that value experience and value language are removed from the epistemic enterprise, but they seem to be placed outside the domain of rationality in their action-guiding functions as well. Indeed "action-guiding" seems to be a misnomer, for on this view of the situation there is no genuine *guiding*, but, as David Falk has felicitously pointed out,[2] only goading. Events, states of affairs, or conditions, with only a structure of pure existence and brute factuality, with no intentional structure, which value experiences are conceived to be on this view, cannot be meaningfully spoken of as rational or irrational, as consistent or inconsistent, as justified or unjustified, as valid or invalid. And if value discourse is only causally related (in the naturalistic sense of social conditioning) to such experiences, either as their effect or as their cause, then there is no room for rational appraisal of value discourse either. And, by extension, the same can be said for action insofar as it is conceived to be the effect of value experience and value discourse. In the opacity of mere existence and factuality, guiding or justifying reasons have no place. There can be only the blind causality of antecedent factual conditions.

And, of course, if the action-guiding function of value experience and value discourse is shown to be illusory and really nothing more than an "action"-causing process, this conclusion must be applied not only to overt behavior but to our so-called cognitive activities as well, where value experiences and value discourse seem to "function" in much the same way as they do with regard to overt behavior. There is excitement, disappointment, feeling troubled, feeling compelled, feeling constrained, feeling that a proposition is worthy of belief, feeling that a given truth is a good reason for believing another proposition, feeling that a thought is justified, etc. If all of this is not what it seems to be on the face of it, but a "thinking"-causing process that is not itself subject to rational appraisal, then the whole epistemic enterprise proves to be an illusion, and everything sinks into the darkness of brute existence and factuality.

4. The causal good-reasons theory of value judgments

We have now traced in broad outlines the slow working out of the implications of the naturalistic way of conceiving and thinking about value experience, that is, taking affective and conative experiences to be occurrences and states subject to being reported, described, and explained in the factual and causal language of empirical science and thus to be of the realm of pure existence and factuality, with no semantic dimension. It was first seen that value language could not have a descriptive-explanatory role in our knowledge of the world, for if value experiences to which it is uniquely related and on which it is dependent are devoid of an internal structure of meaning and have no semantic outreach to the external world, value language cannot have semantic ties to unique features or structures of the world different from those which show up in descriptive-explanatory factual language. Therefore, for descriptive-explanatory purposes value language is at best otiose and completely eliminable. With this realization, value language was taken to have only a descriptive-justificatory function by the classical value naturalist. While value judgments say nothing but what is sayable in factual language, it was said, they are formulated in value language rather than that of empirical science because they are made from within a practical rather than a purely intellectual or knowledge-seeking perspective, where the concern is with decision and justification of action rather than explanation of events or states of affairs. But the descriptive-justificatory theory was torpedoed by the naturalistic fallacy and related arguments, leaving value language only a nondescriptive evaluative action-guiding function, which seems to collapse into a brute factual, causal process, pulling down the house of knowledge and rational action with it. Surely this is a reductio ad absurdum of the purely naturalistic view of value experience. It does not even make room for the wreckers to do their work.

At this point in the unfolding of the implications of the naturalistic assumptions about value experience for value language it was recognized in the philosophical community that room had to be made for rationality both with respect to value judgment and action. In short, even if the descriptive-explanatory function of value language could be dispensed with, the action-guiding function had to be preserved and rendered philosophically intelligible. The so-called "good reasons" school of value theorists and ethicists recognized that in order for value judgments to provide any genuine *guidance* for action the process must not be one of brute factuality and blind causation but somehow intentionality, reason, and knowledge must be involved. A value utterance in a given context, it was seen, cannot be simply an occurrence occasioned by an emotive state, not even a socially conditioned evincing or venting of an emotive state, nor itself a blind causal condition of another emotive state (in an audience) or an action (either of the speaker or another). The utterance must at least commend, condemn, recommend, prescribe, or enjoin against something. A report or description of the linguistic act must mention what is commended, condemned, recommended, or prescribed. The act is internally related to its object. The object is embraced nonexistentially within the structure of the act. In other words, a value utterance, as a linguistic act, must have an intentional structure or semantic dimension so that it makes sense to ask "why?"—not in the sense that asks for an explanation of the utterance as an event, but in the sense that asks for a justifying or validating reason for the commendation, condemnation, prescription, or whatever form the linguistic act takes.

Not only the brute factual, causal view of value talk had to be jettisoned to make sense out of the human enterprise and to show how it is possible for value discourse to be action-guiding, but the strict naturalistic view of action itself had to be called into question. At this point in the ongoing philosophical dialogue, action became a topic of intense discussion. How must it be conceived categorially to make logical room for talk about value-discourse's being action-guiding? If action is subject to rational guidance and rational appraisal, can it have merely a brute factual structure or must it embody a structure of meaning? What is the appropriate form of reports and descriptions of actions and what is their philosophical significance? These are issues we must postpone until later. They are mentioned here because of their intimate relationship to the problem about the action-guiding function of value discourse.

On the view of value utterances as primarily acts of commending, condemning, recommending, prescribing and the like, as distinct from simply reporting or describing, how are they related to value experience? And how must value experience be conceived categorially for it to be related to value language in this presumed manner? Of course in our culture there is resistance to giving up the naturalistic conception of value experience. So it is not surprising to find philosophers operating as though these assumptions need not be disturbed, but it is not clear whether the "good reasons" philosophers have in fact let them lie in peace.

One typical scenario of the "good reasons" school goes something like this. To say "X is good" is to commend X and to say in effect that there are reasons for anyone absolutely or anyone in a certain position (with a certain perspective, orientation, concern, or circumstance) to choose, to support, to promote, or in some way to favor X. And to say to someone "you ought to do X" is "to tell" him to do X and to say in effect that there are reasons for anyone in his situation to do X. It is always meaningful to ask of anything commended, "Why is it good?" and of anything you are told that you ought to do, "Why should I do it?" These "why"s ask for the reasons. Hence, it is argued, a philosopher should not look for the truth-conditions of value judgments, but rather for the arguments which can be brought to back them, arguments which offer reasons for choosing, promoting, or favoring what is commended and for doing what one is told to do or that he ought to do. For factual statements, we can mark a distinction between their truth-value and the arguments that may support them. Indeed the arguments that back them back their claim to be true. No such distinction, it is said, holds for value judgments. They do not have both validity- and truth-values, only validity-values.

The philosopher, of course, is not concerned with producing arguments to back ordinary value judgments, but rather with the nature of such arguments; primarily with what constitutes a reason; how reasons themselves are evaluated as good, bad, adequate, etc.; and how reasons are related to the judgments they back. A prevalent view of the matter holds that a fact, say X is F, is a reason for one in a given position or absolutely to choose, to promote, or somehow to favor X, and therefore a statement of the fact supports the judgment "X is good" if and only if cognition of and attention to the fact X is F would move or incline any informed, rational man in a like position or absolutely to choose, to promote, or to favor X. And the fact X is F is a reason for one in a given position to do Y and a statement of the fact X is F backs the judgment that he ought to do Y if and only if knowledge of and attention to the fact that X is F would incline any informed and rational man in the given situation to do Y and would incline any informed and rational man to approve of anyone in the given position's doing Y. This is not to say that there could not be counter or even overriding reasons, but that the fact in question, if known, would make a difference to a rational, informed, and attentive person.

It seems, then, that value judgments do not have truth-values and that the "reasons" that justify or validate value judgments are facts. So knowledge and reason play an important role in the making of value judgments and in guiding action even though value experience and value judgments do not supplement our factual knowledge of the world available through empirical science, at least not in any way that would lead us to conclude that science is a limited and incomplete method of acquiring knowledge of the world.

But we must not be too hasty. The "good reasons" position, as we have sketched it, in making room for rationality in value discourse and action, recognizes the semantic character of value utterances. And we have suggested that rationality in the area of action is possible only if acts in general also have a semantic dimension or structure of meaning; that is, acts must be conceived and described in terms of the intentions which they embody, if talk about action-guiding and justifying reasons with respect to them is to make sense. This semantic character or meaning structure may itself be something not available to empirical scientific investigation. But we will postpone this problem until chapter 7. We must now explore further how facts can be reasons.

It seems clear, as we have already indicated, that cognition of the facts which are reasons for both favoring something and for the judgment that it is good or for one's doing something and for the judgment that he ought to do it in some way moves people to favor or to do (or to approve the doing of) the things in question and to accept the correlative value judgments. But just how does this work? What is involved? This is a most important problem.

Let us consider some simple arguments.

1. This pen is blue. So it is a good pen.
2. This pen writes smoothly. So it is a good pen.

It is to be assumed, of course, that these are not intended to be conclusive; only that the premise supports the conclusion. Most anyone would reject (1) as having no validity, but would accept (2) as valid. To accept the premise of (1) in no way moves or inclines an informed, rational person to accept the conclusion, but to accept the premise of (2) does move or incline such a person to accept the conclusion. We would not believe that one who rejected (2), saying the premise was irrelevant to the conclusion, really understood the argument.

3. The coffee is cold. So it is not good.
4. The milk is cold. So it is not good.

Here most would agree that the premise in (3) supports the conclusion, but that the premise in (4) does not. The premise in (4), however, is not irrelevant as in (1), but in most situations would count against the conclusion.

The issue we want to explore is the connection between the premises and conclusion of this kind of argument that warrants us in saying that informed, rational men would be moved or inclined in certain ways. Obviously an informed, rational man comes to such arguments with a stockpile of information, memories, principles, assumptions, attitudes, wants, and the like. It might be argued convincingly that this stockpile provides suppressed premises which together with the given premise (or premises) logically yield the value conclusion so that the movement of the mind from the acceptance of the given premise (or premises) to the acceptance of the conclusion is no different from that in arguments involving only factual statements. However, it is widely held, and with justification, that for this to be so the suppressed premises provided from the stockpile must contain what amounts to at least one value judgment.

One who takes this approach will treat value judgments as embracing imperatives and "ought"-judgments, as well as predicative value judgments like "X is good," "X is right," etc. This is not arbitrary. While we would not want to treat an imperative sentence as the expression of a judgment, strictly speaking, there are reasons for counting it a value sentence. For one thing, an imperative premise in conjunction with a factual premise can yield a value-judgment conclusion. For example: Stop when the light is red; the light is red; therefore you ought to stop. Or: Stop when the light is red; the light was red; you did not stop; therefore it was wrong for you not to stop. Or again: Build house H according to the set of blueprints A and the set of specifications B; the set of descriptions C, which consists of a translation of the prescriptions of blueprints A and specifications B into descriptions, are true of the completed house H; therefore, the builders of house H did a good job. Also it makes sense to ask of any imperative "Why?" with the same force as it does of an "ought"-judgment or a predicative value judgment; that is, an imperative sentence can be backed by the same kind of argument. In fact, we may say that an imperative sentence is a lean, stripped down "ought"-sentence. Any imperative sentence, with respect to its semantic function (prescription), can be replaced by an "ought"-sentence. As we indicated earlier, the sentence "You ought to do X" entails "Do X" and says in effect that there are reasons for the person addressed doing X. We would not believe that one had accepted the judgment that he ought to do X if we did not believe that he had accepted the imperative to do X, that is, that he was committed to doing X, or at least strongly inclined to do X. It would not make sense to say "We convinced him that he ought to do X but I don't think that he is at all disposed to do it."

We must be careful to distinguish the strictly semantic function of imperative sentences, their prescriptive functions, from their use as commands. "Do X" has the same semantic function when used to give a command as when used to advise or to instruct. In both cases, the sentence prescribes an act, indeed the same act, but with a different force, defined by the circumstances of the utterance and the intent of the speaker.

Admittedly "ought"-sentences cannot replace imperative sentences in commands, and preserve their force. This is not what I am claiming. But it is revealing for our purposes to examine the conditions of commands. A command requires a position of authority on the part of the one who gives the command vis à vis the person commanded. Such a position is constituted by a responsibility or right to make decisions that obligate those subject to the authority to carry them out. A certain competence is required of one as a qualification for the position, a competence consisting of the knowledge and wisdom to make sound decisions on matters with respect to which the authority pertains and thus to command within reasonable limits only that for which there are objective reasons in the situation for doing. So we may still say that in principle even commands can be replaced with respect to their semantic functions by "ought"-judgments, but not with respect to their force.

Where imperative sentences may in a sense be said to be lean "ought"-sentences, predicative value sentences may be said to be fat "ought"-sentences, fattened with existence claims. To say that X is good is to say that X is more or less the way it ought to be. To say that X is good and to back the claim by citing the fact that X is F is to say in effect that X, in being F, is the way it ought to be. We equate "X ought to be F" with "X would be good if it were F" or "It would be good if X were F." So a "good"-judgment combines an "ought" and an "is" judgment. The same is true for "right" and other value predicates. So there is nothing strained or arbitrary in calling imperative and "ought"-sentences, as well as sentences with value predicates, value sentences. We may with equal ease call them "normative" sentences after the "ought"-sentence. These are three syntactical forms of value discourse.

Let us return to the point that for a factual premise to yield logically a value conclusion there must be a suppressed value premise. This was Hume's point, as we saw earlier, in claiming that we cannot derive "ought" from "is." It was also, as previously remarked, the point of Moore's naturalistic fallacy argument. Yet John Searle has attempted to instruct us in "how to derive 'ought' from 'is'" in a paper with that title.[3] He leads us through the following steps: "(1) Jones uttered the words 'I hereby promise to pay you, Smith, five dollars.' (2) Jones promised to pay Smith five dollars. (3) Jones placed himself under (undertook) an obligation to pay Smith five dollars. (4) Jones is under an obligation to pay Smith five dollars. (5) Jones ought to pay Smith five dollars." I think he is quite right. The derivation is valid. He is also right, I think, in pointing out that the facts stated by the factual premises from which the value conclusion is derived are peculiar in that they are what he calls "institutional" facts, facts "whose existence presuppose certain institutions," the institutions of language, promise making, etc. These are to be contrasted with brute facts, like those asserted by "this thing is blue," "Jones is six feet tall," and the like. Institutions are constituted by rules or, what amounts to the same thing, recognized and accepted general imperatives. Thus institutional facts are high level facts which embrace structures of value, meaning, and fact. Those who claim that value judgments do not follow logically from factual statements mean factual statements which involve only the categories of factuality, those which assert only brute facts. So there is nothing in Searle's argument that counters the point of the naturalistic fallacy argument or Hume's claim that we cannot derive the category of "ought" from the category of "is." His paper is important not for what it shows about values, but for the distinction between brute and higher level facts.

Let us now return to the issue of how a purely factual statement (one that asserts a brute fact, or at least a value-free fact) may provide support for a value judgment. If it is the case, and I think it is, that no purely factual premise alone logically yields a value conclusion, then is it the case that whenever one correctly takes or judges a purely factual premise to support a value conclusion it is by virtue of a suppressed value premise which he provides from his own storehouse in conjunction with the given factual premise so that the validity of the inference is logical in character? There is a certain plausibility in the view that this is so. No one faces a particular fact or set of facts empty minded. No one can simply accept or believe a new factual proposition with which he is presented. There has to be a place for it in his mind. There have to be commitments, assumptions, beliefs, memories, and attitudes which embrace it and welcome it. And if there are commitments, assumptions, beliefs, and attitudes which are disturbed and feel threatened by the new proposition, then either the new proposition will be rejected or room will have to be made for it by either adjustment or dislodgement of some of the prior contents of the mind. Coming to believe a new statement may force extensive, even radical rearrangement of one's mind and this can be a slow and painful process. One may have very compelling reasons for believing a proposition but not be able to do so. Again a given proposition may be eminently believable for one and he may readily accept it with apparently little or nothing to support it. All of this is a matter of what one brings to the consideration of the matter. So it may well be that with value judgments or their equivalents the acceptance of a new factual statement will pull along with it a certain value judgment; that is, given one's commitments, attitudes, assumptions, and all, it might be irrational of him, a matter of logical inconsistency, for him to accept the given factual statement and reject a certain value judgment. If so, he would have to acknowledge that the factual statement backed the value judgment and provided a reason for him to accept it.

If this is what makes a fact a reason for favoring or doing something and the statement of the fact a premise for a value conclusion about the thing or act in question, then reasons and the validity of arguments for value judgments would seem to be relative to those considering them unless it could be assumed with justification that informed, rational men would approach any given situation with a common stock of suppressed premises. Some philosophers have distinguished between what they have called "subjective" and "objective" reasons along these lines. Subjective reasons are said to be those which would be acknowledged by only an individual or group because of his or their peculiar makeup; whereas objective reasons are said to be those which would be acknowledged by any informed, rational man either absolutely or from within a shareable perspective or orientation which anyone could in principle adopt. Adoptable perspectives or orientations which would provide relative but objective reason-generating premises would include anything from games like chess or baseball to institutions like promise-making, marriage, an economic system, a government, or even, according to some, the moral enterprise itself. Reasons which any informed rational man would acknowledge absolutely would depend on value assumptions and factual beliefs one would have to have in order to qualify as both rational and informed; for, on this view, if one failed to acknowledge what was already established to be an absolute objective reason, this fact would count against the claim that he was rational and fully informed about relevant matters. What is involved here is the assumption or thesis that for one to be engaged in knowledge-seeking, information-gathering, or the rational enterprise generally, one must accept certain value judgments or at least operate under certain value commitments. In other words, the rational enterprise is taken to be constituted by certain imperatives or normative principles so that all undertakings or adopted enterprises presuppose them. Therefore all people may be presumed to share them. So on this approach we should recognize subjective reasons, relative objective reasons, and absolute objective reasons.

Two questions suggest themselves: Do we have adequate stockpiles of value premises together with factual beliefs to generate all the reasons we acknowledge? And what about the value judgments in one's stockpile? Are there reasons for them? And if so, are there still further value premises which generate those reasons, and so on ad infinitum? Or just what status do they have?

With regard to the first question, a person can of course quite genuinely explore why a given fact about a situation makes a difference to him. Suppose a poor man should find himself, for example, against a tax reform bill because it would wipe out all inheritance in excess of $500,000. When pushed on the matter of why he counted this fact a reason against the bill, he might after some reflective soul-searching come up with the judgment that a private property system is a good thing and that owner-ship of property or wealth in any form entails the right to transfer the ownership to others, which the proposed bill would compromise. But we could never in this way establish nor falsify the claim that for every fact anyone acknowledges to be a reason for favoring or doing something (or for disfavoring or not doing something), he does so by virtue of some value assumption or prior commitment. If one subscribes to the theory of reasons under consideration, every time he confronts a fact which he "finds" to be relevant or to make a difference to some issue, to count for or to count against some value judgment, he would have no trouble locating the requisite value premise in his storehouse for he would take it to be a presupposition of the reason he acknowledges. And it would be said of the person who does not subscribe to this theory of reasons, that, in his search for the alleged suppressed value premises for the reasons he ac-knowledges, he denies himself the proper access route, namely, the presuppositions of the reasons in question.

The point is that the thesis that a factual statement supports a value judgment only in conjunction with a value premise, suppressed or other-wise, is not an inductive generalization and therefore is not subject to being confirmed or falsified by the examination of instances in search of value premises. It is a philosophical theory about the nature of arguments for value judgments and what constitutes a reason for favoring or disfa-voring something and for doing or not doing some act. The claim is that there is a conceptual tie between a fact's being a reason and a value premise just as there is between a man's being a husband and there being a woman to whom he is related in a certain way. What would be relevant would be a situation in ·vhich we could consistently affirm that a given factual state-ment provided a reason for a certain value judgment and deny that there was a value premise working in conjunction with the factual statement in providing support for the value conclusion. Thus looking at certain situa-tions and exploring what we would and would not say about them can re-veal how our concepts behave and whether the theory in question is true of them. But it is often difficult to make sure that we are giving a theory-free reading of the logical behavior of the concepts in question. We have grounds for suspicion, however, when we find ourselves, as in this case, positing a vast number of value assumptions and commitments which are recognized in no way other than through our acknowledgement of reasons for value conclusions. When this is the case, it behooves us to consider alternative theories.

The question about the status of the value judgments located in or imputed to our storehouse is an even more serious matter. No doubt we do confront any particular situation with a vast stock of value assumptions and commitments. Many of these surely are subject to being reasoned about as well as to being reasoned from. In our recent example of the poor man, he could undoubtedly give a reason for his judgment that a system of private ownership of wealth is a good thing. He might readily say that it is a good thing because it makes for greater independence of the individual. But why is that a reason for the value judgment in question? Clearly, it would be said, he is arguing from the premise that independence is a good thing. Well, why is it? This question seems appropriate, but one is likely to be taken aback by it, for he expects the judgment to be accepted without argument. If the issue is pushed, we are likely to get one of several kinds of answers, none of which is of the ordinary reason-giving type. It might be said that here we are back to a basic value which simply has to be acknowledged as such. Or the response might be that people like to be independent, that they dislike being dependent, that people are unhappy when they are not independent, and the like. Some might say that man is by nature independent so that dependence is an unnatural state or condition for him. And others might say that any informed, rational person would choose to be independent. All of these replies indicate that the fact that a private property system makes for greater independence is an absolute reason for favoring a private property system. This would not mean of course that there are not other considerations, or that making for greater independence is an overriding reason. In fact, some might see in the independence of individuals or of families a threat to communal life and therefore might argue that a system of private wealth is a bad thing because it makes for independence. Here they would be reasoning from the premise that independence is a bad thing. "Why?" asked of this premise would elicit an ordinary kind of reason to the effect that independence undermines and weakens communal solidarity. Underlying this argument is the assumption that communal solidarity is a good thing, which in turn admits to being questioned, in the ordinary reason-seeking way. The reason elicited might be that communal solidarity provides strength and support for each member of the community. The assumption is, of course, that this is good, but why? At some point not far removed, we would be back to something acknowledged to be good, for which continued questioning would not elicit an ordinary kind of reason and the answers would repeat those given above for why independence is good. And so faced with conflicting values, some accommodation would have to be made by finding ways of achieving some measure of independence within a supporting community.

    Both of the above examples of reasoning terminate in absolute reasons, reasons which any rational, informed person would be expected to acknowledge as binding on him. But there are reasons which only those operating from within a certain perspective or orientation could be expected to acknowledge as so binding. For example, suppose A should say to B, "You ought to wear white today," and upon being asked "Why?" he said, "Because your father is dead." This would provide a reason for those operating within the Chinese institution for expressing grief and respect upon the death of a member of one's family. The judgment that one ought to act out his grief and respect in a socially acceptable way upon such an occasion, however, is not so restricted. And the reasons that would back it would lead us to the limit of ordinary reason-seeking questions as in the cases considered above. Even in the case of reasoning about moves within a game of chess, for example, although appeals will be made to the imperatives the players accepted and submitted themselves to in undertaking to play the game, namely, those that define the objective and constitute the rules of the game, at some point these may be transcended by appealing to reasons for playing the game and to principles of sportsmanship in general.

Talk about acknowledgment of reasons for favoring or doing something may be misleading. Some may read it in such a way that for one to acknowledge a reason for an act involves his being inclined or moved to perform that act. This no doubt is true when one acknowledges a reason for *his* doing something. But "acknowledgment of a reason for an act" may include acknowledgment of a reason for someone else to do something or for anyone in a certain situation to do such and such. Indeed the universalizability principle applies to all reasons. If F is a reason for A to do G under conditions C, then F would be a reason for anyone to do G under conditions C (provided C is taken to include the imperatives one is committed to), and to acknowledge the antecedent with understanding is to acknowledge the consequent. Therefore most of the reasons one acknowledges may not incline or move him to do anything, but only to favor or to approve someone else's doing something.

The important point which has emerged from our discussion is that the "good reasons" theory, in the form which we have considered, leaves us with value judgments which cannot be accounted for by the theory, namely, those ultimate value premises for which the ordinary reason-seeking questions go begging and cannot be answered. All the position establishes is that, given certain value judgments or commitments, logic, in conjunction with factual beliefs, can generate further value judgments. And to that extent rationality is possible. But all the important philosophical problems about value language and its relationship to value experience and to the world remain. Are these ultimate value judgments really statements of psychological fact after all as the classical naturalists would have it? Or "expressions" of these states as the emotivists would have it? We have already seen the inadequacies of those positions. There must be some other possibility.

The "good reasons" position, however, has revealed to us two important things to consider. One is the syntactical complexity of value language. Its approach shows, as previously remarked, the logical connectedness and therefore the categorial relatedness of predicative value sentences, "ought"-sentences, and imperative sentences. These belong together and make up the area of discourse with which we are concerned. Insight into the interrelatedness of these forms helps us in understanding the problem with predicative value sentences of the form "X is good" which Moore was wrestling with in the naturalistic fallacy argument. To say that X is good does not, as Moore pointed out, describe X. It does not ascribe to it a characterizing property. Rather it says that X, in having the properties it does have, is more or less the way it ought to be. And to say X ought to be F is to say that there is a good reason for X to be F. So "good"-talk cashes into "ought"- plus "existence"- and "fact"-talk; and "ought"-talk cashes into imperative sentences and "reasons"-talk. This, I think, is an important gain.

The other thing the "good reasons" philosophers have shown us is that, contrary to the emotive theory, value judgments, including even the ultimate value assumptions invoked in arguing for value judgments, stand in genuine logical relationships. They have logical entailments and may be meaningfully spoken of as logically consistent or inconsistent with other beliefs and judgments. This is particularly significant with respect to the stockpile theory of suppressed premises. Many, perhaps most, of the alleged value premises invoked in giving reasons in the manner the theory acknowledges have never been articulated. They are there, if at all, as psychological states or dispositions, but as states or dispositions which, like ordinary factual beliefs, stand in logical relationships and lend themselves to being linguistically formulated or expressed. This opens up the possibility of a new kind of relationship between value sentences and value psychological states which classical naturalists and emotivists did not consider, namely, that of genuine *expression* in the sense of articulation. The classical naturalist had thought of value sentences as being of or about value experiences and their causes. The emotivist had thought of value utterances as "expressions" of value psychological states, but they conceived the latter as pure events, states of affairs, or factual dispositions in such a way that it did not make sense to talk about them as standing in logical relationships or as having a semantic dimension. Therefore they could not make sense out of talk about a value utterance being an articulation or linguistic formulation of the value psychological state or disposition. So "to express" could only mean to vent, to show, or in some way to exhibit the value attitude or state of the speaker. But if the value psychological state or disposition which is unexpressed can stand in logical relationships to statements and judgments in an argument or in logical relationships at all, then it must be the kind of thing that a value sentence can proxy for and the two must in some sense be the same. In other words, our feelings, attitudes, emotions, desires, and the like may be of such a nature that they can be put into language, not in the sense of being reported or described, nor in the sense of being vented, evinced, or shown, but in the sense of articulation or translation. What is semantically in the psychological state or act can be put semantically in value sentences. And it may well be the case that some of these psychological dispositions, states, or acts are dependent on value language in the sense that they would not be possible without the capability of linguistic expression.

We moved from talk about value psychological states and dispositions having logical relationships to their having a semantic dimension. This was suggested by the fact that their being subject to being invoked as suppressed premises in arguments indicates they are the kind of thing for which sentences can be proxies. But the point should be made that it does not make sense to talk about anything in logical terms which does not have a semantic dimension or is at least incomplete or somehow defective if it does not. There can be conflicts and effects in the purely existent, factual world but not logical incompatibilities and implications. These can hold only among intentional acts or structures of meaning. Indeed if the realm of pure existence and factuality as such could embody logical inconsistencies, inconsistency would not be a mark of error in the area of thought, for if some pure facts that obtain in the world were inconsistent, then the several beliefs about these facts would have to be inconsistent to be true. Also if things or states of affairs with no semantic dimension could be logically inconsistent, such inconsistency would indicate nothing about truth or falsity, for these are semantic concepts and as such apply only to things that embody semantic claims. In short, logical and semantic concepts belong to the same team so that the one kind is not applicable to a given subject matter unless the other is also.

It will be instructive for us to consider further the status of the psychological states or dispositions invoked in our arguments for value judgments. We have seen that value sentences can be their proxies. The indications are that these proxies may take on any of the syntactical forms of value sentences. Certainly our efforts at formulating the suppressed premises of such arguments produce imperative, "ought"-, and predicative value sentences. Insofar as these sentences are proxies for or expressions of the psychological states and dispositions appealed to in the arguments, it seems reasonable to think of the psychological states, acts, and commitments involved as having the same syntactical forms as their respective proxy-sentences. A psychological state with the form of an imperative sentence would be a desire, a want, a craving, a longing, an intention, or some conative state. One with the "ought"-form would be a felt constraint or restraint, a feeling that oneself or another is caught up in an imperative, that an imperative impinges on oneself or another, that something is required of oneself or another, or the like. It is a more complex and sophisticated psychological state or disposition than a simple desire or longing in a way that parallels the greater complexity and sophistication of an "ought"-sentence over a simple imperative sentence. The psychological states and dispositions which are parallel with predicative value judgments are those of liking and disliking, favoring and disfavoring, approving and disapproving, and the like. Again there seems to be the same kind of higher level complexity that matches the greater complexity of predicative value sentences. Fundamentally we like or dislike, favor or disfavor, and approve or disapprove what exists. Insofar as we talk about liking (or disliking), favoring (or disfavoring), or approving (or disapproving) something which does not exist, we mean that we would like (or dislike) it, etc. if it were to exist. And this is just the way our talk about something's being good (or bad) or right (or wrong) behaves.

Now let us look at the kinds of ultimate answers the reason-seeking "why?" elicits. In our example about the poor man's opposition to heavy inheritance taxes, we find that he counts personal independence a good thing and that the reason-seeking question about this judgment elicits such answers as "People like to be independent," "They dislike being dependent," "They want to be independent," and the like. These, as we observed earlier, are of quite a different order from the ordinary kinds of reasons that are given. They report what we have called value psychological states or dispositions of the kind for which the value sentence, "Independence is a good thing," may be a proxy. If our analysis of predicative value sentences is correct, to say that independence is a good thing is to say that the independent person is the way one ought to be, and this indicates that it is imperative for a person to be independent. The answer that people want to be independent in response to the question about why independence is a good thing simply reports the common psychological state for which an imperative sentence would be a proxy. Even the reply in terms of the nature of man says that man by his very constitution is under an imperative to be independent. This may be a report of the same imperative that appears at the psychological level as a want or longing and for which an imperative sentence could be a proxy. These are suggestions which have profound and far-reaching implications, but they must await further developments in our enterprise before they can be explored.

We have been considering how value sentences can proxy for value psychological states and dispositions; that is, how we can express or translate psychological states and dispositions into value sentences. It may be illuminating to consider the reverse order. In the case of beliefs, we readily recognize that we can express them in sentences and that in accepting what is said in factual sentences we form beliefs. The same is true for value sentences. If we accept what we are told in value sentences, we form value psychological states and attitudes. To accept what we are told by the sentence "X is good," in many cases anyway, is to form a pro-attitude toward X. To accept what we are told by the sentence "X is right" is to form an attitude of approval toward X. To accept what we are told by the imperative "do X" when it is addressed to us is to form the intention to do X. When a person undertakes in good faith to play a game, he accepts the rules of the game, the general imperatives which define it, and thereby forms a clear set of intentions and commitments which may be invoked or appealed to in reasoning about particular moves or situations within the game. It should also be pointed out that when we reason from some psychological state or commitment in conjunction with some factual beliefs to a new value conclusion, to accept that conclusion is to form a new value attitude or commitment. If this were not so, such reasoning would serve no action-guiding purpose.

That there are value psychological states, dispositions, and commitments with semantic and logical structures which lend themselves to being expressed or formulated linguistically and that they themselves can be formed by the acceptance of what is expressed in value sentences are conclusions of the greatest importance. But what about one's basic psychological states, dispositions, and commitments which are not formed by logical derivation or by acceptance of what we are told? How do they occur or come into being? This is not a scientific question. The answer is to be sought by exploring what it makes sense to say and what it does not make sense to say about such origins.

One way some "good reasons" philosophers have answered the question is this. Some facts count as a reason for a value judgment, not because the value judgment follows logically from a statement of the fact in question in conjunction with a suppressed value premise, but by virtue of the fact that comprehension of and attention to the fact in question causally produces a value psychological state, a nonindifferent response to the fact or to that to which the fact pertains; and that the linguistically formulated value judgment for which the fact is a reason both in some sense "expresses" the nonindifferent response and asserts that the comprehension of and attention to the fact in question caused the psychological state "expressed" in the value judgment and thus implies, by virtue of the generality of the causal relation, that a similar attention to the fact in question would so move anyone. One who subscribed to this theory might claim that to say that personal independence is a good thing, to use our earlier example, is to "express" one's pro-attitude toward personal independence and to say that the pro-attitude thus "expressed" was caused by comprehension of and attention to what it is to be personally independent and by implication that anyone who comprehended and attended to personal independence in this manner would be so affected.

This is a theory about basic value judgments. One who subscribed to it would not deny that further value judgments can be logically derived from a given value judgment in conjunction with factual beliefs. But when confronted with a value conclusion drawn from a set of factual premises without any obvious suppressed value premise, he would not be inclined to search very hard for underlying value assumptions.

If the nonindifferent psychological state caused by the cognition of and attention to the fact in question is conceived naturalistically, that is, as devoid of a semantic and logical structure, so that linguistic "expression" of it can be only a venting, evincing, or showing of it in the manner of the emotivist theory, which all of our earlier arguments for a nonnaturalistic view counts against, then at this point the "good reasons" position is in the last analysis nothing more than a combination of the emotivist and classical naturalist positions. Of course it might be that such a combination combines the virtues of both while canceling out the weaknesses of each. But unfortunately this does not seem to be the case.

One of the weaknesses of emotivism is that it does not account for, indeed it denies, the logical relationships of value judgments; whereas one of the virtues of classical naturalism is that it does acknowledge and make sense out of such logical relationships. And one of the virtues of emotivism is that it acknowledges and tries to make sense out of the emotive state usually involved in accepting a value judgment; whereas one of the weaknesses of classical naturalism is that it does not do so. It might seem that the combination "good reasons" theory under discussion appropriates these virtues and avoids these weaknesses, if we consider only a single value judgment like "personal independence is a good thing." But when we look at arguments involving value judgments trouble arises. The combination comes apart. How can a naturalistic nonindifferent psychological effect caused by the cognition of a given fact and "expressed" in a value judgment be transported by a chain of logical inferences to a value conclusion which involves another fact? If the value psychological states were only naturalistic causal effects of cognitions of facts, it would seem that we would have to investigate empirically to determine whether value arguments could transport such states from premises to conclusions and appropriately transform them in the process. For example, how could the emotive state be transferred and appropriately transformed in our argument: "Personal independence is a good thing. A system of private wealth makes for personal independence. Ownership of wealth involves the right of disposition of the wealth. Liquidation inheritance taxes compromise the right of disposition of private wealth. Therefore liquidation inheritance taxes are bad." Granted the argument could alter our comprehension of liquidation inheritance taxes, and, according to the theory, this might causally produce an emotive response, but we would have to experiment to find out what the emotive effect would be, if any. In other words, the theory cannot make sense out of the value conclusion's following logically from the premises. It is forced back into the emotivist view that the logical inferences involve only the factual statements. A rational person, accordingly, would be one whose feelings, emotions, inclinations, and actions were causally dependent on his cognitions of and beliefs about the facts so that the former were responsive to changes in the latter. But it would make no sense to talk about feelings, emotions, and the like being irrational in the sense of being logically inconsistent and unresponsive to criticism to this effect. Thus this version of the "good reasons" theory preserves one of the foremost weaknesses of the emotive theory (the inability to render intelligible the logical relationships of value judgments) and one of the more telling deficiencies of the classical naturalist position (the inability to do justice to the emotive dimension of value language).

Suppose the value psychological states were conceived nonnaturalistically as having semantic and logical structures so that value sentences might be genuine *expressions* of them or proxies for them. We have argued that the "good reasons" theory has to take this position if it is to do justice to the way arguments for value judgments behave. Now is it possible on this view to hold that some value psychological states, particularly those our basic, logically underived value judgments express, are causally induced by cognition of or beliefs about the facts of the situations to which they pertain? Here we have to be careful about just what is being asked. It is not simply whether the cognition of or attention to the facts in question occasions the nonindifferent psychological state, but the way in which it does so. The issue is whether we are free or in some important sense rational in our emotive reactions to facts and situations semantically present to us. If we take the causal view under discussion, we would have to deny that we are. If the semantic presence of a certain situation to a person causally produces, in the naturalistic sense of causation here intended, a value psychological state which would be expressed by the sentence "X is good," then it would not make sense to say that the person was responsible for his attitude in any way over and above what responsibility might be attributed to him for the cognition of and attention to the facts in the case. We could not fault him nor praise him for his feelings and attitudes except in the sense in which we might praise or condemn him for his natural features; that is, it would not make sense to say he was responsible or accountable for them. Nor could we fault the feelings and attitudes themselves if they were inconsistent among themselves or inconsistent with the emotive reactions of others to the same cognized facts. Remember that the theory holds that these value psychological states have a semantic dimension and a logical structure. But on the naturalistic causal view their occurrence and continued existence are totally impervious to these matters. What occurs or comes into existence by such a causal process simply is. It may be explained, but it is not subject to being assessed as right or wrong, correct or incorrect, justified or unjustified, valid or invalid, rational or irrational. Like dreams or hallucinations, they may have a semantic dimension and logical relationships, but their existence is in tow to occurrences in another causal chain. Insofar as rational appraisal talk would be at all applicable to nonindifferent psychological states, it would, on this view, be indirectly through its application to the underlying cognition of and attention to the facts involved.

This being so, the same problem arises which we encountered above about how value psychological states can be transported and transformed by logical inference from accepted value premises to value conclusions. It seems as though there are some value arguments which are such that if one accepts their value and factual premises and rejects their value conclusions, he is subject not only to having it said of him that he is inconsistent but also that his inconsistency is a fault, indeed the same kind of fault he would have in accepting the factual premises of a valid deductive argument and rejecting its factual conclusion. It is not at all clear how the causal "good reasons" theory could render intelligible how it is possible for value judgments to behave as they seem to in the very argumentation the theory focuses attention upon. This seems to be a fatal defect.

5. The voluntaristic good-reasons theory of value judgments

The existentialist insists that we are free in our value stances toward cognized facts. Like the causal "good reasons" philosopher, he thinks that one is in some way at fault or subject to criticism if he is not informed or makes no effort to be informed about the facts of a situation he confronts or does not attend to them. But given comprehension of and attention to the facts, the existentialist maintains that whether one favors or disfavors, approves or disapproves, or however he looks upon the situation value-wise, it is a matter of choice, his decision. There are no guidelines for him. There is no way he can go wrong or make a mistake, for this kind of talk about one's value orientations or commitments, given that he is fully open to the facts of the situation, makes no sense. There is no room for either justification or causal explanation. This is what freedom means for the existentialist. Raymond Polin, a French existentialist, says: "Whereas noetic consciousness, by means of an act of immanence, is lost in the object, and, by becoming aware of it, expresses its truth and reveals it, there axiological consciousness, by means of the act of transcendence, overcomes the given, invents the unreal, and creates. . . . It belongs to each man to choose the orientation and scope of his own transcendence, and to decide in an essential uncertainty, beyond all determination, on his values and actions. Now, the structure of the act of transcendence is essentially subjective," he maintains. "Man, the power to transcend who invents its unreal values and creates its works, depends at each moment only upon himself. In this creation of the self by the self, he founds himself. With respect to the certainty he acquires and the work he creates, he is a god who is responsible and sufficient. Values and actions are founded *de jure* only within the framework of the subjective human person, and also only for him."[4]

Here we have the existentialist position succinctly stated. The two fundamental modalities of human consciousness are said to be knowledge and action. In the former, there is self-transcendence toward things-in-being and consciousness has to conform itself to things-in-being. This is what constitutes truth and knowledge. In the case of action and the valuations which shape it, however, human consciousness transcends itself toward nonbeing or possibility and the realm of things-in-being is transformed to make it conform to consciousness. This is creativity. It is a matter of going beyond what is through choice and action. There is no place for truth in this mode of consciousness. "If it is true that there is neither a foundation nor an objectivity of values, if they escape all reality as well as all determination, what relationships are there, then, between truths and values? . . . The idea of an axiological truth would be limited to an ethical coherence of an invented value and of an axiological hierarchy that is conventionally accepted. . . . Now, a value is not a real thing which is given; it is essentially imaginary and unreal; it does not contain any reality that is susceptible to being revealed. . . . The evaluation constitutes a deliberate transcendence that brings about a hierarchy and creates, but does not reveal any data."[5] Thus values are taken to be subjective and unreal. It is the task of each man, by virtue of his freedom, to transcend his given situation and the conventional "values" and "norms" of his culture by creating personal values on the basis of his comprehension of the facts of his situation. To do less is not to be an authentic self.

The existentialist acknowledges the intentionality, the semantic character, of our value modes of consciousness and therefore that they lend themselves to linguistic expression or articulation in value language. Since decision, or choice, is taken to be the basic form of value consciousness, the imperative sentence, it would seem, must be regarded as the basic form of value language, even though existentialists are not given to talking in these terms. Although decisions, commitments that have imperative form, may be free from causes and givens, they stand in logical relationships with one another and therefore one must be under some logical constraint in this mode of consciousness, for logically inconsistent imperatives cannot all be fullfilled through action or any other way any more so than logically inconsistent thoughts can all be true. Indeed existentialists recognize the need to be coherent in one's valuations and actions, not only for the reason just mentioned, but also because of their view of selfhood. One invents or constitutes himself by his choices. He is the project his decisions define. So if he is to be a unitary self, his valuations must form a more or less coherent whole. There must be life-constituting decisions, commitment to imperatives that define a life style, with which lesser valuations must be consistent. Otherwise one will not only be defeated in his actions by virtue of undertaking the impossible but he will disrupt his selfhood.

This view of the nature of our basic value commitments, which we may call the voluntaristic "good reasons" theory, avoids one of the chief difficulties of the causal "good reasons" theory. It makes sense out of how commitment to a value premise can be transported and appropriately transformed by logical inference to a value conclusion, for to reject a valid value conclusion while holding on to the value premise would be a decision inconsistent with one's commitment expressed in the value premise. This would be to commit oneself to an impossibility or to divide oneself. The existentialist position, however, has its own problems. While claiming that all valuations are free and personal, it acknowledges the imperative to be consistent in one's valuation as binding on all. This does not seem to be a matter of choice, but an imperative the acknowledgment of which is a condition for being the kind of being who can make choices and thereby constitute himself. We could not make sense out of one's choosing not to be consistent in one's valuations and actions, for we cannot make sense out of talk about one's choosing and striving for what he acknowledges to be logically impossible. The existentialist insists that all valuations are modes of reaching out intentionally to possibilities, not to impossibilities. Any effort so to choose, if we can make any sense out of this, would, on the existentialist view, force division of the self and thereby destroy the choosing self and consequently the choice. So here is a value, namely, consistency of one's valuations and actions, which seems to be given, not created by one's valuation. The existentialist theory has no way of accounting for such a value; and, furthermore, as a comprehensive theory, it seems to be wrecked on this given and universal value.

Existentialism, at least in the form under discussion, draws a sharp distinction between noetic or knowledge-seeking consciousness and valuative, action-oriented consciousness. But surely the cognitive enterprise itself is shot through with valuations. We count inconsistency in thought bad and to be avoided, consistency good and to be sought. We are committed to the pursuit of truth and to the avoidance of falsity in our beliefs. We are troubled by confusion and lack of intelligibility and seek clarity and understanding. We count some propositions worthy of belief and others not. We count some statements as evidence for another, that is, we count them as worthy-of-belief-making statements. Even knowing some fact involves valuations as recognized by most analyses of what it is to know. If all of these valuations involved in the cognitive enterprise should be conceived in the existentialist manner, then "knowledge" in any form would be a purely personal affair and devoid of objectivity and truth, which is to say that there would be no knowledge at all.

And if knowledge is not possible, it does not make sense to talk about reality. And if we cannot talk meaningfully about an objective reality we cannot talk meaningfully about choosing unreal possibilities to be made real through action. So talk about valuation, action, and creativity would collapse into meaninglessness if the existentialist's theory of valuations were true.

If this reductio ad absurdum of the voluntaristic "good reasons" theory is sound, and I believe it is, then is there any other way in which we can account for our basic value orientations toward recognized facts which would avoid its difficulties as well as those of the causal "good reasons" theory? I think that we have shown that the basic nonindifferent psychological responses to cognized facts which are expressed in value premises of value arguments cannot be conceived as causally produced in the naturalistic sense. They must be "free" but in a nonvoluntaristic sense. This may provide a way out of the value-subjectivism trap.

V

Value Realism

Let us review the situation to see just where we are at this point. We have found that the classical naturalist theory, which holds that value language is of or about value experiences and their causal conditions, and emotivism, which holds that value sentences, in their value function, evince or show the emotive state of the speaker and tend to incite or causally arouse similar emotive states in the audience, are unacceptable for compelling reasons. The "good reasons" theory, as we have seen, is an attempt to construct an acceptable theory in light of the virtues and weaknesses of the other two. It recognizes that we argue for value judgments and that facts can be cited as reasons for favoring (or disfavoring) and for doing (or not doing) things. It seeks to understand value judgments in terms of the arguments that back them. It recognizes that value conclusions cannot follow logically from purely factual premises, and that, therefore, whenever a value judgment is logically inferred from apparently purely factual premises there are supressed value premises. These must be, in many cases at least, in the form of value psychological states or dispositions which lend themselves to being "expressed" in value sentences. Some of these may be logically implied by still further premises, but some must lack such backing. Problems arise about our basic, logically underived value judgments. The reason-seeking "why" asked of them elicits reports of value psychological states or dispositions which the judgments in question "express." We have considered several ways of understanding the nature and origin of these valuational states and dispositions of mind. We have explored whether they are nonintentionalistic and causally produced in a naturalistic way, intentionalistic but nonetheless tied naturalistically to causes, or intentionalistic and free in the voluntaristic sense of the existentialist. We have found all these unacceptable for what seem to be commanding reasons. We have, however, concluded that valuational states and dispositions of mind, including the basic ones, are intentionalistic and "free" in some sense. Our problem at this point is to determine in what sense they are free.

1. An epistemological analysis of value psychological states and acts

The first thing that can be said is that "free" in this context means, negatively, that value psychological states and dispositions are not caused in the naturalistic sense of causation. The second point is that "free" does not mean undetermined, disconnected, arbitrary, and the like as the existentialist seems to take it. In our modern culture, we have not been able to conceive or to make convincing any third alternative. This is what we must explore.

The fundamental thing about *naturalistic* causation, for our purposes, is that it is causation conceived entirely in terms of the categories of existence and factuality. This means that the cause of an event or state of affairs is antecedent to it, that nothing but what is antecedently existent can be a causal factor in bringing about an occurrence or state of affairs, that only the factual structure of the existent makes a causal difference, and that given the antecedent causal factual conditions of an occurrence or state of affairs, that occurrence or state of affairs is inevitable. It is important here to emphasize that both the cause and effect, in the strict naturalistic view, are conceived entirely in terms of the categories of existence and factuality. This means that what is conceived in terms of the categories of meaning, logic, and value, unless these are in the ultimate analysis reducible to the categories of existence and factuality, play no part in the causal process.

Those who oppose the doctrine of naturalistic causal determinism of human action have usually argued that it is knowledge and rationality that make us free. What is involved here, I suggest, is not freedom in the sense of indeterministic, free-floating, unconnected acts of will, as some voluntarists seem to think, but the addition of the dimensions of meaning, logic, and value to that of existence and pure factuality. Semantic, logical, and value structures as well as purely factual ones become causally involved in such a way that one is free in that his actions are not simply effects of purely factual antecedent conditions in the naturalistic way. Indeed the semantic, logical, and value structures become the paramount determining factors in human action. Through them the domain of pure existence and factuality is transcended. In an important sense the future, the distant past, the spatially distant present, the abstract and the general, the possible, the required, and the like, as well as past existences and facts causally impinging on a given point in time and space, become causal factors in determining what happens.

Freedom in the area of psychological states, dispositions, and actions in general, then, has to do with processes or changes in which the semantic presence of facts, structures of meaning, logical relationships, and values, especially in modes which embody existential claims and may be correct or mistaken, make a difference. With regard to such occurrences, states, and dispositions, rational criticism—appraisal as rational or irrational, justified or unjustified, correct or incorrect, and the like, along with supporting reasons—is appropriate and meaningful and can be effective in bringing about changes. Wherever the requisite conditions for rational criticism do not obtain there is no freedom.

The "good reasons" position which holds that basic value psychological states and dispositions, whether intentionalistic or not, are naturalistic effects of cognitions of and attention to facts acknowledges that their causes are not, in our terms, naturalistic events or states of affairs. Nevertheless they claim that the *causation* involved is naturalistic in that the value psychological occurrence, state, or disposition, given its causal conditions, is not itself subject to and cannot be changed by rational criticism of it. Of course the theory allows for the rational criticism of its cause, the cognition of and attention to the facts involved, and therefore for change in its causal conditions and thus of the value psychological state itself through such rational criticism. But what is at issue is whether the value psychological state is in its own right subject to such criticism and change with the underlying cognitions of fact left unassailed and unaffected. In other words, can the value psychological response to cognized facts be faulted or approved in rational assessment independently of the cognition of the facts? And can such an assessment work a change in the value psychological response itself?

It is our claim that valuational acts, states, and dispositions of mind are intentionalistic and "free" in the sense that they are proper subjects of and responsive to critical assessment in their own right. We have already seen that they may be logically consistent or inconsistent with one another. For one to come to realize that some value psychological state or disposition of his is inconsistent with some other value attitude he has is usually sufficient for some change to be wrought in one or the other or both. If this were not so, value arguments, especially those that involve only value judgments and do not alter our factual beliefs, would have no function in shaping our value attitudes. Consider the argument: "All men have an inalienable right to life, liberty, and the pursuit of happiness. Therefore, any institution of human slavery is morally wrong." It has convincing power and can change value attitudes and dispositions precisely because the person who subscribes to the premise and rejects the conclusion, that is, one who has a value psychological state or disposition which the premise would express and one which the negation of the conclusion would express, would be guilty of a logical inconsistency.

The existentialist would admit this much, but, as we pointed out earlier, he would here betray his fundamental position by invoking an imperative about which he has no choice, namely, the imperative to be consistent in his valuations. But there are further weaknesses in the existentialist's position. When inconsistency is discovered among one's value dispositions and valuations, there is no way, according to the theory, to assess some as better grounded and others as less so to guide one in making changes to achieve consistency. One would be free to choose, without his choice's being subject to criticism, how he would achieve consistency. One might adopt the principle to achieve consistency with minimal change, another to strive for consistency by maximal change, and still another by purely arbitrary changes. All would be equally free from rational criticism. Another point. Although the existentialist would acknowledge that one should be consistent in his value dispositions and valuations, inconsistency between one's own valuations and those of another would not, according to his position, be in any way a challenge to one's own and therefore would have no place in the critical assessment of one's valuations. Of course the other person's valuation may be a relevant fact among other facts to be taken into account in making one's choices. But this has to do with whether one's valuations are informed, whether they are based on knowledge of the factual situation, not with the critical assessment of them per se.

Here, then, are two issues to explore. Does the critical assessment of our value psychological acts, states, and dispositions go beyond logical appraisal in terms of consistency and inconsistency and, if so, what form does it take? And does the logical appraisal of one's value psychological acts, states, and dispositions take into account their logical relationships with those of others and, if so, why?

With respect to the first question, it will further our inquiry to explore why logical inconsistency among our value psychological acts, states, and dispositions is a fault and consistency a good-making feature. Is it only because inconsistent valuations of whatever form involve or imply inconsistent imperatives of action and therefore condemn us to failure in our undertakings? This would reduce inconsistency to a minimum. There would be no inconsistency, for example, in one's condemning in others what he approves of in himself, or even in condemning in himself at one time what he approves of in himself at another time. Critical assessment on this basis would fault one's valuations only for leading him or tending to lead him to undertake impossibilities. There would be no basis for condemning undertakings which logically could be successfully carried out. Whatever was possible in the area of action would be right. One could not succeed in wrong undertakings.

The only way this could be made at all plausible in light of the way in which logical appraisal language behaves would be to maintain that one has many imperatives he subscribes to and the question of consistency applies only to the whole set. Is it a set which is so constituted that all can, logically speaking, be acted on successfully? If so, inconsistency only indicates that the set taken as a whole is doomed to failure. But then one could always make a proposed act right by withdrawing other commitments to achieve consistency, for on this view inconsistency between two valuations A and B indicates no fault with either one taken singly but only with the conjunction. If A is withdrawn or in some way disappears, then B is left without suspect. And the same is true for A if B is removed. So it in no way matters which one is altered to achieve consistency.

If this were the truth of the matter, consistency among one's valuations would not be a positive good-making feature, only the absence of a bad-making feature. And coherence, the structure which obtains among a set of valuations (or beliefs) if the replacement of anyone with its negative would generate a logical incompatibility, would not be a better good-making feature than simple consistency. Indeed all value arguments would be strictly deductive, for the only reason to accept the conclusion would be that its negative would be logically inconsistent with one's commitments expressed in the premises. There would be no such thing as logical incompatibility short of inconsistency so that we could speak of a nondeductive value argument in which the premises provided inconclusive support for the conclusion.

But our logical appraisal of valuations do not seem to operate this way. It is not at all clear that inconsistency among our valuations always involve logically inconsistent imperatives of action. One may regret a past action about which he was terribly excited at the time. It is not clear that the regret involves any imperative of action, at least not any oriented to the future. It seems to be primarily a revaluation of the action, a valuation inconsistent with the initial excitement which seems to call into question the original valuation and not simply the conjunction of the two valuations. Indeed it does seem to matter in most cases which valuation is dislodged by the exposure of inconsistency. We do critically assess individual valuations and not just whole sets of them. And too a thoroughly consistent set may be faulted.

This leads us into the second issue we proposed to examine, namely, whether critical assessment of one's valuations takes into account their logical relationships with the valuations of other people. We do argue about our value differences with the hope of achieving some measure of agreement. Indeed we test our own valuations by exposing them to the hazard of being contradicted by the valuations of others. We often feel disturbed by such inconsistencies and changes are wrought in our own feelings and attitudes by them. We feel reassured in our own value responses when they are concurred in and shared by others. We talk about bias and prejudice in the valuations of others as well as of ourselves. We give a privileged place to the feelings and sentiments of an informed but disinterested person on an issue.

All of this indicates that logical inconsistency among our value psychological acts, states, and dispositions is a bad-making feature for some reason other than that it would lead us to undertake impossibilities. What can the reason be if it is not that reality cannot be brought through action to conform to our valuations? Could it be that inconsistency is a fault among valuations because it indicates that all of them do not conform in some relevant way to reality? Here of course we do not mean conformity to the purely existential and factual structure of the world but, if at all, to a value structure of reality. In other words, is inconsistency a bad-making feature among our valuations for the same reason it is among our factual beliefs and perceptions, that is, does it indicate falsity of a semantic claim about the world and error in our effort to appropriate reality semantically? If so, this would push critical assessment of valuations beyond logical appraisal. The valuations would be assessed as veridical or not, that is, as true or false, and as constituting knowledge, correct valuation but short of knowledge, or error. This would at least make sense out of the way the logical appraisals go, but does semantic and epistemic appraisal-talk about value psychological acts, states, and dispositions make sense?

Consider a man who with great excitement undertakes to do something but after the deed regrets it. He might say: "At the time it seemed to be a great thing to do, but I must have been out of my mind. It was the biggest mistake I ever made." The important thing here is the introduction of "seeming" and "mistake" talk about valuations. He felt that the act was a great thing to do. This is a way of reporting his excitement about it. It gives the semantic content and structure of his emotive state or attitude. His regret after the act is expressed by the judgment that it was all a mistake, one that a person in his right mind would not make. And speaking from the orientation of his regret, he says that at the time it *seemed* to be, that is, it *appeared* to be, a great thing to do. Wherever it makes sense to talk about what seems or appears to be, it makes sense to talk about the situation's really being, or not being, the way it seems or appears to be. And if one takes a situation to be really the way it appears to be, he may be correct or mistaken. Thus the "seeming-to-be" versus "really is" distinction opens the door to semantic and epistemic appraisals. The man in our example could say after the fact that at the time X seemed to him to be a great thing to do and that he took it really to be the way it appeared to be, but that it really wasn't a great thing to do and that he made a mistake in taking it to be in reality a great thing to do. The mistake here was a semantic error. He took what was semantically present to him to obtain in the world, namely, that X really was a great thing to do.

But his regret after the fact, which he gives a privileged position, contradicts his earlier valuation. So he was then prepared to say that his initial valuation was false and that he had made an epistemic error, whereas his regret was a true valuation and that he then knew that X was not a good thing to do.

The thesis that value psychological acts, states, and dispositions are subject to semantic and epistemic appraisals as well as logical ones is reinforced by the way in which we talk about people being biased and prejudiced in their valuations as well as in their factual perceptions and beliefs. With regard to the latter, we say that a person is biased or prejudiced if he has some prior beliefs or interests which distort his factual perceptions and beliefs about a situation and interfere with his getting at the objective situation as it really is. Bias and prejudice which distort one's view of the facts would of course pervert one's valuations as well since they are dependent upon one's grasp of the facts. But two people in agreement about the facts of a situation might be in radical disagreement in their valuations of it. We might explain such differences by saying that both of them have ulterior interests or concerns which color their valuations. This is to say that their valuations are not "disinterested" and therefore cannot lay claim to being objective. It is easy to become confused here. Of course one's value reaction to the situation is a nonindifferent or "interested" response. To speak of such a valuation as "disinterested" is to say that it is dependent on one's comprehension of the facts of the situation and is not shaped or colored by *ulterior* interests or concerns. When we select a jury panel for a trial in a court of law we want disinterested, fair-minded people, but not people who are indifferent and unresponsive value-wise to all facts. We want people who will be objective both in forming their views of the facts and in forming their value attitudes towards the facts as they comprehend them. If this kind of objectivity were not possible about values, our concern about disinterested, fair-minded, objective, reasonable juries and boards of arbitration would not make sense.

The whole area of perversion talk also supports the view that valuations admit of semantic and epistemic appraisals. A perverse fear, for example, like a grown man's being afraid of any household cat, is a disposition to experience a certain kind of safe animal as dangerous which resists being dislodged by rational refutation. This way of talking would not make sense unless normal fears, which are clearly value psychological states or dispositions, were subject to being rationally confirmed or refuted. And of course we witness in our culture today how the spread of value subjectivism tends to undermine talk about perversion in our value experiences and attitudes. Some even go so far as to challenge the meaningfulness of talk about mental health at all. But this is a sword that cuts both ways. The meaningfulness of perversion talk counts against value subjectivism and whatever counts for value subjectivism counts against the meaningfulness of perversion talk. Perversion talk, however, is a product of our ordinary commerce with human experience in life situations and therefore philosophy has a responsibility to render it intelligible if at all possible. It places a considerable liability on any philosophical theory which must discredit it.

The practice of giving and seeking advice insofar as it goes beyond facts and causal means would not make sense either unless there were value knowledge. Our talk about wise and foolish men is based on the distinction between those who are capable of *sound* value judgments and those who are not. And we expect wise people more or less to agree in their judgments whereas we do not expect the foolish to agree among themselves or with others. Value subjectivism, if true, would wipe out the distinction and rob talk about the wise and the foolish of its meaning. But to the extent this talk is funded with meaning, so much the worse for value subjectivism.

All of these considerations, I think, make a convincing case for the claim that our value psychological acts, states, and dispositions are subject to logical, semantic, and epistemic appraisals. But is value knowledge, which, if our line of thought is correct, is categorially unique, possible unless there are value epistemic encounters with reality? So far we have drawn no distinction in the value sphere comparable to that between justified true belief and perceptual knowledge with respect to facts. Indeed approaching the problem, as we have, through an examination of arguments used to back value judgments may suggest that we have not touched upon anything comparable to sensory perception. Doubt about the possibility of such a distinction is a central factor in generating value skepticism and in calling into question the meaningfulness of value discourse, which is a matter of whether value language has a semantic outreach to an objective value structure in the world. So the issue of whether there are value epistemic encounters with reality is fundamental for our whole enterprise.

If we have located value epistemic encounters in our explorations without having distinguished them from value beliefs or assumptions, it is at the point where we find basic, logically underived value judgments which seem to be grounded in value psychological responses to comprehended facts. Although it is widely acknowledged that value judgments cannot be logically derived from factual statements, it seems as though we do manage in some way to generate some value judgments from purely factual beliefs. We have considered causal theories and the existentialist's creativity theory, but concluded that the value psychological response to comprehended facts is subject to critical assessment in a way that is contrary to both. Indeed we concluded that it is subject to epistemic assessment and may be a case of knowing. But we did not explore whether it has the character of an epistemic encounter.

It will be recalled from chapter 3 that an epistemic encounter, as I am using the term, involves (1) thinking that P, where P is that which is semantically present in the mode of consciousness concerned and thinking-that, regardless of the mode of consciousness in which it is involved, is a matter of taking that which is semantically present to obtain in the world; (2) being correct in thinking that P; (3) being responsible in thinking that P, that is, having grounds or reasons for thinking that P and their being responsible for the correctness of the act of thinking; (4) the act of thinking that P being at least partially self-warranting; and (5) the act of thinking that P being of a mode of thinking that provides an indigenous semantic content, either empirical or categorial.

The crucial issues to be explored in determining whether the value psychological responses to comprehended facts which ground our basic value judgments are epistemic encounters are whether they meet conditions (3), (4), and (5) above. We have already concluded that these responses have a semantic dimension and that they are subject to logical, semantic, and epistemic appraisals, which is to say, in effect, that they meet criteria (1) - (3). But a further word is needed with regard to (3). We must be clear about the distinction between grounds and reasons for a value judgment. Consider our earlier example about the poor man who was against a heavy inheritance tax. He was, it will be recalled, for private wealth because it makes for personal independence. Here the fact that private wealth makes for personal independence is a *reason* which supports the judgment that a system of private wealth is a good thing. But when asked why personal independence is a good thing, the answer given was that people like to be independent, they want to be independent, they are unhappy when they are not independent, and the like. These are what we are calling grounds for value judgments as distinct from reasons in the ordinary sense. The value judgments which they ground are expressions of them. The judgments articulate their semantic content. The value experience is a grounding link between the semantic and the existential realms. Here, if anywhere, are value epistemic encounters.

Turning to criterion (4), are such experiences partially self-warranting? We may translate the statements "People want to be independent," "People like to be independent," and "People are unhappy when they are not independent" respectively in this manner: "People feel that they require independence," "People experience being independent as good," and "People experience the lack of independence as bad." With the reports of value experiences cast in this form, it makes more sense to talk about their being partially self-warranting, for the form of these reveals that the experiences embody a semantic claim for which the fact of the occurrence of the experience could count as supporting evidence. Indeed it does seem that the fact that people want independence, the fact that they like independence, and the fact that they are unhappy when they do not have independence constitute strong evidence that independence is a good thing for people. The reports, as we are dealing with them, indicate that people generally experience personal independence to be a good thing, that is, there is virtually universal corroboration of the matter. But unless each such experience was partially self-warranting, the universality of such experiences would provide no corroboration, for there would be nothing to corroborate.

When comprehension of certain facts alone moves one emotively, a wise man is concerned about whether his response will be steady and continuous or whether a review of the facts will give rise to a contrary response. Otherwise taking time to reflect on and to consider a matter would not make sense. We all think it is the course of wisdom to sleep on an important matter before making firm commitments or acting on it. We also think it is wise for one to check his responses with those of others whom he respects for their sound judgment. All of this indicates that we do think and talk about our basic value responses to comprehended facts in a way that supports the claim that they are partially self-warranting and that they are subject to being corroborated or refuted by further partially self-warranting emotive responses of one's own and others.

The mode in which we comprehend the facts is of no particular importance for determining whether the emotive response is an epistemic encounter. The relevant facts may be semantically present to us through our own experience of the situation, oral or written reports of others, or memory. The important thing is that we have the factual situation before us in some mode of comprehension. If the value response is of such a nature that it may be an epistemic encounter, what it encounters is a value structure involved in and supervenient upon the facts of the case so that the value structure is open for anyone to grasp who comprehends the facts of the situation. We can be delighted or saddened by a situation presented to us in a biography, a play, a film, or a novel as well as one we witness in real life or live through. So the emotive response to a semantically entertained factual situation may be perceptual in nature even in a thought experiment.

A further requirement for this to be so, as our criterion (5) for epistemic encounters indicates, is for emotive responses to comprehended facts to be a source of new ideas, for them to have an indigenous semantic content, either empirical or categorial. We have already concluded that value language is unique and irreducible to nonvalue language and that it is grounded in the intentional structure of value psychological acts, states, and dispositions. We noted how imperative- and "ought"-sentence forms are grounded in conative experience—in desire, longing, felt constraint and restraint, and the like; and predicative value language (e.g., "X is good," "X is right," etc.) in affective experience—in liking, enjoying, favoring, approving, etc. Hence there is an indigenous categorial semantic content in our value psychological responses to comprehended facts. This categorial structure is not simply a structure of our discourse or of our consciousness but an ontological structure, just as the categorial factual structure is not just a structure of our statements or of our consciousness but of facts obtaining in the world. Although value structures are categorial, it is a contingent, empirical matter whether a given thing is good, right, or ought to be. Here of course we have to broaden the concept of the empirical to include that which can be known through affective and conative experiences.

We may conclude, then, that our value psychological dispositions, states, and acts, like our factual holdings, may be divided into those which are experiential or perceptual in nature and therefore provide us with epistemic encounters with reality, and those which are nonperceptual modes of knowing or holding a value judgment. It is the former, of course, that provide the foundation for our value language and our value knowledge.

Because of our approach from the perspective of the good reasons position, which focuses its attention on arguments for value judgments, we have restricted ourselves for the most part to value responses to comprehended facts. This might suggest that value experience as such presupposes and is dependent upon the power to comprehend facts. Indeed we have said that the value aspects of a situation are open to anyone who comprehends the facts of the situation so that even thought experiments will work in value inquiry. But as we pointed out earlier and will develop more fully later, the facts comprehended may not be entirely pure facts in the sense of being structured solely in terms of the categories of existence and factuality. They may involve semantic and logical categories as well and perhaps even value categories. For example, the facts may involve people and their experiences and actions. And we shall argue that nothing can be perceived or grasped under the concept of a person or of an action without involving semantic, logical, and value categories as well as those of existence and factuality. Indeed it may be that we cannot even have something semantically present to us under the concept of an organism without involving value categories, for is it not a logical truth that whatever is an organism has needs or value requirements and may have lacks or deficiencies? So most comprehended factual situations which arouse a value psychological response are conceived in our comprehension of them in a way that involves semantic, logical, and value categorial structures embedded within the facts. But this does not mean that the value judgment which expresses the emotive response to the comprehended facts can be logically derived from a statement of the facts and certainly not that the emotive response involves a logical inference from the comprehension of the facts. But the fact that most middle-size facts the comprehension of which evokes from us a value psychological response involve in some way a value categorial structure indicates that emotive responses at this level, although they may be epistemic encounters, are not our most elemental value epistemic encounters; for, if they were, how could we account for the value concepts embedded in our comprehension of such middle-size facts? In other words, how could we account for our capacity to comprehend something as an organism, as a person, as an action, and the like?

It is perfectly obvious on a moment's thought that our most elemental experiences of all, from a temporal point of view, are value experiences. No doubt one's initial consciousness is a vague discomfort, a vague feeling that something is wrong. At least most of the expressions of infants I have witnessed would have to be read this way. In fact in early days, most infants sleep except when in discomfort. But expressions of feeling good soon follow. Perception of things and facts come later. In learning language, value words are among the first to be mastered. Everything is experienced valuewise. It takes a great deal of training and maturity to grasp simply the facts of a situation. Indeed one's capacity to grasp the facts seems to develop through refining the focus of one's interests and emotions. This may be one factor that gives rise to the idea that a thrust toward objectivity moves us toward pure facts.

We may say that the most elemental mode of consciousness is a vague discomfort, which is an awareness of the normative state of one's body. It takes time, however, for the discomfort to develop until it is, in terms of its own intentional structure, an awareness of one's body, for this requires differentiation of one's body from the world around it. This is part of the refinement of the focus of one's value consciousness. The vague discomfort may become more specific by becoming, for example, hunger or thirst. This is a matter of its becoming more specific by defining what is wrong and what is required. In the case of hunger, it is an awareness that there is a bodily lack or deficiency and that food is required. In the case of thirst, that there is a bodily deficiency and that water is required. The discomfort may take the more specific form that one is wet and cold but ought to be dry and warm. It may take the form of a pain in the stomach. Here it is a perception that something is wrong in the stomach. It may be simply that or it may include awareness of a pressure there.

What I am suggesting is that bodily discomfort, physical misery, or just plain pain are not to be thought of simply as subjective occurrences or states of affairs, there to be noticed and inspected only by introspection and to be reported. They are value experiences of the normative condition of one's body and they have a semantic dimension which is expressible in value language. A pain, for instance, is not, I suggest, something that is existentially in one's stomach, one's head, or wherever it may be. If so it could be located by others probing into the area. If one has a bone in his hand and his hand is over the table, then there is a bone over the table. But if one has a pain in his hand and his hand is over the table, then it does not follow that there is a pain over the table. It would be less misleading to say that one's hand is in pain rather than that a pain is in one's hand. One's hand can be in one's pain in much the same way as something can be in one's visual or auditory perception; that is, the hand is semantically in the pain, it is part of the semantic content of the pain, part of the intentional object of the pain. The other part of the content or intentional object of the pain is that something is wrong with the hand. This way of thinking about pain solves the old conundrum about the man with a pain in his amputated foot. There is no peculiar problem about having a nonexistent foot semantically present in a pain. People often "see" or "hear" things that are not existentially there as well as believe things that are not so. This is a rather common condition for various modes of consciousness.

We do of course talk about pain and misery in a broader sense. We sometimes speak of mental pain or suffering to differentiate it from bodily pain or physical suffering. Of course all pain or suffering is mental in the sense that it is a mode of consciousness. Bodily pain is bodily only in the sense that it is an awareness of the value aspect of one's bodily condition and physical misery is physical only in the sense that it is an awareness of the value aspect of one's physical condition. In like manner mental pain or suffering is an awareness of the value aspects of one's personal life and social life. The same is true for physical pleasure and mental or spiritual joy and delight.

We have our spiritual discomforts and pleasures in much the same way as we do bodily ones but they come somewhat later in time for they have to wait for the development of one's selfhood. There are, though, those vague discomforts which are simply dim perceptions that all is not well with oneself. They may become more specific in various ways. Sometimes a general, indeterminate, spiritual discomfort may turn into loneliness, an awareness of a lack or deficiency of social relationships and that companionship is required. At times it may take the form of shame, an awareness of a self-inflicted injury to one's personal status or dignity; or guilt feelings, an awareness of a self-inflicted injury to one's standing as a human being; and there are the spiritual joys and pleasures, perceptions of our various forms of well-being and well-doing as persons and rational agents.

These various ways of monitoring the normative states and require-ments of one's body and selfhood are not dependent on the comprehension of facts in the same way in which our value responses to an external situation are, for with respect to these modes of value consciousness we are the factual situation and the value structure involved in and dependent on that factual situation emerges into self-knowledge more readily and prior to knowledge of the factual structure. So here value experience is not dependent upon nor responsive to cognized facts. It is the most primitive form of consciousness. To be sure the more sophisticated forms of value self-knowledge require comprehension of one's factual situation both in the mode of self-knowledge and observation-based knowledge.

Value modes of self-consciousness admit of epistemic appraisal as well as our value responses to comprehended facts. We have already mentioned how pain can be hallucinatory or illusory. Remember the case of the man with the pain in his amputated foot. Pains are often illusory. In ordinary idiom we speak of them as displaced pains. We experience something to be wrong at one place in the body when the trouble is really at another location. One can enjoy, that is, experience as good, injury to his body. Consider the masochist who enjoys burning his body with a lighted cigarette. One can have a hunger for food without a bodily deficiency. In some cases, there may be an ego lack which is misperceived as a bodily deficiency. The falsity of the hunger for food is corroborated by the failure of consumption of food to be satisfying. It makes sense to ask of the man who feels guilty whether he really is guilty, and the like. All of these ways of talking support the claim that there is such a thing as self-knowledge of the normative state of one's body and person.

The refinement of our grasp of our environment involves discri-minating in terms of factual, semantic, and value distinctions. Thus the comprehension of most middle-size facts of our human situation which evoke value responses already involve value concepts and therefore we cannot restrict ourselves to such responses in our search for the experi-ential ground of our value conceptual system. Our value concepts are grounded in our value self-knowledge as well as our value responses to our comprehended factual environment.

Thus because it is meaningful to talk about value experiences as having a semantic dimension and as being expressible in language in the way we do, as logically consistent or inconsistent, as being correct or in error, as being corroborated or refuted, as being the source of our value concepts, and the like—because it is meaningful to talk about value experience in terms of this team of semantic, logical, and epistemic terms, we conclude that this dimension of experience is knowledge-yielding and provides us with epistemic encounters with reality in much the same way as factual self-knowledge and sensory experience.

2. The ontological status of value

This opens up for us a whole new dimension of reality, namely, the realm of values. Let me say just a word about what values are. We have seen that value language is not constituted by a set of peculiar predicates, but fundamentally by peculiar sentence forms. A predicative value sentence like "X is good," for example, is reducible to "X is more or less the way it ought to be" or more specifically, "X ought to be F and X is F." Thus the value predicate is eliminable. What we are left with is the "ought"-sentence. It takes two fundamental forms: "X ought to F" and "There ought to be an x that would be F." There is also the imperative sentence, which has several variations: "X be F," "F is for X to be or to do," etc. We pointed out earlier that, for our purposes, the imperative sentence may be regarded as a stripped down, somewhat impoverished "ought"-sentence. "X ought to be F," for example, says in effect that there is a reason for X to be F, that there is something which normatively requires that X be F. So the more perspicuous form would be something like "X, being F, ought to be G," or "If X is F, then X (or perhaps Y) ought to be G," or "If X is F, then there ought to be a y that would be G." In the conditional sentences, the "ought" does not belong to the consequent. It is part of the conditional as such. It goes with the "If . . . then" connective and the conditional can be read, for example, "If X is F, then this fact normatively requires that X be G." It would not make sense to say that a given individual ought to be F and that this was so regardless of what features or properties the individual possessed or what the factual context of the individual might be. It is always meaningful to ask of what is said with an imperative sentence, "why?" and the "why?" asks for the facts or circumstances which do the requiring or make the thing in question imperative. To ask for the reasons is to ask whether there is an objective imperative about the matter at all, that is, whether it really is something that ought to be or to be done. We can render whatever is said with an imperative sentence with an "ought"-sentence even if we cannot perform all of the illocutionary acts with "ought"-sentences which we perform with imperative sentences. So we may settle for the "ought"-sentence as the basic value sentence as we concluded earlier.

Value, then, may be said to be a normative tie or requiredness which . is expressed by the "If . . . then . . . ought . . ." of the perspicuous form of the "ought"-sentence. It is, I suggest, locatable in the structure of the semantic content of our feelings, emotions, and desires. If we fail to look here, which most have done because this dimension of experience is widely taken to be causal reactions to the reality discerned and grasped through sensory observation and thought grounded in it or creative responses of the mind, then we cannot find in either experience or the world what seems to be meant by value language. But I urge that it can be found here and if value experience has the epistemic capability I have argued for, then normative requiredness is an objective categorial feature of reality.

The way in which our discussion has progressed and the way in which we have analyzed "ought"-sentences seem to give an ontological priority to facts over values. Values seem to be involved in and supervenient upon the factual structure of a situation. The requirements of a situation are said to be fact dependent. With regard to any external situation, one must comprehend the relevant facts in order to discern the values involved. As the factual situation changes the values change. This is true even of one's bodily and personal condition of which one may have knowledge of the value structure involved without comprehension of the facts. Yet we have observed that, for the most part anyway, our value experiences are of situations involving middle-size facts which are not pure brute facts. Although they are facts, they involve more than the categories of pure existence and factuality. They have embedded in them semantic, value, and perhaps essential or necessary structures. For example, suppose the relevant facts in a family situation are that the baby has just eaten a handful of aspirin tablets and has a pulse rate of 140 per minute. The mother upon comprehending these two facts may be terribly frightened. But the situation is not one structured solely in terms of the categories of existence and factuality. The baby is not simply an existent with a factual structure; he has a place in the family, he belongs there. This is a normative matter. He has a value structure, conditions in which he ought to be, which means that there are things he ought not to eat, and so forth. The mother upon comprehending the facts is frightened. She discerns the danger, the threatening harm to the child. But the values she perceives do not supervene upon comprehended brute facts. Nor need they follow from suppressed value premises. In comprehending that the baby ate the aspirin, anyone would comprehend that he was a being with a normative structure and therefore was subject to injury, sickness, and death. Therein lies a value structure embedded in the facts comprehended. The question I am raising is whether a situation constituted by brute facts could have a supervening value dimension. It would seem that unless this were so facts would not be ontologically prior to values.

One area in which we seem to experience a value structure among pure facts is that of aesthetics. Consider the matter of decorating a room. When one faces the bare physical structure, there are already aesthetic restraints on what he can do with it, and each decision he makes imposes further restraints on what remains to be done. A choice of colors for the walls narrows his options for the color and texture of the drapes. Once the walls and drapes are determined, they impose restraints on the carpet, and so forth until the last decision is rather narrowly prescribed. Here we have a sense that the brute facts of space, figure, line, color, texture, etc. impose requirements which the interior decorator must be sensitive to and in terms of which his work can be judged. It is true of course that the decorator will consider all of this in terms of what it expresses about and how it relates to the life-activities and personalities of those who use the room. But there is that dimension of aesthetic experience and judgment which is of and about a value structure among what seem to be brute facts, sheer lines, shapes, colors, sounds, and the like. We talk about those with a good aesthetic sense and those who are lacking in aesthetic sensibilities. This is a capacity which is subject to training and education. It admits of marketable expertise.

Even though brute facts may impose value requirements, the value requirements hold among possible facts as well as actual ones. This is the point of the "If . . . then . . . ought . . ." formulation of the philosophically clarified value sentence and what makes thought experiments possible in value inquiry. Contrary-to-fact conditional "ought"-sentences may be false as well as true. What this seems to indicate is that certain properties or clusters of properties are such that whenever they are exemplified they normatively require certain others, or, what amounts to the same thing, some possibilities (possible facts) are such that if they were to become actualities (actual facts), they would normatively require certain other facts. Even though this seems to give the factual structure, the exemplification of properties by particulars, some priority in the realm of existence, there is a sense in which the value structure seems to transcend the realm of existence and perhaps even to have something to do with what facts obtain. It would be difficult to believe that there is a value structure of the kind indicated and yet that it makes no causal difference.

The issue of priority between factual and value structures is even less clear with respect to natural kinds where it makes sense to talk about individuals of a given kind being mature or immature, well developed or poorly developed, well formed or deformed, and the like. Here the concept of what something is embraces not only some of the properties it actually exemplifies but also some of the properties it ought to exemplify. We might formulate such a concept "φ" this way: For all x, x is a φ if and only if x is F and x ought to be G. Of course this whole area is a thicket of philosophical problems for the modern mind. Modern empiricism has as much trouble with natural kinds and objective essences as it does with objective values. But for our purposes at this point we can say that normative structures seem to have a prominent role along with factual structures in at least some natural kinds, however we end up philosophically clarifying talk about objective essences and natural kinds. And if, ontologically speaking, there are objective essences, and there would be a good case for the claim that there are if we could only show how knowledge of them is possible, then a value structure is involved in the very existence of an individual of such a natural kind. Indeed theoretical extension of value structures to the essence of all natural kinds might prove to be warranted even though this might commit us to talking about all the specimens of some kinds as perfect. On such a basis, the properties something ought to exemplify would not be clearly dependent on those it does exemplify. The introduction of essential structures greatly complicates the picture, but the only point I am trying to make at the moment is that if there are, ontologically speaking, value structures in the sense our exploration has led us to believe, they are very basic in the structure of reality.

Our study, then, leads us to believe that there is a distinctive value area of experience, the whole range of affective and conative experience, which is epistemic or knowledge-yielding. It provides us with epistemic encounters with reality. Value language is, we have concluded, that area of discourse which is uniquely grounded in this area of experience. It embraces the imperative, the "ought-" and predicative value-sentence forms, with a predicative value sentence being one whose analysis contains an "ought" sentence. It follows that value language may be used not only to express value experiences but also as a set of semantic tools to extend the semantic powers present in our capacity for value experience and thus to make abstract value thought and reasoning possible. So value language is not necessarily restricted to an action-guiding function in a simple straightforward way. Indeed if there is a value structure to reality of the kind our analysis indicates, it must be taken into account in our efforts to know and to understand reality. Any theoretical account of what is the case and why it is so that failed to come to terms with this dimension of reality would necessarily be partial and distorted.

3. A realistic theory of moral discourse

Thus far we have talked only about value language and value experience in general. Nothing specific has been said about moral discourse, moral knowledge, or moral values. It is possible to be a value realist and yet a moral skeptic or nihilist. It is true of course that in our modern culture the most common reasons for moral skepticism are those for value skepticism in general, but historically the most common form of moral skepticism concerned whether there are unique, irreducible moral values distinct from prudential egoistic ones. One may still hold that there is a value structure to reality and at the same time maintain that there are no moral values, that there are no moral imperatives that impinge on one, that there are no moral reasons for one to acknowledge and to take account of in deliberating his actions and in judging himself and others.

There has been considerable disagreement among philosophers over what constitutes moral discourse. Some seem to conceive it so broadly that it embraces all action-guiding use of value language; some so narrowly that it has to do only with other-regarding attitudes and social concerns. It is generally agreed that one encounters moral imperatives, however they may be ultimately interpreted and analyzed, as felt obligations and restraints, which are distinct from one's ordinary wants, desires, and aversions; and that one has moral feelings of guilt and remorse and of approval and disapproval which are quite distinct from feelings of regret and ordinary liking and disliking. Moral experiences seem to be no respecter of persons. They speak for the interests of others or of society in general or of all mankind as well as for oneself. They are as quick to condemn and to make demands on oneself as others. And to the extent they do not, they are subject to self-condemnation. Furthermore, our moral feelings and attitudes seem to be of a higher order and to take precedence over or to speak with authority with respect to our ordinary wants, feelings, and likes and dislikes. It is the inclusive and overriding nature of moral judgments that generates the peculiar skeptical problems about them. They seem to be set over against and to have precedence over egoistic prudential concerns. So the question is raised: Why should one be moral?

At first glance this looks like an ordinary question asking for a reason, but it is really a very odd question. If one acknowledges that there really are moral reasons which make it imperative for him to do such and such in a given situation, there is no logical room for him to ask further whether there are reasons for him to do the particular thing. The question would really amount to this: Why ought he to do what he morally ought to do? In this form, it is clear that what is at issue is whether one really ought to do the things we say he morally ought to do. In other words, "Why should one be moral?" acknowledges that there is moral discourse and that internally within the framework of moral thought certain moves are made. The question is not asking whether a particular moral judgment in question has been made in the proper way as defined by the rules of moral discourse. It is questioning the status of the whole universe of moral discourse. It is a philosophical skeptical question which challenges the validity of moral judgments, the possibility of moral knowledge, and the reality of moral values. It calls into question the legitimacy of the whole moral enterprise and demands that its claims be made out or that its lack of legitimacy be exposed. In other words, the question calls for a philo-sophical account of moral discourse.

Broadly speaking, there are three possibilities from within the per-spective of general value realism: (1) A realistic interpretation of moral discourse, which involves the claim that man has the epistemic and semantic powers to know and to talk meaningfully about objective moral values and that ontologically speaking there is a moral structure consisting of uniquely moral reasons, moral requirements, rights, and the like;

(2) Rejection of moral realism with a reduction of moral discourse to some form of nonmoral value discourse, most commonly to egoistic prudential talk; and (3) Rejection of moral realism with an explanation of moral discourse which discredits the moral enterprise.

Plato dealt with all three of these positions in the *Republic*. Thrasymachus argues for (3). Rejecting moral realism, he argues, in anticipation of Karl Marx, that moral beliefs are superstitions foisted off on the people by the power structure of the society as a way of inducing them to serve sacrificially the interests of those in power. Thus understanding the moral enterprise, Thrasymachus contends, would liberate one from it, for it would be seen to be a system of oppression and enslavement. This would not, of course, preclude the liberated from using moral judgments to serve their own purposes.

Glaucon, in anticipation of Thomas Hobbes and John Rawls, argues in the *Republic* for (2). He contends that justice is not good in itself and that there are no reasons for pursuing it as such. This is a way of denying that justice is something that ought to obtain in its own right and that everyone has epistemic powers which enable him to acknowledge that it should. But, unlike Thrasymachus, he holds that morality is not something for one to outgrow or to be liberated from. The rational man has good reasons for heeding moral judgments and thus for acting in the manner called "just," but they are egoistic prudential reasons. It is contrary to the self-interest of anyone to be treated by others in the manner called "unjust." The whole system, he contends, is based on a contract among the people of a society to practice mutual restraint in pushing their own advantage against others, a contract each enters into because of the advantages he is to gain from the self-restraint of others. His own self-restraint is the price he pays for these advantages.

The position has been developed most fully in Thomas Hobbes's *Leviathan* and in John Rawls's recent book, *A Theory of Justice*.[1] A word of caution: the social contract theory of ethics must not be confused with the social contract theory of civil government. Hobbes shared a social contract theory of government with Locke and Rousseau but they did not share his social contract theory of ethics. Rawls argues that the basic principles of justice and thus of the moral enterprise are those principles regulating the life and conduct of people in society which all people, cloaked in a veil of ignorance about what their individual positions in society would be, could rationally consent to on the basis of egoistic prudential considerations.* In other words, given egoistic prudential

---

*It is only fair to say that Rawls is somewhat ambiguous on this point. One could read him as contending that the veil of ignorance about one's own circumstances in society is a device to remove all self-serving considerations so that one would be impartial and objective in his assent to or objection to proposed principles of social life. Such a reading would point in the direction of moral realism. But for our purposes we shall take him to be an egoist. The general tone of his book supports this view.

value-truths, however philosophically interpreted, and the facts of social life, ethical principles for which all individuals would have egoistic reasons to follow can be generated. Or turning the matter around, we can say that ethical discourse can be reduced to factual and egoistic prudential value-talk.

Plato's purpose in the *Republic* is to refute (2) and (3) and to argue for (1). He develops a theory of knowledge and a correlative metaphysics which would make (1) possible and gives a strong argument for moral realism itself. His argument turns on both his theory of man and his theory of moral values. He contends that man is by his nature subject to moral imperatives and that moral imperatives are those which impinge on him as a human being, which he can ignore or disobey only with injury to himself as a man. In other words, one cannot be egoistic in an enlightened way without being moral; not because to be moral just is to be egoistic in an enlightened way—that is, not because ethical talk reduces to egoistic talk or ethical reasons to egoistic reasons, but because of what enlightened egoism must be by virtue of the nature of man, because there are irreducible moral imperatives and reasons which one must take account of even in promoting his own genuine egoistic concerns.

I think that Plato was essentially correct about the connection between moral judgments and the nature of man. We evaluate actions in many ways. We may say, for example, that what one did was wrong in a way that reflects on him as a surgeon, as an engineer, a carpenter, or whatever. This would not be a moral evaluation. But if we say that what he did was wrong in a way that reflects on him not as a surgeon, or not as anything else of that genre, but as a human being, then we are making a moral evaluation. We have to be careful here, however. We can evaluate one's action in a way that indicates that he is stupid, for example, and this might be taken to reflect on him as a human being, for we would all agree that it is good for a human being to be intelligent and bad for one not to be, that is, being intelligent is the way a human being ought to be and lack of intelligence is a human deficiency. But this is not a moral matter. It is when we say that what one did was wrong in a way that reflects on him as a person, in a way that indicates that he has acted in a way unbefitting the office of a human being, so to speak, even though he had the requisite capacities for the position, that we make a moral evaluation. So we may say that a moral obligation is any imperative that impinges on one as a human being in such a way that failure to execute it to the best of one's ability reflects on him as a person.

The moral virtues are those characteristics of a person peculiarly related to functioning well in the office of a human being. Being smart or highly intelligent is not a moral virtue. To be sure a certain level of intelligence is essential to being a functioning person at all. But highly intelligent people can be lacking in all the distinctively moral virtues, whereas people of mediocre or relatively low intelligence can possess the moral virtues to a high degree in that they can conduct themselves in the activities they undertake in ways befitting human beings. Their limited intelligence will affect them most with respect to the activities they undertake. To be sure there is something great about undertaking great tasks and performing them well in a manner befitting a human being. But such a person may not excel in moral virtue more than the humble man who performs his lowly tasks in ways befitting a human being. Both can live with dignity and be worthy of moral praise. But perhaps we do need a distinction between moral excellence and moral greatness comparable to that between excellence and greatness in art. If so, moral greatness would seem to require a high level of intelligence and perhaps other talents. The same would be true on the negative side as well. In one sense, an ordinary man is capable of reaching the depths of depravity and the limits of degradation, but it takes a high level of intelligence to be diabolical, to reach greatness in evil.

What is at stake here is the viability of this conception of a human being. It is, as we remarked early in the book, the concept of man as having a position, an office as it were, constituted by certain responsibilities and correlative rights and privileges. The primary responsibility involved is to be self-directing under the guidance provided by the proper exercise of one's rational, semantic, and epistemic powers. This is what the Greeks meant when they defined man as a rational animal. He is an animal who is by his nature under an obligation to assess rationally his experiences, feelings, desires, attitudes, beliefs, intentions, and actions and to live by the judgments and verdicts of reason so that he will stand justified in all of his thinking and doing under rational criticism. He is a being for whom the ascription of irrationality is a condemnation. It is clear that this is not a biological, not even a biopsychological conception. It cannot be grounded and legitimatized within the methodology of any strictly empirical science or set of them. It is a humanistic conception. Its ontological viability depends upon the epistemic character of the modes of experience and thought on which the humanities depend and whether and how this concept of man is grounded in them. We have already argued for the semantic and epistemic character of affective and conative experience and the ontological status of value structures, which constitute two of the essentials here. We will in following chapters consider our epistemic power to grasp structures of meaning and the ontological status of semantic and logical structures. But for now the central problem concerns whether our humanistic conception of man is somehow grounded in our moral experiences or whether our moral experiences are functions of our conception of man.

Few will deny that there is an essential correlation between one's humanistic conception of what it is to be a human being and one's moral feelings—one's felt obligations, guilt feelings, basic self-respect, respect for others, and moral approvals and disapprovals. A change in one's conception of what it is to be a human being in this sense involves changes in one's moral experiences. Ambiguity or uncertainty in one's self-image as a human being, as in adolescence or other serious identity crises, generates moral confusion. The important question is what wags what? Some would say that such conceptions of man are social constructions developed for the purpose of controlling people's behavior and that they are instilled in people by the culture. We cannot deny that one's culture imparts to him for the most part his conception of what it is to be a human being. But we come by all our conceptions this way. The important question is how the culture developed its humanistic conception of man. Is it a pure fabrication or invention? Or is it a product which has emerged from a critical assessment of our epistemic moral and other experiences of self and others through history and which is subject to confirmation or correction by our continuing self-knowledge and interacting experiences with others?

R. M. Hare, in *Freedom and Reason*,[2] contends that moral judgments based on a conception of what it is to be a human being are fanatical for they are not under any kind of experiential control. But if affective and conative experiences in general are epistemic in character as we have argued, what reason is there to doubt that our conception of what it is to be a human being and our ideals of human excellence are grounded in experiences of admiration, contempt, self-satisfaction, pride, guilt feelings, approval, disapproval, and the like? To admire someone as a person, according to our analysis, is to experience him as being very much the way a person ought to be; to feel contempt for one as a person is to experience him as lacking a lot of being what one ought to be; to feel morally guilty for what one has done is to feel that one has done injury to oneself as a human being; and so forth. To be sure ideals, once formed and taught, color and largely shape such experiences. But nonetheless ideals of human excellence are tied to such experiences. They arose out of them and are subject to modification by them. Only a philosophical assumption about the character of this kind of experience which would block such an interpretation would drive us to think otherwise. We have, I think, removed that block and are justified in accepting a realistic interpretation of moral discourse as well as of value language in general.

Thus, if we are right, there is, ontologically speaking, a normative structure to man which includes a moral dimension. Man has by his nature the responsibility to develop and to exercise his powers, according to the constitutional principles of his mind, in semantically appropriating the world and to be self-directing in his actions under the guidance of knowledge of all relevant values and facts in the various situations of his life, with special regard for what is obligatory or unfitting for him to do as a human being; and furthermore he has the correlative rights and privileges that go with this responsibility or set of responsibilities, the areas of freedom which he must have or may safely enjoy in fulfilling his human responsibilities and thus in living a human life. This view, as we have seen, is substantiated by a critical analysis of our various valuations of man and his actions and what it makes sense to say about him.

4. Defense of value and moral realism

There are certain criticisms of value and moral realism which should be considered. Perhaps the most telling consideration against the position for most people is the uncertainty and variability of our affective and conative experiences. Many have felt that such experiences speak, if at all, in too conflicting, confused, and uncertain ways to be knowledge-yielding. We must admit a great deal of variability in this area of experience, but I think it can be accounted for on our view just as easily, if not more so, than on the causal theory, for in the naturalistic causal realm regularities and uniformities are more expected than in the domain of knowledge-yielding experience and thought.

A factor which should not be ignored is that value requirements, according to the position I am urging, are fact-dependent and therefore contextual, with the possible exception of those involved in the essential structure of a natural kind. The context in which a value requirement holds, especially those with which we are most concerned, may be quite complex at several categorial levels and therefore not often duplicated. This makes for what looks like value relativism. It does indeed make values relative to a given kind of context, but this in no way undermines the objectivity of values. In fact, when we consider the variations in the situations in which people find themselves, including the social facts which are not transculturally duplicatable, the differences in their value experiences and judgments do not at all seem to be so devastating for the claim that such experiences are epistemic. This is especially true when we consider that the value experiences are of these complex factual situations as they are comprehended. People's comprehension of the facts in such situations are notoriously diverse. Consider the great debate over the war in Vietnam. There have been many diverse value judgments about America's part in it. But any exploration of these differences quickly reveals an equally diverse set of views about just what it was that America did in Vietnam. Presumably if we could reach an agreement on what the facts were, the diversity in value judgments would be greatly diminished. So a great deal of the apparent lack of agreement in our value experiences and judgments has to be attributed to the fact that they are really of and about different things and situations and therefore may not be really value disagreements at all.

Furthermore, wherever there are seemings or appearances of things, and this is the case in all realms of epistemic experience, there is a great deal of variability and confusion. In fact, for centuries rationalists regarded our sensory experiences to be too fluctuating and uncertain to be a basis for genuine knowledge. Rational appraisal of experience, however, uses just this feature of it, its inherent inconsistencies, in the search for truth. In fact, without such incompatibilities within experience, there would be no inquiry and no higher levels of thought, for it is precisely this kind of conflict which forces the mind to its higher achievements. With a critical method of assessing the conflicts of sensory experiences and a well developed theoretical structure within which to operate, sensory experience has become highly reliable within scientific inquiry. Perhaps our value experiences would not seem so variable and confused from within a highly critical method of assessing them and a theoretical framework which supported and guided them in the manner scientific method and theory are related to sensory experiences. Here, I think, is one of the great weaknesses of our culture. The modern mind, for the most part, has no viable theoretical framework to give direction and intelligibility to our emotions, passions, joys, sorrows, fears, wants, and longings.

S. W. Blackburn, in a recent paper,[3] gives what he takes to be a decisive refutation of moral realism, but it is clear that his argument would apply equally to value realism in general. He argues that two doctrines which he thinks are true and which are widely accepted by moral philosophers cannot be held along with moral realism. The two doctrines are the thesis (S) that moral properties are supervenient upon naturalistic properties and the thesis (E) that "[t]here is no moral proposition whose truth is entailed by any proposition ascribing naturalistic properties to its subject."[4] He defines supervenience in these terms: "A property M is supervenient upon properties $N_1 \ldots N_n$ if M is not identical with any of $N_1 \ldots N_n$ nor with any truth function of them, and it is logically impossible that a thing should become M, or cease to be M, or become more or less M than before, without changing in respect of some member of $N_1 \ldots N_n$." And contrapositively, "a thing remaining the same in respect of all members of $N_1 \ldots N_n$ strictly implies that it remains the same in point of possession, lack of possession, or degree, of M-ness."[5] He maintains that a moral realist "has to say that the truth of a moral proposition consists of a state of affairs, which it reports; that the existence of this state of affairs is not entailed by the existence of other, naturalistic facts; yet that the continuation of these facts entails that the moral state of affairs continues as it is."[6] Even if this could be shown not to involve an outright inconsistency, he says, "[s]upervenience becomes, for the realist, an opaque, isolated, logical fact, for which no explanation can be proferred."[7] He concludes that moral realism is false, and if this is so for the reasons given, then value realism is false also.

I agree with Blackburn on the principles of supervenience and nonentailment and that the realist must not only show that his realism is consistent with them but that it must show why they are so. I think the version of realism we have developed does just that. Blackburn conceives of value realism as taking value sentences to be predicative and as holding that a value sentence, "A is good," for example, "reports" as he says, "the existence of a state of affairs: A's goodness."[8] Thus he regards the realist as holding that values are peculiar properties. It is this assumption about what value realism must be that generates the problems he sees for realism. Our version of realism, however, takes the basic value sentence to be of the "ought"-form which under philosophical clarification becomes something like "If X is F, then X (or Y) ought to be G" or "If X is F, then there ought to be a y that would be G." The "Ought," we have argued, belongs to the conditional as a whole, not to the consequent. The connective "If . . . then . . . ought" expresses the value requiredness that is said to obtain in the objective situation. It is a real connection, one that has to be perceived. There is no logical connection involved. So the value involved is supervenient upon the fact indicated by the antecedent of the conditional and there is no logical entailment between the factual statement of the antecedent and the value judgment (with the possible exception of a value judgment which partially expresses a functional concept or a concept of a natural kind). A predicative sentence like "A is good" would not, contrary to Blackburn, report that A exemplifies goodness, but rather would report that A in having the naturalistic or nonvalue properties it does is more or less the way it ought to be. So there is no mystery at all on this view of value realism about the supervenience thesis along with the nonentailment doctrine. Indeed the power of the theory to make intelligible these two truths is added support for it.

Another argument frequently brought against value realism is that, with its emphasis on objective values and our knowledge of them, it does not account for the practical role of value judgments, how they tie in with our springs of action and move us to do things. Henry Aiken, for example, in commenting on Everett Hall's version of value realism, says: "Hall's attempt to reveal what value is is not only unilluminating, it is also obfuscating. For it leads us to think of the *act* of judgment or appraisal as essentially a passive display of that which ought to be and to think of ourselves, to whom the judgment is addressed, as inactive witnesses to a revelation. In a curious way, it seems to assimilate evaluation to a kind of quasi-aesthetic contemplation of values rather than to a decision which commits us, in appropriate circumstances, to a line of action. Or, to put the point another way, Hall's theory sheds not the slightest light on the fact that when we violate a moral judgment to which we have ourselves assented, we are necessarily remorseful, and assume automatically that we have an obligation to make amends. But this belongs to the essence of a judgment about what ought to be done."[9] B. J. Diggs, in his review of my book, *Ethical Naturalism and the Modern World-View*, says: "Adams somehow fails to grasp 'the practical': he fails to see that an act or rule or practice is really different from anything which the 'language of science' [which can only be read as "language of knowledge"] . . . can effectively describe. Determined to find 'ought,' but missing its habitat, he just begins referring to it as if it were 'there.' "[10]

This kind of criticism arises from within our modern conception of knowledge and of the objects of knowledge which generated value skepticism in the first place. It is true that value realism cannot be maintained within the confines of these assumptions. What we are arguing for requires a radical restructuring of the modern mind, especially our philosophical assumptions about the nature of knowledge and the objects of knowledge. This, as we have seen, forces reconsideration of the modern doctrines that knowledge is a passive state of mind, that knowledge is value-free, that the objects of knowledge are facts, that value language has only an action-guiding function, and that the language of knowledge as such cannot have this kind of action-guiding use.

The value realism we have argued for is grounded in the claim that value language is funded with meaning and that value data are acquired through value experiences—our affective and conative experiences, which are our springs of action. It is our claim that knowledge itself is born when the value requirements of an organism emerge into consciousness and, through awareness of them and a rudimentary perception of the factual situation, action is undertaken for their fulfillment. Furthermore, we contend that our powers to appropriate semantically the value structure of the world are extended through value language. Thus for one to accept the judgment that something is good, with certain exceptions we shall consider later, involves his looking upon it with some favor; for someone to accept the judgment that something he did was wrong involves his having a negative attitude toward it; for one to accept the judgment that he ought to do something involves his having some inclination to do it; and for one to accept an imperative for him to do something is for him to form an intention to do it. It is indeed a credit for our theory that both its account of value language, value experience, and value knowledge and its account of the value structure of reality illuminate the practical, action-guiding function of value language, for it maintains that value language is not only used to express our value experiences but is used also as a set of semantic tools with which we are able to extend our affective, and conative, and volitional powers.

Indeed our position is more likely to be open to the charge that it cannot account for how a person can act contrary to his judgment about what he ought to do. I am prepared to argue that a person is moved to act only by what he judges or takes to be good and that no one ever knowingly does what he at the time takes to be the wrong thing to do. This is not to deny that there are wicked people. But wickedness is a perversion of one's desires, feelings, and emotions so that he is systematically in error in his value judgments. The wicked man may be of strong character and absolute integrity in that he always acts on his best judgment about what is good and right. His defect lies in his evaluative and judgmental powers, not in failing to do what he takes to be good and right. Nor is it to deny that there are people with moral weakness, people with lack of integrity, people who act against their own considered judgments. Such people do things and feel guilty about them. Does this mean that they do things knowing that they are wrong? In a sense, yes; but also in a sense, no. The will is the capacity to form an action-initiating commitment to an imperative or ought-judgment. Such a commitment may be formed directly from a desire or an emotion. It may also occur in a reasoned manner by reflection and deliberation. This does not necessarily require delay. It is a matter of bringing acquired knowledge and wisdom to bear upon the decision; whereas a commitment to action formed directly from a desire or a situation-grounded emotion is devoid of this rational ground. The morally weak man is one who, unlike the wicked man, is capable of sound judgment about what is good and right and yet on occasions will hastily make uncritical decisions largely on the basis of immediate desire or emotion; that is, he takes something to be good or right which in a sense he knows is not. But this further knowledge is the knowledge of his considered judgment which is crowded out and thus is dormant and inactive at the moment. So he does what he, with lack of integrity of mind, takes to be good or right on the basis of a particular desire or emotion, but yet holds to be wrong in his temporarily inactive reflective judgment. There is nothing, then, in the case of either the wicked man or the morally weak man to controvert the thesis that a person is moved to act only by what he judges or takes to be good and that no one ever knowingly does what he at the time takes to be the wrong thing to do. This of course is not to deny that people often act with mixed feelings, doubt, and uncertainty about what they are doing.

But if we accept value realism and take it seriously, value language cannot be restricted to its peculiar action-structuring and guiding function, for our efforts to know and to understand the world would have to come to terms with the value dimension of reality. This would seem to require that value concepts have a place in our theoretical (in contrast with "practical") conceptual system. If there is a normative structure to biological organisms and if the way an individual of a species ought to be has something to do with the way it actually is factually, for example, it would seem that a biology oriented toward simply grasping and understanding the reality of organisms would have to take account of the value dimension of them, even if a biology oriented toward grasping and understanding the structure of organisms in a way that would be useful in manipulating, controlling, or even making organisms could safely ignore it. My purpose here is not to explore just how nor the extent to which our theoretical knowledge would be affected by the acceptance of value realism, but to raise a question about how value language used in a descriptive and explanatory way in our theoretical pursuits would relate to our affective and conative experiences and actions. In other words, value realism seems to require that value language have both an action-guiding function and a theoretical use. The question I am raising is whether this creates a problem for value realism.

First of all a word of explanation. It sounds strange to modern people to talk about value language having a descriptive use. We think of description as the ascription of properties to something and thus as the assertion of facts. But the term "to describe" originally meant to write down or to give an account of something in words. It has been our metaphysical view about what is there in a thing to write down that has generated the restricted meaning of the term in our talk about the descriptive use of language. Given that value realism is true, there is no reason why we cannot liberalize the meaning of the term so that description will include writing down the value aspect of things as well as the factual. Talk about an explanatory use of value language sounds equally strange to us. But if there is a value structure to some things as value realism maintains, surely it makes a difference in some way. It must have something to do not only with what and how things are but also with why some things are what and how they are. In other words, value realism would seem to force a change not only in our naturalistic conception of description but also in our naturalistic conceptions of change and causality, and thus in our conception of explanation.

Now let us return to the question about the relationship between the descriptive-explanatory use of value language and the action-guiding use. If our account of value experience is correct, it is clear that our most rudimentary and primary form of value consciousness and thus of value knowledge concerns the requirements and normative states of ourselves both bodily and personally. Here we have enjoyments and sufferings in many forms which inform us of what is good and what is bad and what is right and what is wrong with ourselves and all with which we identify, whether family, club, business, university, country, or the human race. We have desires, longings, and aspirations which tell us something about what it would be good for us and for whatever we identify with to have, to do, and to be. We have felt constraints and restraints about what we as individuals and groups and institutions with which we identify must and must not do. All these are a form of or an extension of self-knowledge, not only in the sense that it is knowledge which pertains to one's self either as an individual or to one's larger self through his identifications (whatever one is prepared to embrace by "we"), but in the sense that it is a form of or an extension of self-awareness.*

We are able to extend our knowledge of what is available through the mode of self-knowledge through our power of perceptual understanding of the subjectivity of other people and the higher animals, a matter to be discussed later, and through their communications with us. In this way we come to know the normative states and requirements of other selves as they are known to them through their self-knowledge. But we are not entirely dependent for knowledge of values on our own self-knowledge of the value structure of ourselves and our transitive grasp of others' self-knowledge of their own normative states and requirements. We have our own value experiences of the states, conditions, and actions of others. We may be shocked and horrified at their injuries or conditions; we may be indignant at what they do; we may be disgusted with their behavior; we may feel contempt for them; we may find them delightful people; we may admire them; and so forth. But we have such experiences of the conditions and actions of only those beings with whom we are to some extent in an intersubjective relationship and the closer that relationship the more pronounced such experiences are. And for beings who enjoy an intersubjective relationship there is on the part of each at least some imagined projection of oneself into the position of others so that the experiences of others of the kind under discussion are not totally distinct from nor unrelated to self-knowledge.

The point I am making is that value knowledge which is a form of self-knowledge (or is derived from an understanding grasp of the value self-knowledge of another or is of another in a way that is dependent upon an intersubjective relationship with the other and possibly projected "self-knowledge" of his condition and actions or is derived from one or more of these forms) is tied in with our springs of action in a peculiar way and has a distinctive action-forming and guiding function. This is the original habitat of value language, which developed as a way of giving

*Here we need to distinguish between two kinds of self-knowledge: (1) knowledge one has of oneself through specific experiences which could only be of oneself, such as somatic sensations, guilt feelings, etc.; and (2) nonobservational knowledge of one's experiences and activities such as one's knowledge that he is in pain or that he is talking.

expression to such experiences and extending the powers inherent in them—the powers of knowing the normative states and requirements of ourselves and others with whom we can identify which could be righted or fulfilled by our actions and theirs.

Our ordinary value experiences of things around us and of the general conditions of our environment are of them as they relate to our normative conditions and requirements or to the normative conditions and requirements of those with whom we have an intersubjective relationship and with whom we identify in some way and to some extent. The possible exceptions are our aesthetic experiences and our experiences of the sublime. Some would interpret even these as experiences of their objects as fitting or appropriate for our sensibilities or as meeting some deep psychic need. In any case, most of our affective experiences of things are of them as satisfying or frustrating normative requirements of our own existence or of those with whom we identify. Therefore, value knowledge derived from our value experiences of our environment by virtue of its relationship to the value structures known through extended value self-knowledge is also action-guiding.

But we do extend value language beyond the limits of our value experiences. We talk, for example, about a plant's being healthy or diseased, its being mature and well developed or its being poorly developed and deformed. We do not verify such judgments through our affective and conative experiences, for we are evaluating them with respect to their own internal normative structure, the way in which they ought to be by virtue of what they are. And we do not know this internal normative structure through value self-knowledge nor any of its extensions yet considered. If we know the way it ought to be and the way it factually is, we can make and verify predicative value judgments about it, like, for example, it is diseased or healthy, mature, deformed, and so forth. In the case of an artifact, which we evaluate in a somewhat similar way, we know its internal normative structure, like, for example, that a pen ought to write and that it is defective if it will not, by knowing or discovering its design as conceived by its maker. But how do we discover the internal normative structure of the plant?

We have seen how we discover the internal normative structure of man through his value self-knowledge and its extensions through intersubjectivity. This applies to man both as a biological organism and as a self or person, but it is as a biological organism with which we are concerned at the moment. Through sensory observation of organisms alone man would not discover the value structure that is revealed through extended value self-knowledge, for if he could, value language could be translated without loss of sayable content into empirical scientific language. But man, with both extended value self-knowledge of the human organism and the higher animals and sensory observational knowledge of these organisms, establishes sensory criteria for value concepts so that they can be applied to biological organisms on the basis of these criteria alone; and we can verify value judgments about organisms on the basis of sensory knowledge that these criteria obtain. If value realism is true, then, there are empirical scientific criteria for determining, for example, that an organism, even a plant, is diseased or healthy, but the concepts of "disease" and "health" cannot for philosophical clarification be defined in terms of these criteria. What constitutes the states of disease and health involves the value structure of the organism.

The point I am making here is parallel with a familiar one about psychological concepts. It is often said that our subjective psychological concepts, like "pain," "visual experience," etc., have publicly observable criteria for their application but that pain, visual experience, etc., are not constituted by those observable states and that these psychological concepts cannot be defined with respect to them. I don't think we apply psychological concepts to others only on the basis of such criteria. This way of dealing with psychological language will not work because the whole program of establishing language in general requires intersubjectivity. But this method of extending value language grounded in value self-knowledge and its intersubjective extension by sensory observable criteria seems not only possible but the best explanation of our value talk about organisms which is not verifiable through our value experiences as such.

A somewhat similar point, I think, can be made about our causal talk. It is from within the perspective of our own action in an interacting relationship with our environment, which involves self-knowledge of our own actions and of the effects of the environment on us, that we develop and learn the concepts of cause and effect. We learn criteria by which we can apply these concepts to the purely observational realm but we run into trouble, as Hume exhibits, if we try to define the concepts solely in terms of such criteria. Some contend that for these reasons "causation" is an anthropomorphic concept which, like the concept of value, has no place in scientific thought. The same can be said for the related concept of force.

In any case, we seem to have bona fide value discourse which is not reducible to factual discourse and which is not tied in with our affective and conative experiences and is not action-forming and guiding in the peculiar way in which our primary value language is. It is value language whose primary use is descriptive and explanatory. It is still normative and evaluative but in a way that does not involve imperatives which impinge on us and move us to actions—at least not directly. This means that we need to modify our prevailing conceptions of the normative and the evaluative just as we need to alter our conceptions of the descriptive and the explanatory. If we are right about the epistemic character of our value experiences and the realistic interpretation of value language grounded in such experiences, it seems that we have to accept this conclusion.

Furthermore, if there is a value structure to persons and organisms of the kind we have indicated, it would seem that our theories developed to render intelligible the primary realities we discover about the world must reckon with this truth. This would seem to require a more extended theoretical use of value language as well, for it is not at all clear how a theory restricted categorially to factuality could explain data with both factual and normative dimensions.

Our study, then, leads us to conclude that our modern value skepticism and subjectivism are based on a false philosophical assumption about the constitutional principles of the mind, the assumption that our affective and conative experiences are not semantic, logical, and epistemic in character and, therefore, that value language cannot have a semantic outreach to a unique value structure in the world. We saw in chapter 2 some of the consequences of this assumption for our culture and life. Value realism, grounded in the epistemic character of affective and conative experience, opens up the possibility that the descriptive and the explanatory and the action-guiding uses of value language might be combined, and that man might comprehend himself and his world intellectually without suffering disaffection and alienation and might even find a supporting world view and environment for the human spirit. We will return to this prospect in the concluding chapter.

The Antinomy of the Mental

We have from the beginning operated from within and partially presented a philosophy of mind. In the last three chapters we have argued for certain aspects of it. Yet one of the philosophical perplexities of our modern culture which we pointed out in chapter 2 calls into question this whole position. There we saw how the scientific study of man, the extension of the scientific conceptual system to human behavior, challenges the meaningfulness of rational appraisal talk about man and his action. This, as we observed, is a threat to man himself, for it seems to deny, ontologically speaking, the reality of the mental—the reality of meaning, subjectivity, and selfhood. We must now explore this antinomy of the mental in some detail and determine, if we can, how it can be resolved and whether the philosophy of mind we have assumed throughout this work is defensible and true.

Perhaps the least question-begging way to point out the mental is by means of our ordinary set of rational appraisal terms. As we indicated earlier, the mental is comprised of whatever may be meaningfully appraised in a nonmetaphorical sense as intelligent or stupid, as rational or irrational, as justified or unjustified, and so on. The list will include the whole set of semantic, logical, and value terms that are used to make similar appraisals. The mental is also comprised of whatever may be said to be abnormal to the extent these terms do not meaningfully apply. Finally, we take as mental, or at least as having a mental aspect, anything for which the inapplicability of these terms requires explanation. Any philosophy of mind which does not remain faithful to this starting point must justify its departure from it or else be judged unacceptable.

1. Rational appraisal language

"Rational" and "irrational" are certainly two of our broadest rational appraisal terms. We must of course distinguish their appraisal use from certain others. In the expression "rational appraisal language," "rational" is obviously a purely nonevaluative, factually descriptive term. Here "irrational" is not its negative. We also use "rational" and "irrational" to indicate the causal conditions of behavior. We may speak of a person as "not rational" or as "irrational" when his experiences and beliefs are causally independent of and thus unalterable by rational considerations. A delirious person, for example, is said to be irrational. Such a use of the term is valuative, but not in the usual appraisal sense. It ascribes a sickness or morbid condition to the person rather than mistakes or tendencies correctable through criticism.

As rational appraisal terms, "rational" and "irrational" are of course value concepts. To call a belief, attitude, or action "rational" is to commend it, whereas to call such "irrational" is to condemn them. However, they are not pure value terms like "good" or "ought," but rather more like "industrious" or "wise." They have a built-in factual component. To be told merely that something is good or that it ought to have some specified feature is not to be informed of any of its factual properties. But to be told that one is industrious is to be told that he is a hard worker, and to be told that one is wise is to be told that he knows how to solve human problems. In like manner, to be told that a belief, attitude, or action is rational is to be told, among other things, that it is consistent with at least a certain range of other beliefs, attitudes, experiences, or actions. We may mark the difference I am pointing up this way: pure value terms merely tell us that something ought to be or that it is the way it ought to be (or the negative of these), without at all informing us about the way it is, whereas a value term like "industrious" or "rational" tells us something about the way something is and that that is more or less the way it ought to be (or, in the case of a negative value term, like, for example, "lazy," it tells us how something is and that it ought not to be that way).

Some may contend that "rational" and "irrational" are not as extensive in application as such terms as "intelligent" or "stupid," for they may regard the former pair of terms as restricted to that which is subject to being reasoned about abstractly. It is true that to call a belief, for example, "rational" in the appraisal sense is to claim that it stands justified under rational criticism, but this doesn't mean that the subject has carried out the rational criticism or even that he is capable of doing it in any abstract way. We may even speak of our ordinary simple experiences like perceptions, for example, as rational or irrational. We usually assume that simple experiences of this kind are rational in the appraisal sense unless their occurrence is independent of and unalterable by rational considerations. Natural selection has no doubt made this a safe assumption for the most part. However, we do find inconsistencies among even our most elementary perceptions. The distinction we draw between what perceptually appears or seems to be the case and what we perceptually take to be the case indicates that we extend rational appraisal to the most elementary experiential level. In fact, we extend it even to the experiential level of lower animals. We would say that a dog that jumped in a frightened way out of the path of a moving shadow made a mistake in his perception, and to say that something embodies a mistake is to say that it does not stand up under rational criticism.

"Intelligent" and "stupid," however, are perhaps just as broad in application as "rational" and "irrational." Whenever there is adjustive behavior through knowledge or the appearance of values and of existing factual conditions there is the exercise of intelligence and the behavior may be appraised as intelligent or stupid. This is so not only in cases of overt action but even in adjustable desires, feelings, attitudes, perceptions, and beliefs. It may be stupid of a man to want certain things just as it may be stupid of him to believe certain propositions. One can lack the capacity to form desires, attitudes, beliefs, and even perceptions in an intelligent manner just as he can lack the capacity to make decisions and to act intelligently. We must distinguish between desires, feelings, beliefs, and the like which are causally produced in such a way that they are not adjustable in the rational way and those that are correctable through the exercise of intelligence. The former we exempt from rational appraisal. The latter we may appraise as intelligent or stupid according to the degree of intelligence manifested in them.

In addition to these most inclusive terms, rational appraisal language, as I have already mentioned, embraces semantic, logical, epistemic, and justificatory concepts. It is in terms of these that we find the conditions for the application of the broader rational appraisal terms. Let us look at logical appraisal terms first, for they are in a sense central. Indeed the mental may be called the realm of the logical. But, as we shall see, it can also be said to be the realm of the rational, of intelligence, of the semantic, of the epistemic, or of the justificatory. Nevertheless logical appraisal terms will lead us into the others and perhaps they are more clearly understood, at least at the prima facie level.

The same kind of things I said about "rational" and "irrational" applies to "logical" and "illogical." They are themselves the broadest logical appraisal terms. Although some uses of "logical" may be factually descriptive, as in "logical appraisal terms," in the sense in which it contrasts with "illogical," both it and its opposite are logical appraisal terms. To call a belief, argument, action, or anything else to which it meaningfully applies, "logical" is to commend it; it is to say that at least in the respect pointed up it is more or less the way it ought to be. In contrast, to call it "illogical" is to say that with respect to consistency with other beliefs, attitudes, experiences, actions, and the like, it is not the way it ought to be.

Some other logical appraisal terms are "valid," "sound," "cogent," "coherent," "consistent," "compatible," and their negatives. I am not so sure that the latter three are value terms in a very significant sense. For beliefs, attitudes, and actions to be coherent, consistent, or logically compatible is of course for them to be in this respect the way they ought to be and this is universally recognized, notwithstanding Emerson's talk about little minds. But I am not sure that the value element is built into these concepts as such. It cannot be denied, however, that consistency, coherence, and logical compatibility are good-making features in the realm of logical appraisal. They are the basic logical features that ought to obtain in beliefs, attitudes, experiences, actions, and the like, and therefore they are the marks of the logically good in this area. In like manner, their negatives (inconsistency, incoherence, logical incompatibility) are the marks of the logically bad or unacceptable.

Let us concentrate, for a moment, on logical compatibility and incompatibility. They are likely to be regarded as somewhat broader concepts than consistency and inconsistency. At least the latter have long been thought of primarily in the context of propositions and often defined in terms of truth-values. But even if we should take consistency and inconsistency in a broader sense, "compatibility" and "incompatibility" seem to be somewhat weaker concepts. Two propositions may be incompatible without being inconsistent. For example, P and Q may be said to be incompatible if P supports or makes not-Q evident with some significant probability even though P and Q may not be inconsistent. What is more, "consistent" and "inconsistent," at least with regard to propositions, are absolute terms, whereas "compatible" and "incompatible" may be qualified by "more" and "less." Any degree of compatibility of two propositions, however slight, constitutes consistency and absolute incompatibility is inconsistency.

Logical compatibility and incompatibility play a significant role in the rational life of man. They are in one way or another involved in all logical if not indeed in all rational appraisals. The validity of a deductive argument consists of the absolute incompatibility of its premises and the denial of its conclusion. The soundness of an inductive argument is grounded in the fact that the contradictory of its conclusion is less compatible with the premises of the argument than the conclusion itself. A body of statements, questions, rules, instructions, plans, actions, or what have you are said to be coherent or incoherent according to their compatibility with one another and the incompatibility that would be created by replacing any of these with their negatives. In other words, coherence requires not only compatability of the constituents involved but a pattern of mutual support. Even logical truth of a proposition involves the fact that its contradictory would be self-inconsistent. A belief is said to be cogent to the extent its contradictory would be more incompatible than it with a given body of beliefs.

The role of logical compatibility and incompatibility extends even further in rational appraisals. Verification or confirmation of a truth-claim, whether made in some form of discourse or inherent in some mode of experience, consists of coherence of it with other experiences or beliefs, which, as was observed above, involves not only logical compatibility of the given propositional claims but also the fact that the replacement of any of the set with their negatives would give rise to logical incompatibility within the complex. This kind of corroboration of a truth-claim is its justification, which is essential for knowledge. Thus compatibility and its opposite are essential grounds for epistemic appraisals.

Indeed, all justification, moral and otherwise, is grounded in the coherence of value experiences (including desires, wants, fears, anxieties, hopes, wishes, enjoyments, sufferings, emotions, attitudes, decisions, and the like) and judgments. I know of no serious alternative to a coherence theory of verification, confirmation, and justification. This, however, does not commit us to a coherence theory of truth or of the "validity" of a value claim.

Philosophical inquiry, as already remarked, is initiated and guided by conceptual incompatibilities. This is more basic than the logical incompatibility of propositions, imperatives, value judgments, and the like. "A is red" is logically incompatible with "A is nonred," but this does not at all challenge the meaningfulness of either proposition. It concerns only their truth values. But "A was justified" and "A was caused by a brain tumor" are logically incompatible in such a way that the truth of the latter, instead of simply requiring the falsity of the former, indicates that the former is not a meaningful statement in the sense that A, being caused in a nonrational way, is not the kind of thing that can be spoken of as either justified or unjustified. Just as knowledge of logical truth is grounded in propositional inconsistency, knowledge of philosophical truth is grounded in conceptual incompatibility.

Thus a fundamental value judgment presupposed in all rational appraisals is that our semantic claims of whatever kind ought to be logically compatible and harmonious, or, what amounts to the same thing, there ought not to be logical incompatibilities and dissonances among our semantic claims. This entails the imperative: eliminate logical incompatibilities of all kinds. We may regard this as a generalized version of Kant's categorical imperative, which was tailored to the realm of action. The whole rational enterprise—logic, knowledge, morality, action—rides upon this principle.

We must now turn to the kinds of things we may meaningfully talk about as logically incompatible, and thus define the subject matter of rational appraisals. Here we can only consider this problem in a preliminary way and at the prima facie level, for this is one of the central issues we shall have to deal with later. We may begin by pointing out an obvious area in which logical appraisal terms apply and ask what makes them applicable in this realm. There are undeniably logical incompatibilities in discourse. Strawson holds that logical appraisals are restricted to this realm. He summarizes his answer to the two questions, "what is it to which we apply words of logical appraisal? and . . . what makes logical appraisal possible?" in the following way: "We say that the answer to the first question was not 'sentences or groups of words,' but 'statements or groups of statements.' It is statements and not sentences that are inconsistent with one another, follow from one another, etc. We see that the answer to the second question is: the boundaries of application that we draw between one expression and another, the rules we come to observe for using expressions of all kinds. . . . Behind inconsistencies between statements, stand rules for the use of expressions."[1] He goes on to reject "the illusion of an independent realm of logical facts, of which linguistic rules are merely the adventitious verbal clothing."[2] This illusion, he thinks, is grounded in the fact that the inconsistency-rules of a language seem to transcend the particular language in question. But he explains this by the fact that in laying down inconsistency-rules in one language, we implicitly lay down inconsistency-rules for the corresponding expressions in all languages.

This does not seem to me to get at the heart of the matter for two reasons: (1) rules themselves may be logically incompatible—not just statements made by a rule-governed use of expressions; and (2) it ignores the character of the activity which is rule-governed in making statements. With regard to (1), on Strawson's account, the formation or laying down of rules for the use of expressions must at some point transcend or in some way be beyond the range of logical appraisal, for all formation or laying down of rules for the use of expressions cannot be carried out by the use of expressions. At least some rules for the use of expressions must be formed and operational independently of the use of any expressions in order for there to be any use of expressions at all. Are such rules incapable of logical incompatibility? It is true of course that Strawson restricted the application of "consistent" and "inconsistent" to statements. But surely anyone would have to admit that rules may be logically incompatible. Strawson is simply following the classical concern for logic as it applies to statements. There is little to justify this kind of provincialism in logic.

With respect to (2), Strawson does not tell us much about what it is to make a statement or to perform any other linguistic act except that in doing so we use expressions according to rules and thereby may misuse them. But this does not tell us much about the use of linguistic expressions and what logical errors are. There are rules for using the ball in a baseball game; players can make mistakes, they can misuse the ball, but to do so is not to make a logical error.

The rules governing the use of the ball tell us how it can be thrown, hit, caught, and the like. We know what these activities are apart from the rules. They can be performed outside of the game. Is there a parallel with noises and ink marks (we cannot speak of expressions here, for they are elements of a language and as such have a rule-governed use)? There is this much similarity: we use the ink-marks and noises according to rules to *say* something, to *refer* to things, to make truth-claims about them, to ask questions about them, to prescribe changes in them, and the like. Although it may be the case that these particular acts are themselves constituted by rule-governed uses of linguistic expressions, no one could learn to perform these rule-governed acts unless he had experiences of things, recognized things, remembered things, wanted things, wondered about things or was puzzled by them, took things to be one way or another in his experience of them and in his action in relation to them, and the like. I do not mean to suggest that all of these activities develop independently of our linguistic habits and skills. What I am maintaining is that they can and do exist in a rudimentary form without the specific linguistic skills Strawson is talking about and that they make possible the development and learning of language. Although linguistic acts are quite distinct in some ways from experiences, memories, overt actions and the like, they are also remarkably like them in certain ways which are of central importance for our purpose. They are similar in that they have objects—they are of or about things, they embody questions about things, they make truth-claims about them, they identify or classify things, they prescribe changes in things, etc. Experiences, memories, actions, and the like are, as we pointed out earlier, sufficiently like linguistic acts for us to be able *to express* or to articulate the former in language. Such articulation is not at all like reporting or describing physical happenings; it is much more like putting what we say in one language into the words of another. In short, experience has a semantic (meaning) dimension in much the same way as language. There is the semantic content of experience which may be made the semantic content of discourse. What is experienced is what is meant by the language that articulates or expresses the experience in question.

I suggest, contrary to Strawson, that it is in the semantic dimension of language as such, and not simply in rules per se, that we find what makes logical incompatibility possible. Wherever the semantic obtains, in truth-claims, rules, prescriptions, questions, or even just concepts, whether in experience, memory, action, or in discourse, logical incompatibility is possible and rational appraisal is in order. The realm of the semantic is the realm of the logical and indeed the realm of the rational. Nothing which lacks a semantic dimension, which does not mean something in some mode, can be meaningfully spoken of as embodying a logical incompatibility and therefore such things cannot be spoken of meaningfully in terms of any form of rational appraisal language. Hume, although he may have been in error about what has a semantic dimension and about the nature of the semantic as such, saw this point clearly: "A passion," he said, "is an original existence, and contains not any representative quality, which renders it a copy of any other existence or modification. When I am angry, I am actually possessed with the passion, and in that emotion have no . . . reference to any other object. . . . It is impossible, therefore, that this passion can be opposed by, or be contradictory to truth and reason; since this contradiction consists in the disagreement of ideas, considered as copies with those objects which they represent. . . ."[3]

Our strictly semantic appraisal terms are "true" and "false" and their cognates, like "veridical" and "illusory." In their descriptive role, they indicate the good- and bad-making features of statements and perceptual experiences—the correctness and incorrectness of semantic claims. "Meaningful" and "not meaningful" are another kind of semantic appraisal term. They play a most important role in philosophers' work. All of these feature in epistemic appraisals and define major objectives of the rational enterprise. Logical incompatibility, for example, is a bad-making feature precisely because it makes for falsity, illusion, and meaninglessness, whereas logical compatibility and coherence are good-making features in that they are marks of truth, veridicality, and meaningfulness. These are high values in the rational enterprise.

We now have before us a preliminary sketch of what I am calling rational appraisal language. I hope it is somewhat clear how it includes semantic, logical, epistemic, and justificatory concepts.

2. The language of psychology

There is a widespread tendency to locate the mental as an empirical detail in the world of scientific objects. Hardheaded behavioristic psychologists assume that the mental is known through scientific sensory observation in the manner of the subject matter of any natural science and that the language of psychology, insofar as it is fully scientific, is grounded exclusively in such experiences of its subject matter.

"If psychology is a science . . . of conscious experience," B. F. Skinner says, "then it must develop and defend a special methodology, which it has not yet done successfully. If it is, on the other hand, a science of the behavior of organisms, human or otherwise," he continues, "then it is part of biology, a natural science for which tested and highly successful methods are available."[4] "[T]he behavior of the subject, verbal or not," Mandler and Kessen contend, "is an event in the external world of the scientist, just as is the behavior of a rat, the construction of a maze, or the composition of a list of nonsense syllables."[5]

We may illustrate the behaviorist's concern with the purity of his observation language from Skinner. He reports a demonstration in which "a hungry pigeon was conditioned to turn around in a clockwise direction." Students included in their observation reports the following: "(1) The organism was conditioned to *expect* reinforcement for the right kind of behavior. (2) The pigeon walked around, *hoping* that something would bring the food back again. (3) The pigeon *observed* that a certain behavior seemed to produce a particular result. (4) The pigeon *felt* that the food would be given it because of its action; and (5) The bird came to *associate* his action with the click of the food-dispenser."[6] Skinner criticizes the reports for using such terms as "expect," "hope," "observe," "feel," and "associate," for such matters could not be observed scientifically. "The events reported by the students were observed, if at all," he says, "in their own behavior. They were describing what they would have expected, felt, and hoped for under similar circumstances."[7] "The observed facts," Skinner goes on to say, "could be stated respectively as follows: (1) The organism was reinforced *when* it emitted a given kind of behavior. (2) The pigeon walked around *until* the food container again appeared. (3) A certain behavior produced a particular result. (4) Food was given to the pigeon *when* it acted in a given way; and (5) the click of the food-dispenser was *temporally related* to the bird's action."[8]

The psychologist of the persuasion under discussion deals with alleged "subjective" states or acts of his human subjects only through their verbal behavior. Typical observation reports of this kind, according to Mandler and Kessen, are:

"Subject *A* said 'I have a pain in my back.' "

"The subject said: 'I'm depressed.' "

"When the subject was presented with areas *A* and *B* he said: 'I see two shades of green.' "

The intent is to report only what is directly accessible to the community of scientists through sensory observation.

Experience in general, and especially observation, is conceptually structured just as much as discourse. Experience is of objects and they are experienced as one kind of thing or another, as being related to other things in certain ways, and the like. To have a concept, to be a master of it, within the range of our observation language, is not simply a matter of our ability to operate with it in discourse, but primarily our skill in discriminating in terms of it in experience. The delineated structure of the observed is a function of the conceptual framework of the observer. Observation concepts may function in the delineation of the subject matter of a mode of observation other than the one in which they are primary modes of discrimination. For example, from within a warm room, we may *see* the snow storm outside as cold and windy.

The behaviorist, in theory at least, insists on delineating behavior in our scientific observation of it only in terms of concepts which are grounded in primary modes of discrimination for the senses involved. Thus insofar as he maintains that the psychologist has no mode of access to behavior other than what the natural scientist has to his subject matter, he is committed to the view that the observation concepts, and thus the observation language, of the psychologist must not be categorially different from that of the natural scientist. It must be a language of objects as discerned and discriminated by the kind of sensory observation employed in the natural sciences. The concepts of the language must not transcend these modes of experience. The psychologist, according to the behaviorist, must not say anything at the observation level about the "behavior" of an animal, human or otherwise, but what in principle could be verified by direct sensory observation of what is locatable solely as the object of just those sensory experiences. In other words, the psychologist must not say anything about animal behavior but what in principle could be verified by direct observation of a machine or robot.

This ideal of an object language in psychology is very difficult to achieve. Skinner, for example, did not do much better than his students in describing the pigeon's behavior. His report of the "observed facts" include "walked," "appeared," "given," "acted," and "action." The reports of verbal behavior taken from Mandler and Kessen include such terms as "presented," and "said," to say nothing of "I have a pain in my back," and the like. Let us look at some of these for a moment.

"The pigeon *walked* around until the food container *appeared.*" Is this a literal or a metaphorical use of "walked"? Does a wound-up toy literally walk? Does it literally walk around until something happens, especially until something *appears* again? One may walk hurriedly or leisurely, with studied, deliberate steps or absentmindedly, carefully or with abandon, clumsily or gracefully, and the like. We can say of one that it was intelligent (or stupid) of him to walk around until X happened, that he was justified (or unjustified) in walking around until it happened, etc. But we could not say these things literally of a wound-up toy or robot. Therefore, it would seem that we could not say that a toy or robot literally *walks*. It would make no more sense than to say that a doll literally cries.

The pigeon is said to have walked around until the food container again *appeared*. What kind of a pure observation report of an objective event is that! What is it for something to appear? It can only mean that it comes into *view*, or into some field of consciousness.

He also says, "Food was *given* to the pigeon when it *acted* in a given way." Something can be *given* grudgingly, reluctantly, willingly, cheerfully, mistakenly, etc., and the act of giving may be intelligent or stupid, justified or unjustified, right or wrong, and the like. Therefore, a machine or robot does not literally give anything. And the pigeon is spoken of as having *acted* in a certain way. An act may be said to be deliberate or done unthinkingly, to be intelligent or stupid, to be justified or unjustified, to be rational or irrational. Thus a machine or robot cannot be said literally to have acted in a certain way.

Among the observation reports of verbal behavior already cited, we find such statements as "Subject *A* said: 'I have a pain in my back.' " In what sense is "said" a pure observation term? It is meaningful to ask, Does what he *said* make sense? Is what he *said* consistent? Can you put what he *said* differently? Can you translate what he *said* into French? Does he literally mean what he *said*? Is what he *said* supported by evidence? Was he justified in *saying* what he did? Is what he *said* true? and so forth. Can we ask these questions literally of the noises emitted by a machine except insofar as the machine is taken to be the instrument of a personal act?

What about the quotation, "I have a pain in my back"? Mandler and Kessen, as well as Skinner,[9] treat the quotation of a statement of a subject as a name of the subject's verbal behavior. I will not here quarrel with the claim that the quotation is a name. My concern is with the verbal behavior allegedly named. The quotation seems to give us the object of the verb "said." If the report had been simply "Subject *A* said," we would ask, What did he say? and the answer might be "I have a pain in my back." On this interpretation the verbal behavior itself would seem to be what was said. If so, what and where is the act of saying of which verbal behavior is the object? This line of thought is obviously absurd. There is no act of saying of which the verbal behavior is the object. The verbal behavior is itself the act of saying, with its own built-in object. The sentence simply says that subject *A* performed an act of saying, and then instead of giving us its object, it introduces the act in person, as it were, into the report. This would be more literally the case if the report were oral. In the written report, the linguistic act of the subject is introduced in its written version. What is important for our purpose is that the observer reports that the subject *said* something and that he transcribes the oral linguistic act of the subject into its written version.

The position one takes about the observation language of behavior and its experiential ground defines the options open to him at the level of explanation and theory construction. The strict behaviorist has no choice but to operate within the framework of explanation and causality employed in the natural sciences. Observed behavior, regarded solely as sensorially discriminated events in the external world of the scientist, is explained in the manner of any other physical occurrence, namely, by laws observed to hold among specific kinds of external events and observed antecedent conditions. The laws are causal in the sense that they concern the conditions under which a certain kind of event occurs and provide knowledge which would in principle at least enable us to bring about or to manipulate such an event. The concepts of change and causality involved are necessarily naturalistic; that is, they are grounded in and are derivable from strictly sensory observation of changes in external objects. Thus only primary sensorially discriminable conditions and relations enter into the concept of causality and feature in the explanation of behavior.

Any theoretical claims must entail and be controlled by observation statements. Furthermore, the theoretical language must be modeled categorially after the observation language. For example, one cannot move from a naturalistic observation language of objects, from which value concepts and the language of subjects or agents are excluded on epistemological grounds, to a theoretical language which embodies teleological causality and the activity of subjects. It was no mere contingency that Laplace found no need for the God-hypothesis in physics. From within his methodological commitments, it was not a possibility for consideration. He had rejected feelings, emotions, desires, and the like as knowledge-yielding or data gathering modes of experience and thus had eliminated value concepts from his observation language. He also had no place for self-knowledge nor for perceptual understanding as a mode of access to his subject matter and thus no place for agency talk in the description of his observed objects. Thus value and agency talk at any point in his system would have transcended the epistemological limits of his discipline and compromised its integrity. He would have been drawing on extra-scientific foundations. The behaviorist who restricts himself to the methods of the natural sciences is in the same situation. As we pointed out in chapter 2, Skinner, in *Beyond Freedom and Dignity* (1971), acknowledges that there is no more place for persons in his psychology than there was for God in Laplace's physics and for the same reasons.

3. The incompatibility of the two languages

Yet to regard the mental as an empirical detail in the world of scientific objects, open for the purpose of knowledge only to scientific observation, description, and explanation in the way of the natural sciences, seems to be doomed to paradox, antinomy, and philosophical perplexity. We cannot restrict ourselves to the conceptual structure of such a psychology in dealing with the mental, not even in psychology itself, for the psychologist must appraise his own scientific activity, if not the behavior of his subjects, in rational appraisal terms. But to the extent he acknowledges the meaningful application of this team of concepts to his own behavior, he must acknowledge that they are also applicable to the behavior of his subjects. Furthermore, to the extent he holds that his scientific language applies to the behavior of his subjects, he must admit that it applies to his own. Thus the working behaviorist is forced to straddle two languages in dealing with the mental—semantic, logical, justificatory, and epistemic concepts on one hand and the concepts of scientific description and explanation on the other.

The two sets of concepts seem to be incompatible. What we take to be appropriately described and explained in terms of scientific concepts of objects, which we may call, in honor of certain historical controversies, the categories of determinism, we feel is not subject to being meaningfully talked about in terms of rational appraisal terms, also known, perhaps misleadingly, as the categories of freedom. This, it seems to me, is what the problem of freedom versus determinism really amounts to—which of these two teams of concepts, assuming them to be incompatible, shall we accept as indicating the categorical structure of the mental?

We feel almost instinctively that the two sets of concepts are incompatible. In our own cultural past, and in many cultures today, rational appraisal terms are applied to almost everything. People ask for and seek justifying reasons for earthquakes, floods, epidemics, good health, good weather, and for adversity and prosperity in general. But as such things come to be described and explained scientifically and people in general come to think about them in terms of scientific categories, as we observed in chapter 2, the rational appraisal terms are withheld as inappropriate. We think that it is meaningless to ask for the justification of an Alaskan earthquake, an epidemic of smallpox, the sudden death by heart failure of a young man, the good weather that brings a bountiful crop to an enemy, and the like. We also feel that it is inappropriate or meaningless to apply rational appraisal terms to the behavior of a person when we explain it in terms of a brain tumor or a stroke he has suffered. Freud sought to explain human behavior in terms of a "physicalized" version of psychic forces and thus was led to reject as *rationalization* the explanation of behavior in terms of justifying reasons. Most of us, I think, feel some intellectual cramp when the behaviorist insists on placing behavior in general, but especially human behavior, in the sphere of the scientific language of objects, for we feel that the meaningful application of our rational appraisal language is thereby jeopardized and along with it the whole realm of the mental (since we identify the mental by the applicability of the rational appraisal terms) and indeed science itself. Thus we face what appears to be an intolerable situation.

4. Is "the antinomy of the mental" simply a mistake?

Some philosophers insist that the alleged conflict or incompatibility of the two teams of concepts is only apparent and that both meaningfully apply to behavior in a perfectly straightforward way without any genuine conflict. Gilbert Ryle, one of the most forceful advocates of this position, contends that thinkers (theologians and scientists, everyman and psychologists, etc.) are sometimes at loggerheads with one another because "[t]hey suppose themselves to be giving, at least by indirect implication, rival answers to the same questions, when this is not really the case."[10] Such disputes cannot be resolved, he contends, by further work within either discipline, for they are philosophical issues requiring "litigations between lines of thought, where what is at stake is not which shall win and which shall lose a race, but what are their rights and obligations *vis a vis* one another and *vis a vis* also all other possible plaintiff and defendant positions."[11] Once the litigations are completed and rights and obligations of the different thinkers staked out, each goes about answering his own questions in his own way without even the possibility of conflict so long as each party stays clear about his own business. The role of philosophy is that of the judiciary in settling conflicts arising between other disciplines or lines of thought. It has no primary questions of its own.

Ryle contends that many stories can be told about the same subject matter without any conflict between them. He gives as an example the story the accountant in the business office of a college gives of the life and activities of the school. It covers every student, faculty member, administrator, caretaker, library, laboratory, athletic program, new construction, visiting lecturer, etc. But there are other stories to be told about all of this—the stories told in faculty reports, in letters home by students, in biographies of those involved, in histories of the college and various phases of it, in newspaper coverage of events on the campus, and the like. There isn't just one story to be told. The language of the accountant covers the activities of the college, but it does not exclude or conflict with the language of the other stories. Again he makes his point with the languages of card games. In a sense the bridge player and the poker player talk about the same deck of cards, but there is no conflict for the bridge player on a given occasion to call the ten of spades a trump and for the poker player never to do so, for he has no such concept in his framework of thought.

Thus, according to Ryle, the alleged conflicts between religion and science, ethics and psychoanalysis, rational appraisal of behavior in general and behavioristic psychology, and the like are all of the same order. They involve the mistaken notion that two disciplines are giving conflicting answers to the same questions when in fact they are attempting to answer quite disparate questions and thus are not in any way in competition with one another. The disputes involved are grounded in category mistakes. It is the philosopher's task to point out these mistakes and thus to let each party pursue his own questions in his own way without the distractions of interdisciplinary wars.

Our dilemma, the apparent conflict between rational appraisal of behavior and the descriptive-explanatory account of the behavioristic psychologist, could be resolved, according to this position, along the lines indicated by Waismann. He distinguishes between a transition in a calculus and a causal connection. The important thing about a move in a calculus, according to Waismann, is that there are rules in terms of which it can be justified. This does not, in his view, preclude in any way that there is a mechanism or causal connections in terms of which the changes involved can be described and explained. "The calculus proceeds," he says, "no matter what are the causes which determine its separate steps."[12] Concerning language in general, and perhaps he would generalize to behavior as such, he contends that it may be regarded as "a kind of mechanism, to explain the mode of operation of which is a task for psychology. But this is not the way a logician describes language . . . we look upon language not as a mechanism, but as a calculus."[13] However, he goes on to say, "It wouldn't be correct to say: language is *not* a mechanism, it *is* a calculus. There is no question that words produce many various affects and are in their turn caused by various processes. All we want to maintain is that the logician considers language, not as a mechanism, but as a calculus. In saying this, we are not making any statement about language, but are giving the point of view from which the logician wishes to consider language."[14]

Some would push the analogy between computers and the human mind. The computer may be regarded as making transitions in a calculus and thus may be talked about in rational appraisal terms. Yet no one doubts that its operations can be described and explained in the language of mechanics and electronics. Why not, then, admit that from one perspective and for certain purposes, we regard human behavior as movement in a calculus and thus subject to rational appraisal and yet from another perspective and for different purposes we view behavior as an empirical detail in the world of objects in the manner of the behaviorist? Stuart Hampshire says, in support of such a position, "At the present time one can only point to the purposes which . . . scientific explanations of human conduct, and of mental processes, are expected to serve, and the contrasting purposes which our deliberations about actions and attitudes now serve. No metaphysical absoluteness, or finality, need be claimed for the distinction between the usefulness of different kinds of discourse."[15]

I agree with Ryle, as I have already indicated, that philosophical reflection is initiated and spurred on by felt incongruities and logical oddities in the ways we experience and think about things. But I am not so sure that these apparent conflicts arise solely from confusion about the boundaries of categories, teams of concepts, or disciplines resulting in trespassing and that the task of philosophy is to settle the territorial disputes by demarcating the boundaries so that each discipline may get on with its domestic affairs in its own way. This is a version of the Lockean underlaborer's view of philosophy according to which its task is to clear away confusions, false issues, meaningless expressions, and the like so that other disciplines may tell their own stories in a better way.

I do not share this view. The philosopher, troubled by conceptual incongruities and oddities and guided by what it is meaningful and conceptually compatible to say, as we argued in chapter 3, attempts to get at, to lay bare, and to understand our conceptual structure and its involvement in experience and thought and its relationship to reality. This involves identifying concepts that function together as a team, distinguishing the major teams of concepts, determining team compatibilities and rivalries, locating the function and experiential ground of the various teams of concepts, explicating or giving a detailed analysis of certain basic, key concepts, and the like. Furthermore, the philosopher is concerned with the conceptual structure as a whole, including what it is (as revealed by an analysis of what it is meaningful and not meaningful to say about it), its involvement in experience and action as well as in thought, and its relation to the structure of reality. Of course some philosophical perplexities may be resolved without going very far in such an exploration of the conceptual just as some of our ordinary factual inconsistencies may be solved short of the full development of science. But this is the realm to which we are introduced by philosophical perplexity.

Thus it is part of the task of philosophy, as I understand it, to construct a philosophical view of the world by an analysis of the categorial structure of language, thought and experience and that of which they are of and about. It must tell us what kinds of things there are in the world: whether there are physical objects, or only sense data; whether there are such things as we talk about in theoretical language or only those things we talk about in observational language; if there are such things as we talk about in theoretical language, are there only those things of this kind as we talk about in the theoretical language of science, or are there also those things that we talk about in the mythical language of religion and the theoretical language of theology; whether there are nations and the like, or only people; whether there are only subjective, private worlds, or one objective, public world; whether there are universals or only particulars; whether there are objective necessary connections in the world, or only contingent ones; whether there are only physical relations, or also semantic, logical, value, and social ones; whether there are only facts, or values also; if there are values, whether there are unique moral values, or only prudential ones; and the like. These matters are to be decided, as we argued in chapter 3, by an analysis of the various modes of experience through an examination of the ways it is meaningful to talk about them to determine which, if any, are epistemic or knowledge-yielding; an analysis of the various kinds of discourse to determine if, and if so how, they have semantic ties to items and features of the world; and an analysis of the categorial structure of the items and features of the world semantically appropriated by examination of the categorial form of the appropriating experience and thought and the language that expresses them and what it makes sense to say and does not make sense to say about the items and features themselves.

If this view of philosophy is correct, Ryle's interpretation of the apparent conceptual conflicts or dilemmas which give rise to philosophical reflection must be rejected. The theologian and the scientist, the moralist and the psychoanalyst, everyman who talks about behavior in rational appraisal terms and the behavioristic psychologist, and the like, are in fact, contrary to Ryle, "giving, at least by indirect implication, rival answers to the same questions," namely, to metaphysical questions. Ryle could locate only the questions of the theologian and the scientist, the moralist and the psychoanalyst, everyman and the behaviorist. He is quite right that the apparent conflicts are not genuine if these are the only questions involved. But, as I have tried to indicate, the conflicts are grounded in implied answers to metaphysical questions concerning the categorial structure of the segment of reality concerned.

The conflict between rational appraisal talk about behavior and the behaviorist account may be pinpointed on the metaphysical question concerning the nature of mental causality. As we have already indicated, the strict behaviorist has no choice but to regard the causality of behavior as naturalistic, as the kind involved in the purely factual realm. Yet rational appraisal language seems to contain its own concept of causality. Rational appraisal deals in justificatory reasons for judgments, beliefs, feelings, attitudes, decisions, actions, and the like. In ordinary discourse, our explanatory reasons for what we do are often justificatory reasons also. We explain why we believe something by citing evidence that supports the belief. A university explains why it dismissed a professor by giving reasons which tend to justify its action. When we offer evidence in support of a proposition, we expect it to affect our audience, to convince them of the truth of the claim. When we give advice, when we tell a person why he shouldn't do a proposed act, we hope that our advice will influence his behavior. To the extent it does not, we feel that we did not convince him of what we said. Reasons, whether for or against beliefs, attitudes, or actions, cannot be known or acknowledged without influencing us. Inconsistency, for example, is a reason for changing one's beliefs, attitudes, plans, actions, or whatever it is involved in, and when known by the person involved actually works a change.

The realm of freedom is the realm in which changes are wrought in this manner. It is not a matter of indeterminism or lack of causes, but rather the kind of causality involved. Known, believed, or felt facts and requirements are causally operative, or at least tend to be, in bringing about what appears or is taken to be required. The freedom involved is the freedom of the mind, indeed the freedom of behavior in general, from blind naturalistic causality and even from simple teleological causality in which knowledge and rationality in general play no part and make no difference.

We hold that rational appraisal terms apply only where reasons are or may be causes. Whenever we discover that reasons are ineffective in a person's behavior, that what he experiences, thinks, and does are causally independent of and unresponsive to truth, logic, and rational considerations in general, we withhold rational appraisal of him. We say that he is not a free, responsible agent. His "behavior," if we may continue to call it that, is totally caught up in the nonsemantic causal nexus.

We cannot, in the manner suggested by Waismann, regard human behavior as transitions in a calculus for purposes of rational appraisal and as a system of scientific objects involving only naturalistic causation for purposes of psychology. These two views, as I have tried to show, genuinely conflict in that we cannot count changes in a system as transitions in a calculus unless we take reasons to be causes at some point in the system. The case of the computer is deceptive. We take its operations to be transitions in a calculus because we place it in a wider system which includes the designers, manufacturers, programmers, and the like. In this wider system reasons are causes and the computer is an instrument of human computation. The fact that we can describe and explain the happenings in the computer in the language of mechanics and electronics does not in any way compromise its status as a tool or instrument in the performance of personal acts. It, as a closed system, no more thinks or calculates than a telescope sees. But if we should extend the language of mechanics, electronics, and the like to the whole universe as a closed system, including human behavior, assuming for the moment a privileged position outside the universe to make this possible, we could not without conceptual conflict, if the rational appraisal and naturalistic causal teams of concepts are distinct and irreducible, acknowledge any changes anywhere in the universe to be transitions in a calculus. To do so would be to give, at least by implication or presupposition, what appears to be rival answers to the same metaphysical question; namely, to the question, "What kind of causality is involved in the transition?"

There are other points of apparent conflict between the two teams of concepts in terms of their implications or presuppositions for philosophical questions concerning the categorial structures involved. But it seems that most of the others are involved in one way or another with the question about causality. Genuine ontological freedom, in contrast with naturalistic determinism, for example, seems to require that human beings and their behavior involve a threefold categorial structure of fact, value, and meaning. Thus the causal question is a very fundamental issue.

By way of summary, then, we have urged that the applicability of rational appraisal terms is the criterion of the mental. We have argued that it is behavior delineated in terms of our commonsense behavioral language, behavior as the acts of agents for whom reasons are causes, that is subject to rational appraisal in terms of semantic, logical, epistemic, and justificatory concepts. Furthermore, we have contended that if behavior is conceived, for the purpose of knowledge of it, entirely in terms of the language of scientific objects in the manner of behavioristic or physiological psychology, then our rational appraisal terms seem not to apply, with the consequence that the mental seems to be denied, and along with it knowledge of every kind, even that of psychology. We have examined Ryle's claim that this apparent conceptual incongruity is not genuine and that the illusion of conflict is grounded in the mistaken notion that rational appraisal of behavior and behavioristic or physiological psychology are giving rival answers to the same questions. We have argued, contrary to Ryle, that the two approaches do involve implied or presupposed answers to the same philosophical questions which appear to be rivals. Therefore the dilemma seems to remain.

VII

Naturalistic Theories of
Rational Appraisal Language

We concluded in the last chapter that if rational appraisal language and the scientific language of behavior are really what they appear to be, then the antinomy of the mental is genuine and we are left committed to both freedom and determinism. The scientific party, it seems, can maintain the determinist's position only by showing that the two modes of discourse about human behavior only seem to offer conflicting answers to the same metaphysical questions but really do not. If we admit the legitimacy of the metaphysical questions, as we have argued, it would seem that the only way the conflict could be shown to be merely apparent would be to show that the two modes of discourse, appearances not withstanding, do not really imply or presuppose conflicting answers to these questions: that when these apparently conflicting answers are philosophically clarified, they will be seen to yield the same or at least compatible answers. Such philosophical clarifications usually proceed by reducing rational appraisal language to some form of the scientific language of objects or by explaining its use in such a way as to show that the ontology of the former is not different from that of the latter.

What is of fundamental importance for this enterprise, over and above the value aspect of rational appraisal language, is the ontological significance of semantic and logical talk. And of these the semantic is primary, for, as we have already observed, logical concepts apply to nothing but what has a semantic dimension or is somehow incomplete or defective to the extent it does not. Having already explored in chapters 4 and 5 the ontological significance of value language in general, and our results there indicate at least partial failure of the enterprise under discussion, the fundamental issue we must now consider is whether there is ontologically a structure of meaning. The issue concerning the ontological status of logical structures will have to wait for a solution to this prior question.

1. The reducibility of meaning talk about language to psychological talk

We are more familiar with semantic or meaning talk in discourse about language. This is the proper place for our inquiry to begin. H. P. Grice, in three papers,[1] has attempted to show that sentence meaning and word meaning can be explicated in terms of what he calls utterer's occasion meaning, and that utterer's occasion meaning can be explicated in terms of psychological concepts, specifically in terms of the utterer's intentions about psychological effects on his audience. His 1957 analysis of utterer's occasion meaning was put this way: " 'A meant$_{nn}$* something by X' is roughly equivalent to 'A intended the utterance of S to produce some effect in an audience by means of the recognition of this intention,' and, we may add," he says, "that to ask what A meant is to ask for a specification of this intended effect" (p. 385). He in 1957 took the intended effects of indicative utterances to be beliefs on the part of the audience and those of imperative utterances to be actions. In the last two papers he modifies this somewhat in ingenious and complicated ways in order to meet certain counter examples.† But for our purposes, nothing is changed. He still reduces meaning talk to psychological talk—to talk about intentions of the utterer and intended psychological effects on (or responses by) an audience.

Paul Ziff[2] has attacked Grice's first step in the reduction, namely, his claim that standard or timeless meaning of expressions can be explicated in terms of utterers' occasion meaning. He gives what he takes to be counter examples. George, an irritable academic, in taking a mental test in the army, answers the examiner's question about how he would identify himself with

(1) Ugh ugh blugh blugh ugh blug blug;

or again with

(2) pi. hi. y. hi. y. ("I don't know" in Hopi).

Ziff says that, according to Grice's theory, George meant something by

---

*The subscript "nn" is an abbreviation for "nonnaturally." Thus "means$_{nn}$" is in contrast with "means naturally," which is the sense of "means" in such expressions as "smoke means fire" and "red spots mean measles."

†Essentially the modifications are these: "the M-intended effect [an M-intended effect ('M' for 'meaning') is an effect one intends to produce in another by the other's recognition of that intention] common to indicative-type utterances as being, not that the hearer should believe something (though there will frequently be an ulterior intention to that effect), but that the hearer should *think that the utterer* believes something"; and "the M-intended effect of imperative-type utterances as being that the hearer should *intend* to do something (with of course, the ulterior intention on the part of the utterer that the hearer should go on to do the act in question)" (in John Searle, ed., *The Philosophy of Language*, [London: Oxford University Press, 1971], p. 59). Here, it would seem, the parallel modification should be: the utterer intends that the audience think that the utterer wants the audience to intend to do and indeed to do X.

(1), but that it is clear that he did not. All we can say, according to Ziff, is that George meant something by uttering (1), not by (1). In the case of (2), however, he says George both meant something by it and by uttering it. He charges that Grice's mistake consists of having conflated and confused "*A* meant something by uttering *X*" with "*A* meant something by *X*."

But what is the distinction here? Consider the following:

(3) George meant something by *X*.

(4) George meant something by the utterance (or inscription) *X*.

(5) George meant something by uttering (or writing) *X*.

(6) George meant to do something by uttering (or writing) *X*.

(7) George intended to do something by uttering (or writing) *X*.

There is no significant difference between (3) and (4) nor between (6) and (7). And to the extent (5) differs from (4) and thus from (3) in any important respect, it is similar to (6) and therefore to (7). In the sense in which one *means* something by the utterance *X*, for example, "I don't know," one cannot *mean* something different by *uttering X*, such as, for example, "I would identify myself as Napoleon." So to the extent George meant something by *uttering X* as distinct from what he meant by *X*, he meant or intended to insult, to impress, to warn, to call attention to himself, or the like. But in the primary sense one cannot mean semantically something different by *uttering X* from what he means semantically by *X*.

One can mean something in uttering (or by uttering) *X* either according to the standard meaning of *X* or by bending *X* to one's private purposes in such a way that one's audience would understand what was said. And of course there are those situations in which one makes mistakes, but nevertheless means such and such. E.g., one may utter "John" but mean Tom and be understood to mean Tom. And there is the case of the code. One may utter "Tomorrow is Marie's birthday" and mean that *X* will launch a military attack on *Y* tomorrow.

Thus it seems that Ziff's accusation that Grice has conflated "*A* meant something by *X*" with "*A* meant something by uttering *X*" is grounded in his own conflation of "*A* meant something by uttering *X*" with "*A* meant (or intended) to do something by uttering *X*." I see nothing in his argument to indicate that we cannot philosophically explicate word and sentence timeless meaning in terms of utterers' occasion meaning.

Words and sentences have uses or functions. They are primarily tools or instruments for the performance of semantic acts. When we say, "The adjective 'ungulate' means having hoofs," to borrow one of Ziff's examples, we mean that it is a word constructed for use in saying of an animal that he has hoofs; or the word, in a standard use, means has hoofs; or the word is a standard way to mean has hoofs. But in a very important sense, the word not in use doesn't mean anything. Perhaps it has a meaning, namely, a semantic use, but this is not actually to mean something.

But words and sentences are not merely tools or instruments. They are social tools or instruments. Indeed a language is an institution. We cannot get at the reality of institutions apart from the life they inform and structure. And the life informed and structured by the institution of language is the semantic acts of utterers (or writers) on particular occasions, acts which can of course be frozen on tape (or in ink) for repeated hearing (or reading). Otherwise language is a mere abstraction, form without substance. Therefore, it is only in utterers' occasion meaning that we find actual concrete meaning. And this is what we want to know the categorial nature of in our philosophical quest.

So far, then, Grice seems to be on sound ground. But what of the second step in his program? Can we reduce the language of utterer's occasion meaning to psychological language?

It would seem that we could not explicate the meaning of an expression in use, that is, what the expression means as used in a given context, in terms of the utterer's intended psychological effect on his audience. What one uses an expression to mean on a given occasion seems to be quite distinct from any intended effect on his audience. One may not even have an audience, but, if one does, one's primary intention vis à vis his audience is that the audience understand what one means by his utterance. Indeed this would have to be contained in the intention that a certain psychological effect be produced in his audience by *recognition of that intention*. But one's primary intention vis à vis his speech act *is* to mean some specific thing. One may intend to mean *M* by uttering *X* but fail to do so. *X* may not be an appropriate instrument, or one may use it in such a way that he fails to mean what he intended to mean. So why not recognize acts of meaning in various modes as things people do and intend to do and may be understood as doing? The answer must be that many people have philosophical assumptions which block such an acknowledgement; more specifically, they have epistemological assumptions according to which we are unable to fund the language of meaning except indirectly through the language of psychology.

But even if we were able to explicate the language of meaning in terms of such psychological concepts as "intending," "thinking," "believing," etc., we would, I suggest, have to reintroduce semantic concepts to explicate adequately these psychological concepts. Thus such an explication of semantic concepts would be simply the explication of semantic concepts in terms of semantic concepts and whatever was philosophically problematic about semantic concepts as such would remain problematic. Indeed, I suggest that the philosophical gain from any attempted reduction of the language of meaning to the language of psychology might be a revelation to the effect that the language of psychology is itself part of the language of meaning.

2. Psychological language is the primary language of meaning

An exploration of subjectivity will help us understand the relationship between psychological acts and meaning. Everyone recognizes that the psychological realm involves subjectivity in some way. Even those who reject subjectivity feel compelled to develop elaborate theories to explain it away and to make sense out of psychological talk without it.

We can gain a starting point with the underlying concepts of subject and object. Linguistically speaking, we talk about the subject and object of transitive verbs, but we may speak of an act designated by a transitive verb as itself transitive, as having an object. When a knife cuts, it cuts something. When acid etches, it etches something. It is, however, with respect to mental transitive verbs that the linguistic subject-object distinction is most clearly extended to that which the language is about, for the structure of language and the structure of psychological states and acts are much the same.

Psychological states and acts are, like mental verbs, transitive. They are constituted, I suggest, by a structure of meaning involving a subject and an object. It is not that the subject and the object exist and that some relation obtains between them as in the case of acid etching a metal plate. The object is an intentional object—something *meant* in some mode of meaning, and the question of its existence is a further matter. This, of course, presupposes a broader view of meaning than that now fashionable, but I would contend that it is in experience, memory, imagination, and "action" that we find our primary structures of meaning. Abstract thought is possible only through the use of language, but language is not the original home of meaning. It has its meaning only through its use in thought, in the performance of semantic acts. And the semantic acts of thought differ from the semantic acts of experience, memory, imagination, and "intention" (the primitive kind possible without the benefit of language such as the higher animals may be capable of) primarily in that they make use of semantic tools and therefore are capable of almost unlimited refinement and extension.

We may say, then, as a first approximation, that a subjective state or act is one that is at least partially constituted by intentionality; it is a state or act with an intentional object, which has to be mentioned or described in a full report or description of the state or act itself.

There have been a number of efforts in recent literature to specify what is meant by "intentionality." Most of the criteria proposed have been formulated linguistically in terms of the marks of intentional verbs and sentences, but the term is applied also to the states, dispositions, and acts located by such expressions. I shall give only a brief summary of the major proposals.

(1) Intentional acts can take for objects not only things designatable by nouns and descriptive phrases but also facts, states of affairs, and possibilities locatable by substantival clauses, and infinitive and participial phrases. Cognitive verbs, Hall says, "can take as objective complements clauses and phrases which can be made into independent sentences themselves by suitable modification of their verbal constituents. . . . This is not true," he says, "of verbs expressing ordinary physical action; they must always take nouns or pronouns, never 'sentences,' that is, substantival clauses, as objects."[3] E.g., I may see a man and I may see that the man is bald. I may hear your father and I may hear him coughing. But, while I may strike a man, Hall says, I cannot strike that he is anything.

(2) Intentional acts, unlike physical ones, do not require the existence of their objects. "A simple declarative sentence is intentional," Chisholm says, "if it uses a substantival expression—a name or a description—in such a way that neither the sentence nor its contradictory implies either that there is or that there isn't anything to which the substantival expression applies."[4] Thus, "Diogenes looked for an honest man" is intentional, but not, according to Chisholm, "Diogenes sat in his tub." A noncompound sentence which contains a propositional clause is intentional, according to Chisholm, "provided that neither the sentence nor its contradictory implies either that the propositional clause is true or that it is false." For example, neither "James believes there are tigers in Africa" nor its negation implies anything about whether there are tigers in Africa.

(3) The nonextensional identity of the objects of intentional acts as indicated by the nonsubstitutability of different names and descriptions of them. This is the most widely accepted criterion. Chisholm puts it this way: "Suppose there are two names or descriptions which designate the same things and E is a sentence obtained merely by separating these two names or descriptions by means of 'is identical with'. . . . Suppose also that A is a sentence using one of those names or descriptions and that B is like A except that where A uses the one B uses the other. Let us say that A is intentional if the conjunction of A and E does not imply B." His example is "Most of us knew in 1944 that Eisenhower was the one in command (A); but although he was (identical with) the man who was to succeed Truman (E), it is not true that we knew in 1944 that the man who was to succeed Truman was the one in command (B)."[5]

(4) Objects of intentional acts may be indeterminate. Anscombe illustrates the point this way: "I can think of a man without thinking of a man of any particular height; I cannot hit a man without hitting a man of any particular height, because there is no such thing as a man of no particular height."[6]

(5) The ineffectuality of intentional acts. Although an intentional act is directed upon an object, "it does not make sense to suppose," Hall

says, "that anything is done to the object by this action."[7] Kenny illustrates: "If Peter has painted his house, then Peter's house must now be different from what it was before he painted it; but if Peter has looked at his house, it may now be exactly the same as it was before he looked at it."[8]

(6) The nonobservability of intentional acts. "[W]hen we say we see others see or hear things," Hall writes, "what we mean is that we see them take characteristic postures of looking or listening, not that we literally see them see or hear."[9]

(1) suggests, as indeed it was apparently intended by Hall, that any intentional act (or, linguistically speaking, any intentional verb) can take a fact or state of affairs (or linguistically speaking, a substantival clause or an infinitive or participial phrase) as its object (or objective complement). But this seems questionable. Consider these expressions: "John looked at Mary," "John loved Mary," "John embraced Mary," "John fought Mary," "John hated Mary," "John mentioned Mary," "John was thinking of Mary," etc. The list could be extended indefinitely. Some of these acts may not appear to be intentional by the criteria listed, but a case will be made for their intentionality below. The acts indicated seem to take individuals for their objects and it is not at all clear how facts or states of affairs could be their objects. Therefore, (1) seems unacceptable as a necessary condition but may be all right as a sufficient condition.

Kenny objects to (2) as a necessary condition for intentionality, and it should be said that it was not intended to be such by Chisholm at least, on the ground that it would rule out epistemic verbs such as "know" and its cognates and that intuitively they belong to the family under consideration. They are, as Chisholm points out, brought into the fold by criterion (3). But it is not clear that (2) as a necessary condition would exclude epistemic verbs and their correlative acts; indeed it is not obvious but that they are brought under the concept of intentionality with (2) as a sufficient condition. Epistemic verbs are not purely descriptive, but, as Ryle would say, achievement verbs. It is by virtue of their achievement character that they imply existence of their objects. It is the semantic acts involved in such achievements that have intentional objects in the primary sense, and these acts themselves, especially in the case of knowing, do not require the existence of their objects. Concentration on the intentionality of verbs and sentences as such rather than on the acts located by the verbs or reported by the sentences is likely to mislead us on this matter. We may say that a verb or sentence is intentional if the act it locates or reports is intentional.

But what about the acts reported by such sentences as were mentioned above in connection with (1), namely, "John looked at Mary," "John loved Mary," etc. They, unlike epistemic acts, seem to require the existence of their objects in a straightforward way. Nevertheless, each is complex in its own way. Consider "John looked at Mary." The act reported seems to require the existence of its object and certain physical relationships between the subject and the object. Nevertheless, the sentence admits of several possible uses. It could be used in appropriate circumstances to make statements with the following truth-conditions: (1) $(\exists x)(x=$Mary and John looked at $x)$*; (2) $(\exists x)$ (John looked at x; John, in looking at x, took x to be Mary; and $x=$Mary); (3) $(\exists x)$ (John looked at x; and John, in looking at x, took x to be Mary [whether or not $x=$ Mary]); and (4) John had the experience of looking at Mary (whether or not Mary or anyone else was there). "John looked at Mary," with the truth-conditions of (1), is not, strictly speaking, a report of an act of John. It is more a statement about Mary. The passive voice, "Mary was looked at by John," would be a more appropriate form for its meaning. (2) and (3) both report behavioral acts which involve physical relationships between the subject and object in a way that requires the existence of the object. Furthermore (2), but not (3), entails that John was correct in taking x to be Mary, which implies the existence of the object. (3) is a report of a more subjective act than (2) but a less subjective act than (4), which is a report of a purely subjective act. Nevertheless there is a subjective dimension to all four with its intentional object.

What about "John mentioned Mary"? This is not to be understood as "John referred to Mary by name" but rather in the more general sense of "John spoke of Mary," which in many ways parallels "John thought of Mary." It is a report of an act which may have been performed in any one of several ways. The point is that he made an identifying reference to her, however it was accomplished. Our problem is whether making an identifying reference to something is an intentional act. It is almost universally agreed that such a reference requires the existence of its object. An attempted act of identifying reference without an existent object would be said to fail and therefore not be an act of reference. Does this mean that an identifying reference is something that one does to an existent object, like some acid's etching a metal plate; that it is a transaction or relation between two existents, involving only externality, with no internality or subjectivity? I think not. But can we distinguish between an intentional object and an existent object here?

An identifying reference, whether by name, description, demonstrative, or pointer, semantically locates something and takes it up into one's consciousness for thought or discourse about it. Therefore, by its very nature an act of identifying reference requires an object, one that is in a sense internal to the act of reference. This is to be contrasted with, let us say, the physical spotlighting of a thing where the thing spotlighted is only contingently and "externally" related to the beam of light. The beam of

*The logical expression "$(\exists x)$" is read: "There is an x such that . . .;" and "$x=$ Mary" means x is (identical with) Mary.

light could exist without the thing spotlighted being there and it could be reported and described without mention of the thing. Not so with an act of identifying reference. The object is "internal" to and constitutive of the act. This kind of an involvement in a semantic act seems to be at least part of what we mean by "intentional object." A further requirement for an act of identifying reference is that its object have some status other than being the intentional object of that act of reference. But must this status be that of existence? Of course a uniquely referring expression like "The present king of France," by virtue of its own terms, could semantically locate only an existent in the physical and social space-time world, and if it fails to do so, it fails to appropriate anything semantically. Therefore, if it were used by a person at the present time in an attempt to make an identifying reference, the attempted act, it would seem, would have no intentional object and would be faulty for that reason. But an attempt at making an identifying reference can succeed without the existence of its object. The intentional object, however, must have some kind of independence; if not existence, then it must be at least the intentional object of some other intentional act. We have no trouble mentioning a particular character in a novel either by name or description. We can mention the person in Bernadette's vision, or even Macbeth's dagger or the big rabbit in the play *Harvey*. What is required for an identifying reference is for there to be independently something to be semantically located and appropriated, for making an identifying reference is semantically picking out or spotlighting something already there in some sense. This can be done with the intentional objects of other semantic acts as well as with existent things.

I want to stress the point that whatever is semantically located and appropriated by an identifying reference is with respect to that reference an intentional object even if it must have some kind of an independent status as well. In this respect, reference is like an epistemic act. But there appears to be an important difference. Although an epistemic act, like an act of reference, requires the existence or at least an independent status of its object, there is in an epistemic act a constituent semantic act, what I have called the act of thinking that P, which does not require that P obtain in the world. It is the correctness of that act that requires existence. But the act of identifying reference itself seems to be a semantic act whose object must have an independent status. Indeed this seems to be true of general reference as well. "Some kings of the United States were assassinated" appears to be faulty in the same way as "The present king of France is bald." It would seem that neither semantically locates and appropriates anything to make a statement about. Yet there seems to be nothing wrong with such statements as "George believes that the present king of France is bald" and "George believes that some kings of the United States were assassinated." They could even be true. But how could George accept as true what is not in effect a statement? Could it be that reference is complex somewhat like knowing and that there is a component semantic act that may or may not be correct or successful, with the existence of its object being required only for the correctness or success of it?

Modern extensional logic, for the most part, reduces reference to a kind of assertion. The sentence "Some kings of the United States were assassinated" would be analyzed not as failing to make a statement for lack of a semantically appropriated subject, but as asserting that at least one thing was both an American king and assassinated. And "The present king of France is bald" would be interpreted as asserting that one and only one thing is presently king of France and that it is bald. Quine reduces even reference by proper name to assertions.[10] This involves converting names into adjectives or general terms. So "John mentioned Mary" would be interpreted something like this: "John said that one and only one person [within the context of my discourse] Maryizes and she. . . ."

So on this view the pure act involved in an act of reference is an assertion which may be true or false and therefore does not imply the existence of its object. But if the assertion is false, the reference fails. We would not say that a person who said either "The present king of France is bald" or "Some kings of the United States were assassinated" actually referred to anything. There is an achievement aspect to reference as there is to knowing. So to make an identifying reference with the expression "the present king of France" one would have to assert truly that there is one and only one thing that is presently king of France. We could conclude, then, that reference, like knowing, is intentional because its constitutive semantic act, which does not require existence of its object, is intentional.

I am not entirely happy with this analysis. It results from analyzing statements in terms of their truth-conditions. It is true that "The present king of France is bald" is true if and only if there is one and only one thing that is presently king of France and it is bald. And "Some kings of the United States were assassinated" is true if and only if at least one thing was both king of the United States and assassinated. But this way of analyzing a statement has no way of sorting out what a statement asserts from what it presupposes and entails. When one utters the sentence "The present king of France is bald" with the intent of making a statement, he does not strictly say or assert that there is one and only one thing that is presently king of France; he presupposes it and the attempted act of identifying reference cannot succeed unless this presupposition is true. But it seems to me that the act of reference is the semantic location and taking up of something in person, so to speak, into thought or discourse. But even if we do not know the success of an attempted reference, or if we know that it failed, we know from the conceptualization in and the presuppositions of the act something of the object that would have been located and appropriated if the attempt had been successful. This constitutes what we may call the secondary intentional object of the act. When we simply report "John mentioned Mary" we say that he made an identifying reference to Mary and our report entails that Mary exists, for it presents her as the primary intentional object of the act of reference. But when we say "John said that Mary was there," our report does not say, at least on one reading, that he made an identifying reference to Mary and it does not entail that Mary exists. But it does report an apparent identifying reference with its secondary intentional objects.

Philosophers talk about intensions and extensions of expressions with intensions identified with what expressions mean and extensions with what they refer to. From within this way of talking intentional objects are usually identified with intensions, that which is meant as distinct from that which is referred to. But reference is itself a semantic act, a mode of meaning, as is describing, asserting, questioning, prescribing, etc. So my line of thought leads me to consider both intensions and extensions as intentional objects. What are more commonly called intentional objects are pure intentional objects in that they may have intentional status only, that is, they may be nonexistent; whereas what are usually called extensional objects have an independent status. But I have argued that they are still intentional objects in that they have an intentional or semantic presence over and above and distinct from their existential or independent status.

It should be clear that intentional and existential objects are not two kinds of objects in the sense that they have different defining properties so that descriptions of them would be different. It is that they differ in their mode of being, the one having a semantic presence and the other an existential status. The intentional object as such not only does not exist, it does not exemplify the properties in terms of which it is described, for properties can exist in or be exemplified by only existent things. But it would not be right to say that the properties are semantically in the intentional object. It is rather that the object along with its properties are semantically present whether or not they are existentially present also.

So "John mentioned Mary" reports an intentional act even though the statement does imply that Mary exists, not from the fact that the word "Mary" is a proper name but from the nature of the act of mentioning or uniquely referring to Mary.

Therefore, the absence of an implication of existence cannot be accepted as a defining mark of intentionality but it does appear to be a sufficient condition.

What about overt behavioral acts such as mailing a letter, sitting in a tub, or embracing a lover? All the criteria mentioned, if taken as necessary conditions, would seem to exclude them. Yet, as Sellars points out, intentionality "lurks in such notions as that of 'behavioral' (as contrasted with geographical) environment, and in the non-technical use of such terms as 'goal,' 'anticipatory,' and 'expectancy.' " Indeed reference or aboutness is encountered, he maintains, in the explication of "all characteristically human states and dispositions above the level of mere sensory conscious-ness."[11] I would question the exemption of even sensory awareness, a matter we shall discuss later.

There is a sense in which we want to distinguish between, for example, an act of mailing a letter and an act that unknown to the agent actually results in a letter's being mailed. Suppose one intends to throw away an addressed, stamped letter by putting it in what he takes to be a trash can on the street but what is actually a mailbox. At no time could he correctly report "I am mailing a letter" in response to the question, "What are you doing?" Nor at any time would the statement, "He is mailing a letter," be a correct report of what he was doing. Also consider the case in which one intends to mail a letter and places it in what he takes to be a mailbox but what is actually a trash can. In spite of the fact that he did nothing that resulted in a letter's being mailed, it would have been correct in an important sense for him to have reported at the time, "I am mailing a letter." Indeed it would in the same sense have been correct for another to have reported at the proper time, "He is mailing a letter." In the sense under discussion, a primitive person with no concept of a letter or of postal service, if suddenly placed in our society, could not perform the act of mailing a letter even though he could deposit an article which was a letter in a container which was a mailbox.

Also consider Diogenes sitting in his tub. There is a sense in which for this to be a human act, as distinct from the location and position of a body, Diogenes has to be about something and he has to know what he is about. He has to take it to be his tub, to be sitting in it intentionally, and to have self-knowledge of what he is doing. There is even a sense in which if he took himself to be sitting in his tub, even though there was no tub and he was only sitting in the corner, we might say that poor old Diogenes was sitting in his tub again.

It looks like ordinary behavioral acts have a subjective dimension which renders them quite similar to those considered clearly intentional and quite different from purely physical acts such as some acid's etching a metal plate or a bag of potatoes sitting in Diogenes' tub. It seems reasonable and fruitful to use the concept of intentionality to order these similarities and differences. In fact, we are working with an intuitive grasp of intentionality throughout this discussion that brings these cases together and makes it seem artificial to separate them. This is not to deny that there are differences, but only to affirm the importance of the similarities for achieving intelligibility.

What is this concept of intentionality we dimly grasp and are groping for? The heart of the matter seems fairly clear intuitively, but adequate formulation is difficult. We have already seen that of the criteria gleaned from the literature (1) and (2) are at best only sufficient conditions. Concerning (4), (5), and (6), behavioral acts, which seem to have an intentional dimension, appear to have determinate objects (as do some acts of reference) and to be both effectual and observable. We might be able to distinguish between the subjective (or intentional) and physical dimensions of such acts and attribute their determinate objects and effectuality and observability to the latter. But even so, (4), (5), and (6) would be left suspect or misleading as defining criteria.

What of (3), the nonsubstitutivity of extensional identity principle? Consider the following substitutions:

A   (1) John looked at Mary.
     (2) Mary is Mrs. Thompson.
     (3) John looked at Mrs. Thompson.

B   (1) John embraced Mary.
     (2) Mary is Mrs. Thompson.
     (3) John embraced Mrs. Thompson.

Most of us would, no doubt, on first thought allow the substitutions and hold that the inferences in A and B are valid. Yet, as we indicated earlier, sentences like A (1) [and B (1)] may be read in at least four ways, having the following truth-conditions.

(1) $(\exists x)$ $(x =$ Mary, and John looked at $x)$;
(2) $(\exists x)$ (John looked at x; John, in looking at x, took x to be Mary; and $x =$ Mary);
(3) $(\exists x)$ (John looked at x; and John, in looking at x, took x to be Mary [whether or not $x =$ Mary]); and
(4)   John had the experience of looking at Mary (whether or not Mary or anyone else was there).

Clearly the substitution holds and the inference goes through in A (and in a parallel way for B) only on the basis of the first reading of A (1) and the parallel reading for A (3).

Thus A and B can be reformulated:

A'   (1) Mary was looked at by John.
     (2) Mary is Mrs. Thompson.
     (3) Mrs. Thompson was looked at by John.

B' (1) Mary was embraced by John.
        (2) Mary is Mrs. Thompson.
        (3) Mrs. Thompson was embraced by John.

What this translation shows is that, if the inferences hold in A and B, (1) and (3) are not so much *report* statements of John's acts as descriptions of Mary or Mrs. Thompson. Therefore, the names "Mary" and "Mrs. Thompson" do not appear in intentional contexts and the substitutions hold.

But what about "John mentioned Mary." Consider this argument:

C (1) John mentioned Mary.
        (2) Mary is Mrs. Thompson.
        (3) John mentioned Mrs. Thompson.

Here, as indicated earlier, we are talking about an act of reference which requires the existence or some independent status of its object. The identifying reference locates the individual as she is in her independent status and semantically appropriates her in person, so to speak, not under some *limited* description or conceptualization. This would be true even if the reference had been achieved by using a descriptive phrase such as "the wife of Ed Thompson." So any expression which can be used to make an identifying reference to the same individual can be substituted for "Mary" in C (1) not only without altering the truth-value of the statement, but without changing what is fundamentally said. Therefore the inference in C is valid.

We must conclude then, either that mentioning and other acts of identifying reference are not intentional acts or that criterion (3), the inapplicability of the substitutivity of identity principle, is not a necessary condition for intentionality. We have already remarked that an act like John's mentioning Mary takes Mary as an object in a peculiar way, quite unlike lightning's striking Mary or anything of that kind. One way of putting this, although not very enlightening, is to say that Mary in her concrete individuality is the "internal" object of the act of reference. Mentioning Mary, or speaking of Mary, is, we said, much like thinking of Mary. In fact, it is to think of her out loud. The very act of mentioning her is one of thinking of her. It does not sound at all odd to say that when one is thinking of Mary, Mary is in his thought. And so why not say that when one uniquely refers to Mary that Mary is in his reference? The "in" here is a semantic "in," not an existential one. This is something of what we mean when we say that the object of the act is "internal" to the act. There is subjectivity involved. The object is somehow inexistentially taken up into the subject and must be taken account of in a description of the subject in terms of his states and acts. This is something of what we want to indicate when we speak of intentionality. The nonsubstitutivity of extensional identity, taken as a mark of an intentional object, would not help us identify an intentional object that had to be, by the very nature of the case, an existential object as well (or at least have some independent status). And this is just what we have found to be the case with the objects of identifying reference.

Thus, like all the others, the nonsubstitutivity of extensional identity principle, although a sufficient condition, cannot be taken as a necessary condition for identifying intentional acts. Simple acceptance of it would have led us to conclude that "looks at," "embraces," and the like are not intentional in structure, but this conclusion does not seem to be warranted. Certainly John's looking at Mary has its own "internal" structure with its intentional object which has a certain kind of independence of the actual state of affairs in the "external" world of public space and time in a way in which the sun's shining on Mary does not. And even acts of reference, which require the actual existence or some independent status for their objects, embrace them inexistentially within the subject. It is in terms of this problematic structure that the intentional idiom has its meaning. Perhaps the principle of nonsubstitutivity of extensional identity, like the principles of propositional objective complements, nonexistence, indeterminacy, ineffectuality, and unobservability, would be adequate for identifying what we may call pure intentional acts, those which involve no overt action and do not require the existence or independent status of their objects. But some acts that would be excluded by these criteria are too closely related in important categorial ways to the so-called pure intentional acts to be excluded. The distinctions between them are not basic categorial differences.

The criteria (2)-(6) were all designed to show that the objects of intentional acts are not as such existent objects, but they did not take into account the possibility that some intentional objects, by virtue of the nature of the acts of which they are the internal objects, have to be existent as well. This is not to reject what these criteria were pointing to, namely, that intentional objects are not as such existent objects, but somehow internal to the states and acts of which they are the object. The picture that emerges is that intentional objects are not to be thought of as peculiar entities to which people are related in mental acts, but rather ordinary things, properties, facts, and the like "taken up inexistentially" into mental states and acts, whether or not they exist or obtain in the world, and form part of the structure of the mental state or act. So what exists or obtains in the world are intentional states and acts, not intentional objects. To ask whether intentional objects exist would be like asking whether existential objects exist, for the adjective "intentional," like the adjective "existential," indicates a status of objects, not a kind of object. Of course it makes sense to ask whether objects which have an intentional status exist also. But this is quite a different matter.

As a first approximation, then, let us say that a state or an act is intentional if and only if a proper (philosophically clarified) report or description of it must be in terms of *a conceptual delineation of or reference to something else as part of the structure of the state or act in question.*

But this formulation of the concept of intentionality may be too broad, for according to it, if there are objective necessities and value requirements, for example, they would seem to be embraced under intentional states (or "acts"). Given that a necessity would be reported by some such locution as "X in being F necessitates that Y be G" and that a requirement would be reported thus, "X in being F normatively requires that Y be G," any proper report of either would seem to involve a conceptual delineation of something as part of the structure of what was being reported. For example, suppose that situation S in 1973 normatively requires that the president of the United States authorize the sale of one hundred fighter planes to Israel. This is not a situation that requires the 1972 Republican candidate for president to authorize the sale of one hundred fighter planes to Israel. Nor is it a situation that requires Richard Nixon to do so. It requires that a person who happens to be Richard Nixon authorize the sale. This is not unlike King George, in believing the author of *Waverley* was Scotch, believed that a certain person (who happened to be Sir Walter Scott) was Scotch but did not believe that Sir Walter Scott was Scotch. Any proper report of the value requirement mentioned above must say that the situation requires *the president of the United States* to authorize the sale. And it is fighter planes, not passenger planes or anything else, that the situation in question requires the president to authorize the sale of. In other words, what is required by the situation is required under a particular conceptual delineation or description and any proper report of the requirement has to appropriate that particular conceptual delineation. This seems to make the language (conceptual system) of the report responsible to what looks like an internal conceptual structure of what is being reported.

But what of the criteria of intentionality gleaned from recent literature? Do "necessitates" and "normatively requires" meet them also? They take substantival clauses or infinitive or participial phrases for their objective complements. "Acts" of necessitating and normatively requiring facts or states of affairs do not depend on or "presuppose" the existence of their objects. This is obviously the case with normative requirements, for otherwise whatever ought to be would be and there could be nothing bad or evil. It may seem that if X's being F necessitates that Y be G, then, given that X is F, Y's being G must obtain. But it need not obtain all the time it is necessitated, for it may be that X's being F at T_1 necessitates that Y be G at T_2. Here we are conceiving the objects of "acts" of necessitating and requiring as facts or states of affairs. If we should conceive the object of such an act as a particular rather than a fact, the picture would be more complex. A situation S may be said to necessitate or to normatively require that there be an x that would be F. Obviously this does not presuppose the existence of an individual who is required to be F. But we may also say that situation S necessitates or normatively requires that some x among existent particulars be F. In such cases, the existence of the individual is involved because of *what* is necessitated or required rather than the nature of "acts" of necessitating and normatively requiring as such. But this, as we shall see in a moment, may be sufficient to validate some inferences based on extensional identity.

Concerning the indeterminacy criterion, neither necessitated nor normatively required objects, whether facts or particulars, must be determinate except where *what* is necessitated or required involves an existent particular. Also necessities and normative requirements are not "observable" in the usual sense of sensory observation, which is what Hall seems to have had in mind. This leaves two criteria, namely, ineffectuality and nonsubstitutivity of extensional identity. It is not clear what we should say about whether "acts" of necessitating and normatively requiring affect in any way their objects. Clearly they do not change or alter them in any ordinary way, but the "act" of necessitating might be said to bring about or to bring "into existence" the fact necessitated, and indeed those who believe in teleological causality might say the same thing about some "acts" of normatively requiring a fact or state of affairs. But if this kind of effectuality should be granted, it would obviously be of a different order than that intended.

What about the nonsubstitutivity of extensional identity? We, in effect, discussed this earlier but not in just these terms. Consider the following argument:

D   (1) Situation S requires the president of the United States to do A.
_____(2) Richard Nixon is the president of the United States.
    (3) Situation S requires Richard Nixon to do A.

Is this argument more like E or F below?

E   (1) P believes that the president of the United States will do A.
_____(2) Richard Nixon is the president of the United States.
    (3) P believes that Richard Nixon will do A.

F   (1) The president of the United States weighs 180 lbs.
_____ (2) Richard Nixon is president of the United States.
      (3) Richard Nixon weighs 180 lbs.

My intuitions tell me that D is more like E than F. Yet many would accept the inference in D as valid but not in E. In other words, they would take D to be more like F than E. But there is a peculiarity about the inference in D that differentiates it from F. In D (1), the president of the United States as the president of the United States occurs essentially in the requirement reported, but in D (3) Richard Nixon as Richard Nixon is not so involved. Suppose the argument was this:

D'   (1) Situation S requires Richard Nixon to do A.
_____ (2) Richard Nixon is the president of the United States.
      (3) Situation S requires the president of the United States to do A.

Clearly D' (3) is not synonymous with D (1). We might read D' (3) this way: "Situation S requires one, who happens to be the president of the United States, to do A;" whereas D (1) might be read: "Situation S requires one *qua* the president of the United States to do A." A similar reading of E (3), namely "P believes that one, who happens to be Richard Nixon, will do A," would allow the inference to go through in E in exactly the same way as it does in D.

    Therefore, we may conclude that in a strict sense the substitutivity of identity does not hold in D. Although substitution allows the inference to go through, it significantly alters what is said about situation S. The *requirement* reported in D (1) is different from the one reported in D (3). Such an alteration in meaning is not occasioned by the substitution of identity in F. The ambiguities here constitute a further consideration against taking in a simple way the nonsubstitutivity of extensional identity as a defining mark of intentionality.

    Nevertheless, it seems that with the possible exceptions, and then only in a qualified way, of the ineffectuality and the nonsubstitutivity of identity criteria, the "act" of normatively requiring (and also the somewhat parallel "act" of necessitating) comes out as intentional under the criteria from the literature as well as under my formulation. And, therefore, my proposal is at no special disadvantage from this embarrassing development.

    Yet we cannot be satisfied with the result if we are to define subjective states and acts in terms of intentionality, for it would mean either that normative requirements and necessities are restricted to the subjective realm or that the subjective realm is far more extensive than its prima facie limits. We must either impose a further restriction on the concept of intentionality or distinguish different species of it.

Chisholm, in a later article and in a reply to criticism by Robert S. Sleigh, Jr.,[12] wrestles in a tortuous and inconclusive way with the blurring of the distinction between psychological and certain other nonextensional modal concepts by his earlier criteria of intentionality. He restricts his attention to the logical behavior of quantified statements containing nonextensional prefixes. Even if some pattern of implications among such statements could be found that would differentiate the psychological prefixes from the others, this would leave nonmodal psychological concepts unaccounted for. As our discussion has already indicated, these too seem to be intentional. In fact, Chisholm himself seems to be committed to the Brentano thesis that intentionality is the defining mark of the mental. This seems to be what drives him to look for criteria of intentionality which would exclude nonpsychological concepts. Therefore, even he must regard any set of criteria which does not embrace the whole realm of the psychological as inadequate.

But why must intentionality be restricted to the mental? There seems to be some merit in the wider concept as we have formulated it, for it brings together and points out certain common features of necessities, value requirements, and structures of meaning as distinct and different from the realm of physical states and events. I shall speak of semantic intentionality to differentiate the specific concept in terms of which I am trying to define subjective states and acts.

But what is semantic intentionality? How is it to be differentiated from intentionality in general? I don't see how we can do any better than to say that a state or act is semantically intentional if indeed it is semantic, if it embodies and is at least partially constituted by a semantic relation to something; that is, if something (a thing, a fact, a state of affairs, a requirement, or what have you) is semantically present in some mode in it. Modifying our original formulation, we may say, then, that an act (or state) is semantically intentional if and only if a proper report or description of it must be in terms of a semantic act, an act of reference or conceptual delineation in some mode, and its object as inexistentially present in the structure of the act itself: in the case of reference, the object's being inexistentially present in person so to speak; in the case of conceptual delineation, the object's being inexistentially present just as conceptually delineated and in no other way.*

*It should be noted that the same expression may in one sentence be used to refer and in another only to delineate conceptually. For example, suppose A should say "The president is in California" and B should say "A said that the president is in California." "The president" is used as a referring expression in the first and as a conceptually delineating expression in the second.

But what is it for one thing or state of affairs to be semantically present by reference or conceptual delineation in the structure of something else? Here we seem to be up against basic categorial concepts that cannot be explicated in terms of any other area of discourse. Brentano, who revived the thesis of intentionality (and he was concerned with what I am calling "semantic intentionality"), maintained that intentional idioms are irreducible. And I think he was right. But perhaps we can show something about the semantic factor here that is absent in other kinds of intentionality.

Reconsider the value requirement case: Situation S requires that the president of the United States do A. We can say, and did above, that the situation requires whoever comes under that conceptual delineation to do A and that therefore any report of the requirement must contain that conceptual delineation as part of the structure of the requirement being reported. There is another way, perhaps more perspicuous, to say the same thing, namely, "Situation S requires that one *qua* the president of the United States do A." What this indicates, I think, is that normative requiring (or necessitating) involves a thing or state of affairs as subject to a certain conceptual delineation and which must be so conceptually delineated in a proper report of the requirement, but that the requirement itself does not embody either a reference to or an actual conceptual delineation of that of which such a delineation would be true. But in the case of semantic intentionality, the act in question is semantic and actually locates and holds its object through an act of reference or conceptualization. In other words, the object of the act is not, as in the case of an "act" of requiring or necessitating, what a given description is or would be true of, but what is "present" in the act through reference or a given conceptual delineation.

Perhaps the best mark of semantic intentionality is its expressibility. Whatever state or act that has semantic intentionality may be meaningfully spoken of either as an expression or as subject to being expressed. In linguistic expression, what is semantically present in the state or act is put into words. This is not a matter of describing the act or state; it is a translation of it. The state or act and the sentence that expresses it may be said to be "synonymous." "Acts" of requiring or necessitating do not stand in this relationship to language. They may be reported but they cannot be expressed. They cannot be said to be synonymous with any sentence.

Furthermore acts or states with semantic intentionality may stand in logical relationships with one another. They may imply or presuppose one another, be logically consistent or inconsistent, etc. What about objective necessities and normative requirements? Could they be logically inconsistent? It does seem that two requirements, for example, could be such that it would be logically impossible for both to be fulfilled. But the issue is whether two such *requirements* could obtain in the world, not whether the facts required could obtain. Suppose situation S requires that A be F and situation S' requires that A not be F. The question is whether situation S and S' requires both that A be F and that A not be F. If this were possible, then inconsistencies among our desires, feelings, attitudes, and value judgments would not be a basis for rejecting any of them as invalid, unfounded, or irrational. The situation is parallel with that of factual beliefs. If inconsistent facts could obtain in the world, inconsistency among our beliefs would be no indication of error on our part and we would be robbed of the basis of corrigibility. So logical concepts like consistency and inconsistency seem to apply only to that which embodies a semantic dimension.

With this refinement of the concept of intentionality, our original characterization of a subjective state or act must be modified accordingly. We may now say that a subjective state or act is one that is at least partially constituted by semantic intentionality, or, what amounts to the same thing, a structure of meaning. This helps illuminate our ordinary talk about the "inner world," which is an often misunderstood metaphor. The "inner realm" is not existential but semantic; its contents are not peculiar entities that exist in a special, private space, but ordinary things, properties, facts, value requirements, and the like semantically present in some mode in the states and acts in question.

The sensuous element in experience may be considered a serious challenge to this view of subjectivity. It has long been regarded as an area in which the distinction between the semantic and the existent collapses. This was the fundamental idea back of the subjectivistic phenomenalism of the British empiricist tradition. Berkeley came down on the side of the semantic in his famous dictum "esse est percipi." Hume favored the existent with his view of sense impressions as original existences with no representative quality about them. Even today friends of the semantic theory of the mental often resist an intentionalistic interpretation of sensation. Both Chisholm[13] and Sellars,[14] for example, develop an intentionalistic theory of thought and sensory perception, but feel compelled to regard sensations as subjective phenomenal states and occurrences, somewhat like what Herbert Feigl calls "raw feels,"[15] that defy an intentionalistic analysis. Chisholm regards sensing as an objectless occurrence. "Sensing blue with respect to X," for example, is analyzed adverbially and causally. Blue is said to be one of the ways in which sensing becomes determinate in somewhat the way in which it is also one of the ways in which being colored becomes determinate. And the phrase "with respect to X" is given a purely causal analysis. This leaves sensing, although phenomenal in that it is open to reflexive awareness, a candidate for identification with neurophysiological processes. Cornman develops Chisholm's position in this direction.[16] Sellars says that a sensation of a red triangle, for example, is "a non-conceptual episode which *somehow* has the perceptible qualities which the corresponding conceptual episode [perception], i.e. the propositional attitude takes to be exemplified in the world of perceptible things."[17] He tries to avoid dualism by identifying phenomenal states and occurrences, insofar as their inherent properties are concerned, with neurophysiological states and events; not in the simple straightforward way of some others,[18] but as neurophysiological states and occurrences may be ultimately conceptualized in scientific theory. Sensations, he maintains, are neurophysiological states and occurrences, in the sense indicated, conceived by analogy with their external causes.

Romane Clark[19] charges that this view of sensations in no way explains the role they play, according to Sellars's own theory, in sensory perception. Taking Sellars's theory that a sensory perception is like a sentence, Clark argues that sensations are to sensory perceptions as predicates are to sentences; that is, they, in sensory perceptions, ascribe "sensuous qualities to the objects of perception." Therefore, he concludes, contrary to Sellars, that sensations as well as perceptions are semantic in character. Nevertheless Clark seems to hold on to the view that sensations in their own existence are phenomenalistic and private. He says that they, like words, are "items which can occur in isolation, which can be savored for their own characters, and which can be reflected upon in abstraction from their occurrences in the contexts of perceptual judgments." Furthermore, he says that "the ascription of any perception to an agent entails that there exists a sense impression the agent experiences."

In taking sensations to be private phenomenalistic existents with a semantic function, Clark is right back with the Cartesian-Lockean representative theory of perception, except for the fact that he has a more sophisticated view of how the phenomenalistic states or occurrences relate semantically to external objects and their properties. In contrast with their physicalistic copy model, Clark thinks of sensations in their semantic "role" by analogy with predicates in sentences. He takes them to be natural semantic "tools," so to speak, in the way in which hands might be regarded as natural "tools" for physical action. But there is this difficulty with his model. One has to be *aware* of his sensations, not only "to use" them semantically in perceptions, but even for them to exist. "Unfelt or unsensed sensations" still sounds like a contradiction and I gather that Clark would agree. So what is the nature of this awareness? We speak of it as having an object, namely, the sensation. Does this mean that it is semantic and that the sensation is semantically present? Do we, with Berkeley, collapse the *existence* of the sensation into its semantic presence? Or, with Hume, collapse its *semantic presence* into its existence? If we are aware of sensations and they in turn semantically present physical properties of things in somewhat the way in which words on a page may be perceived and they semantically present objects and their features to us, then there is no direct semantic presence to one of anything external. The picture Clark seems to have in mind is that of an "ego" shut up within us reading but believing selectively a phenomenalistic ticker tape which is printed by physiological occurrences caused by external impacts. This does not seem to be much of an improvement on Descartes's and Locke's model of an "ego" monitoring and believing selectively a phenomenalistic television screen operated by physical impacts on the body.

The model might be made more sophisticated by having the "ego" caught up in and partially constituted by the semantic functioning of sensations in perceptions. Here we might think of the neurophysiological states and occurrences caused by physical impacts on the body as analogous to ink marks; the "correlated" phenomenalistic states and occurrences as analogous to words, phrases, and sentences; and perceptions analogous to sentences used to make assertions. The fundamental point here is that phenomenalistic states and occurrences are to their physiological counter-parts as words, phrases, and sentences are to ink marks and noises and that perceptions are to phenomenalistic states and occurrences as statements (or illocutionary acts in general) are to the sentences uttered or written in making them. Thus descriptions of phenomenalistic states and occurrences would not be like descriptions of ink marks, noises, and the like in physicalistic concepts, but like descriptions of words and sentences in linguistic concepts.

Such a view might make philosophical efforts at identifying phenomenalistic states and occurrences with neurophysiological states and processes somewhat easier and the results more believable, for many philosophers, contrary to my own convictions, find it acceptable to reduce words and sentences to ink marks and noises for ontological purposes.

Even though this is perhaps a more plausible model, there are difficulties with it. There is no reason to think that we are aware of the neurophysiological states and processes involved in sensation and sensory perception in any way analogous with our awareness of ink marks or noises in our own writing or speaking, which is perhaps the only appropriate analogy. The model would seem to require that being aware of sensations and perceptions would be like being aware of the words and sentences one was uttering without being aware at all of the noises one was making.

Another problematic point with this way of interpreting the phenomenal aspect of sensation and perception is the fact that we use to a large extent the same words to describe subjective, private phenomenal states and occurrences as we do to describe the objects of perception. This is what seems to be back of Sellars's claim that sensations are neurophysiological states and occurrences *conceived by analogy with their external causes.* Clark might explain this by saying that the use of the same words in describing phenomenal states and physical objects (e.g., "The pen is *blue*" and "I have a *blue* sensation") is grounded in a confusion similar to that of failing to distinguish between words and what they are of or about. But once this distinction is made on Clark's model, do we have any words for phenomenal characteristics of sensations? In other words, does not the alleged phenomenalistic description of sensations collapse into descriptions of the objects of sensations? This would suggest that the phenomenalistic theory of sensations is based on mistaking what is semantically present in sensation as existentially present. What is existentially present in sensation might be a neurophysiological process which is in no way semantically present and such linguistic-like properties which a structure of meaning could exemplify and might be discerned in reflective analysis. But the usual so-called phenomenal or sensuous aspect of perception, i.e., sensation, would be the direct (unmediated by semantic tools) semantic presence of physical properties.

I suggest that this is indeed the most plausible view. In sensory perception, accordingly, physical objects and their properties are not only semantically present but are taken to be existentially present in the world. But much of what is semantically present in perception is not directly semantically present but present as signaled or meant by properties which are directly present semantically. What has been called "sensation" is the direct semantic presence of physical properties without any claim that they are existentially present in the world. What is existent about a sensation is at one level a neurophysiological process which is not open to reflective analysis and at another level a structure of meaning whose intentional object is a physical property. The structure of meaning itself exemplifies linguistic-like and logical properties which are open to reflective analysis. But there is no inner private realm of phenomenal existents with purely factual structures.

Sensation-talk of the kind we have been discussing is restricted for the most part to philosophical discourse. In ordinary language, sensations are somatic perceptions, perceptions of our bodily states and processes by a kind of "internal" sense. Itches, tickles, aches, pains, throbbings, and other internal sensings are constituted, I suggest, by the semantic presence to one of states and processes in regions of his body or of his body as a whole and usually, but not always, their being taken to obtain existentially in the body. Any effort to reflect upon the sensation focuses upon its object. It is this which tempts us to describe the sensation as its object. But if my analysis is correct, neither the sensations philosophers talk about in connection with external perception nor bodily sensations involve phenomenal existents with a purely factual structure. The "inner" phenomenal world open to reflexive awareness and reflective analysis is purely semantic in structure, exemplifying only grammatical and logical properties. All else present in it is only semantically present. The purely factually structured existents involved are bodily in nature and they make their appearance in consciousness only through somatic sensation, external perception, or thought. They are not open to reflexive awareness or "introspection" directly.

We may conclude, then, that the sensuous element in experience is not an exception to our semantic theory of subjectivity. The so-called "inner realm," except for existent structures of meaning with their exemplified grammatical and logical properties, is semantically rather than existentially populated.

3. Physicalistic reduction of psychological language

We have now, I think, shown that we cannot reduce the language of meaning to psychological language and thereby establish that the language of meaning is without special ontological significance, for, if our argument is sound, psychological language is the primary language of meaning. But it might still be maintained that the language of meaning, including psychological language, can be reduced or explained in such a way as to show that it has no ontological significance over and above physicalistic or purely factual language. Indeed it might be argued that we have furthered the cause of physicalism ourselves by eliminating sensations or raw feels as purely factually structured subjective states or occurrences, for these have been taken by many to constitute the most difficult problem for physicalism.

The language of semantic intentionality, like value language, is philosophically problematic for the modern mind because from within our naturalistic assumptions about the epistemic powers of the mind it is not clear how we can have knowledge of structures of meaning or fund the language of meaning with meaning. Hempel states the case boldly in these terms: "There is taken to be an absolutely impassable gulf between the natural sciences which have a subject-matter devoid of sense and the sciences of mind and culture, which have an intrinsically meaningful subject-matter, the appropriate methodological instrument for the . . . study of which is 'insight into meaning.' "[20] Rejecting the view that we have the power of "insight into meaning," and thus the notion of an intrinsically meaningful subject-matter as unintelligible, Hempel says: "We find in Behaviorism . . . an attempt to construct a scientific psychology which would show by its success that even in psychology we have to do with purely physical processes, and that therefore there can be no impassable barrier between physics and psychology."[21] Here Hempel is looking to success in behavioristic psychology to show that the language of semantic intentionality can be dispensed with in the study of behavior in much the same way that many cite the success of Darwinian biology as proof that value language has no descriptive-explanatory use in the study of organic structures and processes. But he was not content to leave the matter there. He, along with Carnap[22] and Morris[23] and others, attempted to show by philosophical analysis that the language of semantic intentionality is translatable without loss in sayable content into a physicalistic language. This thesis, sometimes known as logical behaviorism, states, according to Carnap, "that a definition may be constructed for every psychological concept (i.e. expression) which directly or indirectly derives that concept from physical concepts."[24] So, it is claimed: "All sentences of psychology describe physical occurrences, namely the physical behavior of humans and other animals."[25]

What is operating here is the claim that all language must be grounded through sensory observation and that all truth-claims can be confirmed or falsified only by such observations. So the philosopher, in trying to explicate the meaning of psychological sentences, must look for their truth-conditions in terms of what is available through sensory observations. It follows of course that the truth-conditions can be only physicalistic, purely factual conditions, for under the governance of these assumptions, he could not possibly find anything else.

But it is now almost universally recognized, even by some of the earlier proponents of the theory, that this kind of simple physicalistic reductionism will not do, for it does not account for the obvious features of the language of semantic intentionality. Without attempting to review all the difficulties that have been recognized, let it suffice for us to mention a few basic problems with the position.

First-person psychological statements (e.g., "I want to go now," "I see him," etc.) present a special problem for the theory. No one learns how to apply psychological terms to himself on the basis of sensory observation of his bodily states and movements. No one makes or confirms psychological statements about himself on the basis of such observations of himself. Even if one is in a certain physical state or condition whenever he says truly "I want to go now," his statement does not report that physical state or condition. Some would argue that what one has self-knowledge of as *his wanting to go now* may in fact be contingently or theoretically identical with some complex of physical states and events; but even if this were true, it would not help us in explicating the statement "I want to go now." This seems to present a serious difficulty for reductionistic physicalism.

And if the theory is inadequate for first-person psychological statements, it would seem to be inadequate for second- and third-person ones as well, for the logic of the two types of statement are interlocked. "I want to go now" said by me at a given time and place is true if and only if "Maynard wants to go now" said by another at the same time and place is true. So it would seem that if a physicalistic reduction would fail to capture the meaning of the first it would also fail for the second.

Furthermore, there are independent reasons for suspicion of physicalistic translations of second- and third-person psychological statements. We don't simply observe others like we do things. We are in an intercommunicating, interacting, intersubjective relationship with them. We have a sense of their 'inwardness," their subjectivity, their perspective. We relate to them with sympathy, which is to be aware of and in a sense to share their subjectivity. We are aware of ourselves as in their presence, as being caught up in their subjectivity. We don't simply discern their behavior through sensory observation as we do things. To listen to someone talk is not like listening to the noises of an engine. We "read" the behavior of others, whether verbal or nonverbal. This is to grasp its "inwardness," its semantic intentionality. We could no more learn to apply psychological concepts to others on the basis of pure sensory observation than we could to ourselves. Nor could we verify or falsify psychological statements about others on this basis. Suppose we were concerned with the statement, "Jones wants to go now," in a given situation. We could accept any complex description of the physical states, movements, and changes pertaining to Jones and his environment and still have logical space to ask meaningfully "But does Jones *want to go now?*"

Something important is lost, namely, semantic intentionality, in physicalistic translation of psychological discourse. Also something is added, physical facts not caught up in psychological discourse as such. What we have at best is a "shotgun" translation forced by the naturalistic dogma, which even present-day naturalists do not seem to have a stomach for.

4. Quine's rejection of the intentionalistic idiom

Quine, who is thoroughly committed to naturalism, admits that the language of semantic intentionality, which he conceives more narrowly as restricted to propositional attitudes, is irreducible. "One may accept," he says, "the Brentano thesis [of the irreducibility of intentional idioms] either as showing the indispensability of intentional idioms and the importance of an autonomous science of intention, or as showing the baselessness of intentional idioms and the emptiness of a science of intention. My attitude," he says, "unlike Brentano's is the second."[26] The reason for his choice is clearly given: "In the strictest scientific spirit we can report all the behavior, verbal and otherwise, that may underlie our imputations of propositional attitudes, and we may go on to speculate as we please upon the causes and effects of this behavior; but, *so long as we do not switch muses* [italics added], the essentially dramatic idiom of propositional attitudes will find no place."[27] Committed to the view that science is the only muse worthy of consideration, Quine concludes: "If we are limning the true and ultimate structure of reality, the canonical [philosophically clarified] scheme for us is the austere scheme that knows no quotation but direct quotation and no propositional attitudes but only the physical constitution and behavior of organisms."[28]

Quine feels that there is no particular problem in explicating a psychological statement in physicalistic terms so long as it concerns a relationship between the bodily states and behavior of an organism and some physical thing, state, or occurrence in the environment. It is only relationships involving intentional objects that trouble him. With language pruned of indirect quotations and the whole idiom of propositional attitudes, he proceeds with great ingenuity to develop a highly complex naturalistic philosophy of language. In spite of his brilliance in constructing epicicle upon epicicle to save his basic theory in face of difficulties, he accepts in the end the indeterminancy of translation, the indefinability of "synonym" and "analyticity," the murkiness of meaning, and the inscrutability of reference, as well as "a sense of genuine loss"[29] at jettisoning the intentional idiom. These appear to be heavy burdens for a theory to have to bear.

It should be noted that Quine restricts what we are calling "semantic intentionality" to propositional attitudes, to what is reported by mental verbs that take indirect quotations or propositional clauses as their grammatical objects. The criteria he uses are nonsubstitutivity of extensional identity and the lack of an implication of existence. What bothers him, as previously remarked, is the inexistential or nonextensional object. We concluded earlier that objects with an inexistential status, even though they may also exist, are involved more widely than Quine recognizes; indeed that this is true of extensions as well as of intensions. This means, if true, that reference as well as meaning (in the narrower sense) and that all psychological states and acts, not just propositional attitudes, have semantically intentional objects. So it is with respect to the whole psychological and linguistic idiom that, if we insist on specifying its meaning in terms of purely physical states and occurrences, we have "a sense of genuine loss." And the burden that Quine's theory must bear becomes heavier. But he cannot give ground or relent, for to do so would violate his ideal of intellectual respectability, which he exhibits so clearly in the statement: "Sometime, whether in terms of protein or colloids or nerve nets or overt behavior, the relevant branch of science may reach the stage where a similarity notion can be constructed capable of making even the notion of intelligence respectable. And superfluous."[30]

5. Explaining away the apparent ontological import of semantic intentionalistic language

Rather than probing deeper into the problems Quine encounters by discarding the intentional idiom, I shall focus on a theory which acknowledges and professes to do justice by semantic intentionality from within a general naturalistic perspective. Wilfrid Sellars has attempted the ambitious task of trying to fuse into one stereoscopic vision our commonsense view of things, what he calls our "manifest image of man-in-the-world," and the scientific account,[31] which he says are "two pictures of essentially the same order of complexity, each of which purports to be a complete picture of man-in-the-world,"[32] "two whole ways of seeing the sum of things,"[33] both "equally public, equally non-arbitrary."[34] He recognizes that "man is what he is because he thinks of himself in terms of this [manifest] image"[35] and that "[t]o the extent that the manifest [image] does not survive in the synoptic view, to that extent man himself would not survive."[36] Yet he maintains that the scientific view gets at reality the way it is.

It is clear that the domain of semantic intentionality, which Sellars recognizes as embracing perceptions, thoughts, intentions, actions and even persons and social institutions, falls within the manifest image. And so all these things must have a place in the stereoscopic view, but not as part of reality, not as part of the metaphysical account of the world. The problem is how to make this out.

Several assaults have been made on this problem. One that has received considerable attention in the past decade or so is the contingent identity theory referred to in our earlier discussion of sensations.[37] It maintains that what we talk about in our commonsense personal language as experiences, thoughts, intentions, actions, and the like are in fact identical with what science talks about in its more refined, sophisticated language in the same way as what we talk about in our commonsense language as water, salt, silver, and the like are identical with what science talks about in the theoretical language of physics and chemistry. The claim is that the identity is a scientific discovery, not a philosophical one, but that philosophically we must give priority to the scientific descriptions of this sector of reality over our ordinary commonsense ways of talking about it. The philosophical debate has centered on whether the alleged contingent identity is a possibility.[38] Much of the discussion assumes that our personal and mentalistic discourse is straightforwardly factual and descriptive but grounded in introspection and that in using it we refer to particulars, states, and occurrences and describe them. It is these that are said to be identical with what science talks about in physicalistic language grounded in sensory observation.

In this simplistic form, the identity theory does not take account of the peculiar characteristic of mental talk—its semantic intentionality. It treats the subjective domain as a realm of "inner" states and occurrences with purely factual structures. We have already attempted to expose the error of this way of thinking. Dennett,[39] accepting the view that there are no mental states and episodes of this kind, for mentalistic language, he maintains, contains no referring expressions (a wrong reason, in my judgment), argues against the identity thesis on the grounds that mentalistic talk locates nothing to be identified with what is referred to and described in scientific discourse. So he classifies the identity theory along with dualism as an attempt to solve a pseudo problem.

Nevertheless Dennett takes the thesis of intentionality seriously. He holds that intentional language cannot be reduced to the nonintentional and that we cannot get along without it. And yet an intentional psychology, he says, "would entail a catastrophic rearrangement of science in general,"[40] something that is unthinkable for him. So he proposes an *ascriptive* theory of intentionality. His model here is value talk in biology. We talk about the reason for different structures in an organism in terms of their function; that is, according to Dennett, we *ascribe* functions and reasons to the structure of the organism as a heuristic device. But this is not *description*. This kind of talk, he maintains, does not report scientific findings nor provide scientific explanations. In like manner, he talks about *ascribing* content or semantic intentionality, but "[t]he content one ascribes to an event, state or structure is not . . . an extra feature which, along with its other, extensionally characterized features, allows one to make predictions. Rather," he continues, "the relation between Intentional descriptions of events, states or structures . . . and extentional descriptions of them is one of *further interpretation*."[41] But not an interpretation that enlightens us about the reality involved. "If we relegate vitalist and interactionist hypotheses to the limbo of last, desperate resorts, and proceed on the assumption that human and animal behavioral control systems are only very complicated denizens of the physical Universe," he argues, "it follows that the events within them, characterized extensionally in terms of physics or physiology, should be susceptible to explanation and prediction without any recourse to content, meaning, or Intentionality."[42] But the scientific story, he admits, would be mute about actions, intentions, beliefs, desires, for these can be told only in the intentional idiom. Nevertheless the intentionalistic story about them is not "about features of the world *in addition to* the features of the extensional story."[43] "[E]ndowing events with content," he says, "is like giving an interpretation to a formal mathematical calculus or axiom system, a move which does not affect its functions or implications but may improve intuitive understanding of the system."[44]

Just as biologists look to evolution for the generation of structures which lend themselves to the ascription of functions, reasons, and the like, Dennett looks to evolution for the generation of patterns of afferent and efferent nerve impulses that lend themselves to being interpreted in terms of the language of semantic intentionality. But there is one important difference. The ordinary man and the biologist have the language of purposes, functions, reasons, and the like from the area of human action and production of artifacts to ascribe to biological structures and processes. But there seems to be no comparable area for the independent generation of the language of semantic intentionality. Language is the only possible candidate, but, as I have tried to show, it does not have the same independence of the psychological that the production and structure of artifacts have of the structures and processes of biological organisms. Besides, Dennett regards the language of semantic intentionality as only *ascribable* to speech and language themselves. The language of semantic intentionality seems indigenous to the psychological realm. The problem is whether it is possible for us to generate as part of a natural language a categorially distinctive sector that has only an ascriptive function. We can ascribe the language of *A* to *B* and thereby interpret *B* as *A*. But can we ascribe a language which has no native area to anything? How can it be taught and learned? What makes it a language at all? More of a story has to be told than we get from Dennett.

Sellars provides us with one of the most complex stories that has been told in his effort to maintain a version of physicalism and yet preserve the manifest image in his steroscopic view. He defends a complicated version of the identity thesis and gives what amounts to an analysis of the language of semantic intentionality in terms of value language.

Conceptual thought is at the heart of our problem. Sellars would agree, I think, that if the identity thesis along with a convincing account of the semantic intentionality involved cannot be maintained here then it cannot be defended anywhere. The argument that thoughts cannot be physiological processes because we have direct introspective knowledge *that* we are thinking and *what* we are thinking without knowing anything about nerves, Sellars says, "presupposes . . . that knowledge must present what is known in *propria persona*. Once this principle is abandoned," he contends, "there is no absurdity in the idea that what we know *directly* as *thoughts* in terms of *analogical* concepts may in *propria persona* be neurophysiological states."[45] He contends that the concept of a thought is a concept by analogy with speech. And he considers as of decisive importance "the analogy between speech and what sophisticated computers can do, and finally, between computer circuits and conceivable patterns of neuro-physiological organization."[46] "Thus our concept of 'what thoughts are' might, like our concept of what a castling is in chess, be abstract in the sense that it does not concern itself with the intrinsic character of thoughts, *save as items which can occur in patterns of relationships which are analogous to the way in which sentences are related to one another* and to the contexts in which they are used."[47] "Now if thoughts are items which are conceived in terms of the roles they play," he concludes, "then there is no barrier *in principle* to the identification of conceptual thinking with neurophysiological process. There would be no 'qualitative' remainder to be accounted for."[48] "I submit," he says, "that as belonging to the real order . . . [the intellect] is the central nervous system."[49]

Much of what Sellars says on this matter is, I think, defensible and even right. We might say, as we remarked earlier, that speech is thinking out loud or in public; or that thought is silent or private speech. Speech involves cerebral, muscular, and oral activity that disturbs the air in certain fixed ways, whereas silent thought does not disturb the environment in noticeable ways and may involve only cerebral bodily activity. One might say that there is this difference: we cannot perceive or even have self-knowledge of speech without being aware to some extent of the physical processes involved, but we do have self-knowledge of our own thoughts without knowing anything about cerebral activity. But I am not sure that this is entirely so. Self-knowlege of our own thoughts, at least on some occasions, involves knowing that something is going on in our heads. G. E. Moore once said that it felt to him that his thinking took place about two inches beneath the surface of the center of his forehead. Perhaps this is why Descartes thought the mind was located in the pineal gland. In any case, we have good scientific evidence that cerebral processes are involved in both thought and speech. If the identity thesis can be made out for speech, it should also be acceptable for thought.

Sellars's identity thesis about thought and speech turns upon the assumption that the description of them that gets at their intrinsic character would be in terms of their physical qualities alone. He explains the remainder in terms of the roles the physical events play. He speaks of a thought as analogous with a castling in chess. Our concept of a castling does not include the physical properties of the castle involved except as the physical item used in the castling. Apparently he would say that the castling was identical with the physical pieces' change in location on the board and that the description of this would leave no qualitative aspect of the castling unaccounted for.

This seems very odd. To describe one's speech in terms of the physical qualities of the noise one makes or to describe one's essay in terms of the physical qualities of the paper and the ink marks would seem to change the subject rather than to describe the alleged subject in terms of its intrinsic qualities. Description of the speech or essay as such would involve at one level linguistic terms like "sentences," "nouns," "verbs," "subjects," and "predicates"; at another level, words like "clear," "confused," "coherent," "incoherent," "intelligible," "unintelligible," "consistent," and "inconsistent"; and at still another level, expressions such as "about X, Y, Z," "descriptive," "critical," "evaluative," "true," "false," "fiction," "history," "science," "philosophy," etc.

Sellars would say that to conceive of the speech or essay in such a way that these descriptions would be appropriate would be to conceive the noises or the ink marks in terms of the roles they play rather than in terms of their intrinsic qualities. But, as just remarked, this changes the subject. His epistemological commitments prohibit him from acknowledging that the speech and the essay are entities in their own right in which noises and ink marks have roles.

On his basis, I find the concept of role highly problematic. He speaks of the analogy with the sophisticated computer as decisive. No one would deny that the computer is a physical system and that in a sense its operations or products may be spoken of as having semantic and logical roles. Yet I submit that this makes sense only insofar as the computer is thought of as an instrument in a wider system that includes designers, programmers, and the like. In short, it has to be placed in a context of thought in order for *role* talk to make sense.

Even function talk about a purely physical system is philosophically problematic, for it is, as we observed in chapter 5, a form of value discourse. The function of a thing is what it is for, what it ought to do, the requirement which it exists to fulfill. Such talk about a physical system conceived in terms of the categories of modern science is either metaphorical or involves thinking of the physical system as an artifact that places it in a wider context involving thoughts and actions.

But the concept of role is much more difficult for a strict empirical science than that of function, for a role, in the literal sense, is an *assumed* or *accepted* function. In a somewhat extended sense, something may be said to have a role by virtue of its having been given or taken to have a certain function and its being used accordingly. In either case, having a role involves having a function within a system of activity and its fulfilling activity being guided by knowledge of its function. Thus roles presuppose thoughts in such a way that we cannot reduce thoughts to physical states or events and their roles.

Furthermore, we can say only that some physical states and events, e.g., noises and ink marks, have roles in public thought, i.e., speech and writing, but brain states and events, indeed most neurophysiological processes, have only functions, not roles, in thought. Certainly our brain processes are not used in thought according to our knowledge of their function. Indeed, they are not used at all, but they do function in thinking. Their function, however, cannot be understood except in terms of thinking activity. Therefore, we cannot reduce thought to brain processes and their function, for this would be no reduction at all. It would be simply to say that thought is brain process and the fulfillment of its function in *thought*.

Sellars would, I think, acknowledge something of what I am saying but insist on putting it in his own terms. His account would go something like this. Physical structures, whether covert as in thought or overt as in speech and writing, have functions and roles in representation by virtue of certain of their intrinsic features. Functions, he would say, are constituted by "criticizing" rules, "ought-to-be's," and roles by "doing" rules, "ought-to-do's."[50] Thus things with roles would be rule-governed, but things with merely functions would not be.

Jay Rosenberg, who shares Sellars's basic orientation, puts the matter succinctly in these terms: "To say of a particular sentence that it is a particular claim—e.g., the claim that Albany is west of Boston . . . is to characterize what is, ontologically, an inscription—an array of atoms, if you will—as belonging to a pure normative kind. That kind is wholly constituted by a set of rules. . . ."[51] "In both the case of overt speech and the case of thoughts," he continues, "the linguistic behavior consists in *the production of some item in the natural order*, a natural linguistic object,"[52] which would have a representing role or function. Thus Sellars and Rosenberg are left with both representation- and value-talk for philosophical clarification.

In an overly simplified form, but one that presents the salient features that need discussion here, their account of representation goes something like this. There exists in the physical world two sets of structures, natural linguistic objects (neurophysiological patterns, sounds, ink marks, etc.) and the extralinguistic items of the world. The linguistic objects have been developed through a long evolutionary process (including the cultural domain) so that they have physical features which give them in some sense an isomorphic structure with the extra-linguistic world. But this in itself does not constitute representation. A normative structure is needed, a set of rules for projection of the natural linguistic structures on to the extralinguistic world and for intralinguistic transformations.

So allegedly the language of meaning is reduced to physicalistic and value language. Ontologically speaking, then, there are no structures of meaning. But are there physical *and* normative structures?

Sellars proposes a purely naturalistic theory of value language. The bare essentials of his position is that valuings and intentions, like thoughts, are neurophysiological processes conceived by analogy with certain speech-acts; the former with "would that . . ."s and the latter with "I shall . . ."s. Rules, both the "criticizing" and "doing" varieties, are, according to him, constituted by or derived from shared valuings and intentions of a community.

Apart from the difficulties with naturalistic theories of value language, which we essayed in chapter 4, Sellars's position seems to suffer from incoherence. On his account, valuings and intentions, as well as thoughts and speech-acts of all kinds, presuppose and indeed are partially constituted by a normative structure consisting of rules and yet rules are derivative from valuings and intentions. Here the snake is swallowing itself. It seems that both a naturalistic theory of meaning and a naturalistic theory of value are not possible.

6. A realistic theory of rational appraisal language

But even if we accept the value realism I argued for in chapter 5, I see no alternative but to acknowledge that "X means F" indicates a basic categorial feature of the world parallel with that indicated by "X is F" and "X ought to be F," for we cannot explain the *functions* and *roles* of neurophysiological processes, noises, and ink marks in thought and discourse solely in terms of value structures. These physical structures have their functions and roles in *semantic activity*, which is the psychological, just as the roles of the physical objects in chess are in terms of game behavior. Without game play there would be no roles for the physical pieces. In like manner, without the meaning dimension there would be no roles for the noises in speech nor functions of the neurophysiological events in thought. The semantic dimension is no more reducible than the value dimension to the existential and the factual, but certain elements of the existential order have their functions and their roles in terms of semantic or mental activity. These functions and roles, value structures, seem to be unintelligible apart from meaning as a coordinate dimension of being along with existence and value.

But even this is an oversimplification. It still identifies the existent with the purely factual or physical, which is too restrictive for what has already been acknowledged. Thoughts, not just physical processes, occur, and they not only have objects (individuals, properties, facts, value requirements, other thoughts, etc.) semantically present in them, but they exemplify properties of their own. For example, as mentioned earlier, they may have any of a variety of syntactical structures, be clear or confused, be consistent or inconsistent, and the like. And although they share these features with speech, there is nothing to indicate that these concepts are applied to silent and unexpressed thoughts only by analogy with speech. Even if speech were the natural habitat of such concepts, they would still be unintelligible in terms of physical processes and the "roles" they could have in a purely factual system, for in such a system there could be no roles at all. Speech itself, as we have said repeatedly, can be understood only as a form of thought. The categories of speech are the categories of thought.

There is no reason to think that thoughts are not present to us in *propria persona* in self-knowledge, for they appear to us in the same form when we encounter public thoughts. It is true of course that we are only dimly aware, if at all, of the neurophysiological structures involved. But these are not the "person" of thoughts, but their bodies.

Rational appraisal language, then, is stubborn. It refuses to yield to naturalistic reduction and its ontological import defies being explained away. We seem compelled to admit that, ontologically speaking, there are semantic and logical as well as purely factual and value dimensions of the world.

VIII

Resolution of the Antinomy
of the Mental

We have seen some of the difficulties with naturalistic "solutions" to the antinomy of the mental. Indeed we have concluded, for what seem to be compelling reasons, that no naturalistic solution is possible and that we must admit that there are unique, irreducible structures of meaning with inherent logical features. This means, if our conclusion is correct, that there is a domain of subjectivity inaccessible to a psychology dependent on scientific observational methods; and, therefore, that the language of psychology is not categorially appropriate for its subject matter.

We must now explore whether our realistic theory of meaning and logic can be epistemologically validated. Of course the problem about the reality of structures of meaning and the existence of thoughts and other semantic acts arose in the first place because of our insistence on sensory perception (and perhaps "introspection" conceived by analogy with it) as our only epistemic power(s) for gathering data and establishing semantic ties to items and features in the world. So we are brought back once again to our assumptions or views about the constitutional principles and powers of the mind. The issue is whether we have the capacity to perceive or to discern actions which are constituted essentially by structures of meaning. This is not a matter of whether we can perceive physical things and take them as signs or signals of something else through association like we might take smoke to mean fire or clouds to mean rain, but whether we can perceive or be aware of acts in such a way that correct reports would be in terms of an embodied structure of meaning in the acts themselves. We have seen something of the difficulties generated by a negative stand on this issue.

Self-knowledge of one's own subjectivity and what we may call "expression-perception" or "perceptual understanding" seem to be our most likely candidates for such epistemic powers. We have self-knowledge, nonobservational knowledge, of our own personal acts. This is not so much an "introspection," a peering within, as it is how we do things. Of course some activities are so routine or peripheral that we do not have self-knowledge of them. We could give no reports of them except perhaps under hypnosis. Like breathing, they hover in that border between autonomic and personal acts. But there is a level of activity where self-knowledge is essential to the experience or activity. We would not say that one was in pain if he did not have self-knowledge of it. If we were to describe a person's behavior as playing chess and then discovered that he didn't know that he was doing it (and it was not simply a matter of his ignorance of the word "chess"), we would take back our claim that he was playing the game. No distinction can be drawn between the self-knowledge and the experience or the activity. They are not two things. We can of course reflect on an experience or activity but this is a separate act and it interferes with the first. Ordinary self-knowledge does not. Reports of our experiences and activities, for the most part, give their semantically intentional structures. For example, "I see a green color band above a blue one," "I want to go now," "I am on my way to have lunch with Phyllis." Of course we do give such reports as "I have a pain in my shoulder," "I am depressed," and the like. But even these, as I tried to show earlier, may be translated respectively, with a gain in clarity, into "I feel something wrong in my shoulder," "I feel that things in general are not well with me." Thus self-knowledge is one ground of the semantically intentional idiom, the language of meaning. But it does not stand alone and indeed it may not be the basic one.

Expression-perception, our capacity to discern the embodied structures of meaning in the bodily, linguistic, and artistic expressions and actions of others, is perhaps more basic than self-knowledge. At least it is not derivative from the latter. They are no doubt distinct but interdependent and mutually supporting powers. Our most primitive world, speaking experientially, is social. We have felt needs and discern personal responses to them. We learn to discriminate love and hostility, concern and indifference, and the like. The infant responds more readily to the subjectivity of those around him than to their physical structures as such. It is only as he senses the feelings and attitudes and understands the actions of those around him and enters into an interacting and intercommunicating relationship with them that he can come to grasp the meaning embodied in their verbal behavior. Without a prior intersubjective basis there could be no learning of language. Verbal behavior has to be understood, if at all, as an extension of antecedently understood nonlinguistic behavior. If our only power for epistemic encounter with the external world were pure sensory perception, if we were simply *observers* of behavior in the stripped down, filtered scientific sense of the term, we could not learn a language, all forms of culture would be impossible, and we would not be human beings at all. The theory that language acquisition is by a conditioning process in which fortunate random sounds of the infant are reinforced by the behavior of adults provides no genuine alternative, for this process is intelligible only on the assumption that the child *understands* the reinforcing behavior of his teachers and acquires an *understanding* of his own verbal behavior in relation to his own experiences of himself and his environment and his successful communications with others.

Our self-knowledge and perceptual understanding of the expressive behavior of others, the experiential grounds of the language of meaning, are not only reportable in the idiom of semantic intentionality but are themselves linguistically expressible. They stand in logical relationships and are subject to semantic and epistemic appraisals. They are partially self-warranting. They are the source of new ideas, the concepts of semantic intentionality, which are unique and irreducible. A little reflection along the lines we followed with respect to affective and conative experiences in chapter 5 will reveal the truth of these claims. Therefore we seem to be justified in concluding that self-knowledge and expression-perception are coordinate modes of epistemic encounters (although "encounter" may not be quite the right word in the case of self-knowledge) and that semantic intentionality is, ontologically speaking, a structural feature of the world.

Now just a brief word about logical categories and our knowledge of logical structures. As we indicated earlier, structures of meaning are embodied in existents with factual and normative structures and they themselves have properties exemplified in them and are themselves entangled in normative structures. In other words, every structure of meaning has on one hand a physical base with its own normative structure, e.g., some bodily state or process, configurated ink marks, sounds, etc., with a factual structure fitted to a semantic function or role; and on the other hand properties exemplified in it and a normative structure concerning the existence of the structures of meaning in question and the properties that ought to be exemplified in them. What concerns us here are the properties and relations which are or ought to be exemplified in structures of meaning. They are logical in character. We say this not to illuminate what they are but rather to elucidate what we mean by "logical," for being a property or relation which may be exemplified in structures of meaning is just what it is to be a logical property or relation. Some of the key concepts here are structural ones like "subject," "predicate," "connective," "proposition," "imperative," and "argument" and such concepts as "consistency," "inconsistency," and "entailment."

Our knowledge of logical structures is derived from self-knowledge and expression-perception. There is some awareness of logical structures in our ordinary exercise of these powers, enough for us to learn some of our logical vocabulary. But ordinary self-knowledge and expression-perception do not focus on the logical features of structures of meaning. We can, however, learn to bring them into focus and reflectively examine them. This is what the logician and the philosopher do. We may conclude, then, that semantic structures involve logical ones and that both must be given a place in our ontological account of the world.

There are those who would still contend that, even though we have to admit that meaning is a categorial feature of the world, there is no logical incompatibility involved in applying both rational appraisal language and the language of empirical science to human behavior because structures of meaning with their inexistential content and logical features have nothing to do with causation and change. "Naturalism," Ernest Nagel says, "does not maintain that only what is material exists, since many things noted in experience, for example, modes of action, relations of meaning, dreams, joys, plans, aspirations, are not as such material bodies. . . . [W]hat naturalism does assert as a truth about nature is that though *forms* of behavior or *functions* of material systems are indefeasibly parts of nature, forms and functions are not themselves *agents in their own realization or in the realization of anything else* [italics added]."[1]

To think of experiences, thoughts, and actions as effects of causal conditions in the body and the physical environment would mix categories in an inappropriate way. It would combine together within the range of the category of causality such radically different logical subjects as brain states and events, electrical impulses, muscular changes, and the like on one hand and personal acts on the other. A person thinks, feels, hears, sees, desires, enjoys, suffers, decides, and acts. To link causally entities of these diverse categories without any reshaping of them for the role involves a kind of logical mistake. And to tailor the psychological categories for the role involves a physicalization of the mental and the generation of insuperable problems, which we have already explored to some extent. If the arguments of this and the last chapter are correct, we have no alternative but to try to understand mental causality within the framework of the full-fledged native categories of the mental, which are, as we have seen, personal, semantic, logical, and normative as well as factual.

If we take the personal form of psychological statements seriously, and I urge that we do, any philosophical clarification of mental causality must involve elucidation of what it is to be a person. We can only indicate in very broad strokes a line of thought on the subject.

Of course a person has a bodily dimension, for we say such things as "I am on the sofa," "I weigh one hundred and sixty-five pounds," "You are taller than he," and so forth. But a person is not just a physical object in physical relations with his physical surroundings. His physical dimension is a living, functioning body. It has a normative structure. He may be physically mature or immature, well formed or deformed, healthy or unhealthy, and the like. He also has a semantic and logical dimension. He experiences things—he sees, hears, touches, feels, enjoys, suffers, and desires things; he thinks about things—he raises questions about them, he describes, explains, and predicts them, he evaluates them, he chooses and rejects them, he pursues and avoids them, etc. Furthermore, a person has a peculiar rational normative dimension. He is by his nature under an imperative to be rational in his experiences, thoughts, and actions. This defines a special position or office for him with rights and privileges which impose normative limitations on the actions of others. He is subject to and stands justified or unjustified under rational criticism.

We might say that a mind is a language which functions on its own. It denotes things, it describes them, it asserts facts, it questions, it prescribes, etc. It means in all the ways in which language means. The neurophysiological events and muscular activities are to the mental what ink marks or noises are to written or spoken language. We talk about a conventional language in semantic, logical, and normative terms, but not in epistemic and justificatory categories. We have to add these to the way we talk about an automatic language, for it can be said of such a language that it acts, that it shapes up into assertions of what is the case, prescriptions of what is required, etc., and that it does these things in a responsible or an irresponsible way and that it succeeds or fails in what it tries to do.

It would be a mistake to think of our automatic language solely after the model of factual discourse. We must include value language also, which means emotively. This is not to suggest the so-called emotive theory of value language. As I argued in chapter 5, feelings, emotions, attitudes, desires, and the like, the total range of our affective and conative experiences and attitudes, are modes of meaning that their objects have value, that if they exist, they are good (or bad), and if they do not exist, they ought (or ought not) to be. To mean in this way, in most instances, motivates and tends to initiate action on behalf of what is taken to be good or ought to be and to eliminate what is taken to be bad and to prevent what is felt ought not to be. Consequently the mental, and thus our automatic language, embraces the whole of behavior. Every human action, regardless of how physical, is not merely physical. It has a mental or semantic dimension. It can be correctly described as an action only in terms of its intention, the accepted imperative which "informs" the act. The act itself is a part of the system of thought of which its intention is a part and it can be understood only when placed in this context.

The automatic language in its fully active role in experiencing, thinking, and behaving embraces the body and has rights and obligations. This complex is the person.

A person, then, is a multidimensional but unitary being with physical, organic, semantic, logical, and value dimensions. His center of gravity, however, is in his semantic, logical, and value dimensions. A human being as such is uniquely constituted by a set of normative principles, semantic powers, and responsibilities which define an office, as it were, or a social position, one constituted by certain responsibilities, certain imperatives one is under by virtue of what he is, and their correlative rights and privileges, areas in which he must be free or may safely be left free to act at his own discretion if he is to have a chance to fulfill his responsibilities as a person. An individual person consists of his defining or constitutional principles, semantic powers, responsibilities, rights, and privileges as concretely actualized in beliefs, attitudes, skills, competences, memories, expectations, intentions, plans, responsibilities, rights, privileges, and the like to form a unitary functioning being. It is this self-functioning, self-regulating complex system with its semantic, logical, normative, and factual dimensions that is a person and expresses itself as "I."

We now come to the central problem concerning mental causality. How does an automatic language function? What kind of causality is involved in determining what one thinks, feels, desires, perceives, etc.? This is a very complex matter. I can only make a few suggestions. Thoughts, feelings, desires, decisions, and even perceptions do not occur in a vacuum. They occur in a complex semantic field with a conceptual and logical structure. The infant can hardly be said to perceive and to desire, to say nothing of to think and to decide. But he has the foundations on which to build. Some of his biological requirements are felt, and thus a rudimentary consciousness is born. With a push from the biological and a pull from the cultural this bridgehead is enriched and extended. A conceptually "informed" semantic field develops. It comes to have many strata of assumptions, presuppositions, beliefs, attitudes, biases, habits, intentions, and the like. This is the formation of a personality.

In the early formative period of a personality it can hardly be said to be free. It is influenced and shaped too much both from the biological and the social sides. But once it reaches a certain level of development, we speak of it as self-directing, responsible, and free. Yet it is only a matter of degree. Some people never seem to have a mind of their own. They are pulled this way and that by their biological requirements and the beliefs and attitudes of the people with whom they associate. They have no stable semantic field which constitutes their own personality.

The picture I am urging, however, is that a person is a semantic field with a bodily dimension and a normative structure. Given certain assumptions and beliefs, for instance, certain others are normatively required; some others ought not to be, and still others ought to be questioned. I suggest that in the realm of the mental, such normative requirements work towards their own realization. The normative require-ment of a thought within a logically structured semantic field tends to create it. The appearance and knowledge of what ought to be, in the form of impulses, desires, attitudes, and emotions, constitute the springs of action. Perhaps self-knowledge of our thoughts, which cannot be distinguished from clearly thinking them, extends to their normative relations and thereby moves us to think the further thoughts normatively required by them. Reasoning is a process of showing a claim to be justified within a context of other beliefs. To discern such justification while subscribing to the other beliefs involves embracing the justified claim. The human mind cannot by the very nature of the case be indifferent to or unmoved by the discernment of inconsistency, error, evidence, truth, and the like. A person is moved in all realms of thought by value considera-tions just as he is in decision-making that issues into overt action. He is moved by the pull of the ought, by normative requiredness. A semantic field, which constitutes a mind, tends to generate the further thoughts, feelings, emotions, desires, and the like which it normatively requires. It also tends to dislodge such mental states which ought not to be in it. Thus the normative structure of the mental either directly or through self-knowledge, and I am not sure any genuine distinction can be made here, is creative. Its causality is teleological.

It is a common experience for those who write articles or books to find it very difficult to make a beginning. Many starts are likely to be made that refuse to go anywhere. But all the false starts and fussing enables one finally to make a beginning. At first it is hard going. But after part of the work is forged by sheer labor, it gets easier. When it is well on its way, ideas come thick and fast with the greatest of ease. In fact, the work may seem to write itself. It simply unfolds. One idea gives birth to another. This is the creative process. It is the mind at work. One cannot have new and worthwhile ideas in a vacuum. Like capital, it takes ideas to create ideas.

It may be objected that even if my account of mental causality seems to be true of abstract thoughts, it is not true of experience, especially sensory perception. No doubt it is true that sensory perception involves a physical encounter with its object. The body is causally affected in a physical way. But this is only an occasion, a necessary condition, for a perceptual experience. How or even whether one experiences the object which causally affects one's body is a function of one's semantic field. One often sees what one's semantic field normatively requires one to see even though it is not there. Also one may fail to see something that is there because one's semantic field does not require the experience. And without a semantic field, regardless of how and in what ways one's body is causally affected by one's physical surroundings, there is no perception.

I have said nothing to imply that there are no correlations between brain states and the semantic field. In fact brain states constitute an important part of the physical dimension of the automatic language. The question arises, if the brain states and electrical impulses studied by the neurologist are caught up in this total personal complex which involves a teleological causality, can they be adequately described and explained within the framework of the neurologist? This is not a question to be answered by the working neurologist. It is a philosophical question to be settled by philosophical work. The central point is whether there is any incompatibility involved in embracing the brain events under a teleological causality grounded in the mental dimension when talking in personal language and under a "naturalistic" causality when talking the language of the neurologist.

I think the answer must be something like this. The neurologist can delineate his subject matter for his own purposes in terms of the concepts appropriate to his own method of investigation. But since his approach and method are restricted, his categories are inadequate to the subject matter from the philosophical point of view. Events in the neurological and muscular systems which are necessary conditions of the teleologically caused mental states and personal acts must also come under the category of teleological causality. And by extension through personal behavior much of what happens in the physical world around us is brought under teleological change.

Rational appraisal talk, then, not only involves ontological commitments about value, semantic, and logical structures in the world, but also ontological commitments about the nature of causality in the realm of experience, thought, and action. It indicates that value, semantic, and logical structures, as well as purely factual ones, enter into the causal process in the psychological realm and participate in shaping what happens. Scientific descriptive-explanatory talk about behavior involves ontological commitments about only purely factual structures and indicates that they alone are involved in the causal process. Therefore we must conclude that the antinomy of the mental generated by the extension of the scientific conceptual system to man is genuine. We cannot solve the problem by rejecting rational appraisal language, for this would make knowledge in any form, including science, impossible. Therefore, we are driven to the conclusion that we have no alternative but to reject the scientific framework of thought as adequate for the study of man and the naturalistic philosophy of mind it generates. And we have, I think, demonstrated the legitimacy of the indigenous categories of the mental in terms of the epistemic powers of the mind.

IX

The Humanities
and Cultural Renewal

It is now time to review and to see our project as a whole. The concepts of culture, cultural mind, cultural derangement, and cultural therapy have been central. A culture, as we have used the term, consists of a people's way of semantically relating to and appropriating reality and the product of such activity, namely, reality as semantically appropriated and represented. Thus the culture of a people includes their language, symbols, myths, legends, art, ethics, normative social and political thought, history, theology, philsophy, science, and the like. A cultural mind, we have said, is that fundamental part of a culture consisting of a widely shared set of philosophical assumptions or views, whether ever articulated or not, about the constitutional principles and the semantic and epistemic powers of the human mind, which shape or influence how the people exercise their powers in their efforts to know and to cope with reality and thus determine or influence the overall culture they generate. A deranged cultural mind, according to our view, is one which embraces false philosophical assumptions or views about the principles and powers of the human mind and thus gives rise to systematic error, creating a gap between the culture and reality, and thereby thwarting the people in their efforts to cope with the world and to live successfully.

From within a cultural mind, we maintained, derangement may show itself in two ways: through a general pervasive sense or feeling of cultural malaise or spiritual depression, especially in the face of successful living as judged by the criteria of the culture; and the particular philosophical perplexities which the culture generates and the difficulties in and the consequences of trying to solve them from within the general cultural perspective. But the final judgment on the possible derangement of a culture is to be made, we have contended, on the basis of detailed examination of the philosophical assumptions constituting the cultural mind in light of a direct philosophical exploration of the constitutional principles and powers of the mind themselves to determine the truth about them.

Although a deranged culture may regain its health as a result of historical forces which right the people's culture-generating attitude toward the world (but this unaided by reason is an unlikely, precarious prospect), philosophical analysis can be not only diagnostic, but, as we have argued, also therapeutic, especially at the time of a widespread feeling of cultural malaise and when historical forces are at work calling into question the people's basic stance toward the world.

Our inquiry into the spirit of life lived from within the perspective of our modern Western culture, both in terms of the conclusions of those who analyze and comment on the spirit of the age and the revelations of modern art and literature, revealed a progressive, deep-seated alienation, anxiety, and despair about life in general; and we found an explanation for this spiritual plight of modern man in the philosphical perplexities our culture generates and the subjectivistic interpretations of various sectors of culture which have been developed to save the basic commitments of the modern mind. Thus we see how the life-supporting dimensions of the culture have been undermined with the resulting spiritual impoverishment, anguish, and despair.

Furthermore, we have examined in some depth our naturalistic assumptions and theories about the constitutional principles and powers of the human mind and the reductionistic, subjectivistic, and nihilistic views and theories they generate about value language and the language of meaning and their respective sectors of culture; and we have found them to be incoherent and self-destructive when fully developed and systematically thought through and false in terms of our philosophical examination of the principles and powers of the human mind.

Naturalism, as it is here understood, holds that it is only through sensory experience under scientific refinement and thought grounded therein that we acquire knowledge of the world and that reality is structured as it is conceptually delineated in philosophically clarified scientific thought. Thus if value judgments and talk about meaning make genuine truth-claims, they must be in principle expressible in empirical scientific language. Otherwise they must be subjectivistic and noncognitive. In other words, both value language and the language of meaning must be grounded to the world, if at all, through sensory experience. And, if not funded with meaning in this manner, then they are not objective; that is, they do not have a semantic outreach to items and features of the world. They are in some way subjectivistic without ontological significance.

In chapter 4, we reviewed the major ways of interpreting value language as a mode of empirical factual language and also the major theories that interpret value discourse as noncognitive. Both types of theory, we found, do violence to the logic of value language and to the nature of the psychological realm with which value language is essentially involved. We found that the "ought"-sentence is basic in value discourse and that it is neither reducible to nor derivable from the "is"-sentence. Such a reduction would involve a category mistake and generate new philosophical perplexities. Thus value judgments cannot be, as the classical naturalists in value theory claimed, reports and descriptions of affective and conative psychological states and their causal conditions. Nevertheless, contrary to the emotivist, value judgments do stand in logical relationships and may be backed or opposed by rational arguments. Our examination of the nature of arguments for value judgments turned up basic value judgments which are grounded in certain affective and conative experiences. An exploration of the nature of such experiences and the way in which the value judgments in question are grounded in them led us to reject both the emotivist's and existentialist's positions and to conclude that such experiences are, like sensory experiences, semantic and epistemic in character. Indeed they are, we contend, along with such value experiences of the self (whether body or ego) as hunger, thirst, pleasure, and pain, a mode of epistemic encounter with the world. The primary reasons for this conclusion are (1) our nonindifferent experiences lend themselves to linguistic expression or articulation so that the sentences expressing them are synonymous with them and serve as proxies for them; (2) they have a logical structure, stand in logical relationships, and are subject to logical appraisals; (3) they are subject to semantic and epistemic appraisals as veridical, illusory, or hallucinatory, as corroborated or refuted, as rational or irrational, and the like; and (4) they are the unique source of value concepts. Through these experiences, under critical assessment, we semantically appropriate a dimension of reality that is not othewise available to us. Therefore, we contend, there is value knowledge as well as factual knowledge and a value structure of the world as well as a factual structure. Thus it is shown that our modern value skepticism and subjectivism were generated by false assumptions or views about the nature of our nonindifferent experiences. The elaborate reductionistic and subjectivistic theories of value language were developed to defend and to protect these false views and assumptions. But our work, if sound, liberates us from these false and perverting restrictions and allows us to function with these semantic and epistemic powers unfettered in our efforts to know and to cope with the world.

In chapter 7, we explored, in a somewhat parallel way, the language of meaning. We found that there is no easy solution to the apparent antinomy which we pointed out in chapter 2 and developed in chapter 6 between rational appraisal talk about human acts and a scientific descriptive-explanatory account of behavior. The only way, we concluded, that the apparent antinomy could be shown not to be real would be to show that rational appraisal language can be explicated in terms of the language of empirical science or explained in some way that shows that it does not have any ontological import over and above or at least incompatible with that of the science of behavior. Within rational appraisal talk, we found the language of meaning to be fundamental. Efforts to reduce semantic talk about language to psychological talk were of no avail, for ordinary psychological talk indicates that psychological states and acts themselves have a semantic or intentionalistic dimension. Attempts to purify the language of ordinary psychological talk to show that the psychological realm has only a factual structure as indicated by the language of behavioristic and physiological psychology proved to lead to absurdities. Again the culprit is our naturalistic assumption that it is only through sensory experience under scientific refinement and criticism that we can semantically relate to and appropriate reality. And here we find that the implications of this thesis cut the foundations out from under itself, leaving only a world of blank factuality, with no meaning, no truth, and no knowledge at all. So there must be semantic and epistemic powers other than sensory perception and thought grounded in it if there are any at all.

We had already concluded in chapter 5 that our value experiences are semantic and epistemic in character. But they would not suffice for the language of meaning. We concluded that it is through self-awareness of our own psychological states and acts and our powers of expression-perception and perceptual understanding of behavior, which are themselves semantic and epistemic in character, that the language of meaning, including psychological language in general, is funded with meaning in such a way that it is unique and irreducible. This means, or so we contend, that, ontologically speaking, there is an objective structure of meaning with inherent logical features and relationships somewhat parallel with the structures of fact and value.

And, lastly, we have concluded that there are persons—concrete individuals with a multidimensional categorial structure of fact, value, and meaning, with all three dimensions caught up in the causality and change of human acts, both covert and overt.

The modern Western mind, as we observed in chapter 2, was generated by the great revolution in Western civilization, the shift in our culture-generating attitude toward the world. This was a shift from a dominant concern with man's place in the world and with fulfilling the requirements that are inherent in his position and that impinge upon him to preoccupation with getting what he wants, conquering the world, and imposing his will upon it. This reorientation turned Western culture inside out and upside down. Values grounded in our wants and desires, largely materialistic in nature, took over the helm of our civilization from moral and spiritual values grounded in our higher emotions and rational powers. This not only worked a social revolution, elevating those who enhance our material well-being to the top social stratum and crowning them with material riches, and yet another social revolution which knights the workers as the real creators of our material welfare; but more significantly it forced a reconception of knowledge, and therefore of the whole intellectual enterprise, to fit it into the service of the new values. Modern science was born and, as it came to dominate the intellectual life of the age, the naturalistic image of man-in-the-world emerged. In the continuing struggle for consistency within the foundations of our culture, the remnants of our classical heritage have been all but eliminated. We have reached the point where for a great many of the youth of today, as well as for many of the older generation, the moral, political, and religious ideals and symbols that once gave meaning to life and elevated it, justified our institutions, and bound us together as a nation are just so much rhetoric with all the meaning drained out.

In our present cultural crisis, with our materialistic values being called into question, there are indications of some loss of faith in science. Indeed some see it as a god that failed. There are signs of new interest in the humanities, in those arts and disciplines which draw especially upon our experiences of value and meaning and the language and symbolism appropriate thereto in semantically appropriating and representing reality. Many are turning to humanists in search of understanding, wisdom, and guidance. But the humanities long ago sold their birthright in search of respectability in the scientific age. They have been in disarray with loss of identity and direction ever since the demise of theology as a serious intellectual discipline and philosophy became the handmaiden of science. The arts have come to be regarded at best, for the most part, as productive of works for aesthetic contemplation and for commercial value. The academic humanities, with the exception of philosophy and religion, have become the history and aesthetic criticism of the arts and study of and instruction in artistic skills. And religion, as an academic discipline, is a complex of textual, linguistic, historical, sociological, and psychological studies of religious literature, leaders, institutions, and experiences. Studies of man, culture, social and political institutions, and history anxiously brandish their scientific credentials, having broken from the ranks of the humanities long ago and proclaimed themselves behavioral and social sciences. So the humanities in their present state, although they are not without value, do not offer much help for overcoming our cultural derangement and spiritual malaise. Indeed they constitute much of the problem.

The only intellectual developments from within the humanities in modern times which provided indigenous leadership and direction were the idealistic philosophy of the romantic revolt and twentieth-century existentialism. But these were not truly indigenous humanistic developments, for they resulted from the impact of and reaction to scientific naturalism and were largely shaped by the opposition. Idealism, although preoccupied with the humanistic perspective and the humanities, was a peculiar turn in the modern subjectivism generated by the naturalistic extension of the categories of existence and factuality to the realm of meaning and subjectivity. Also existentialism, which is primarily a humanistic mode of thought, is perverted, in my judgment, at least in its most pervasive form, by holding on to and defending subjectivity and selfhood in a world otherwise conceived naturalistically. It accepts totally value subjectivism and a world of factuality, leaving the existential self, in the words of Camus, "a stranger," "an exile," "an actor divorced from his setting," with a feeling of meaninglessness and absurdity.

We have in this study, I think, offered serious arguments and considerations which, if sound, go a long way toward validating both epistemologically and ontologically the central humanistic categories of value and meaning. It is urgent, I believe, for the humanities to reassert themselves in their own authentic, indigenous categories and to reclaim their rightful place as man's natural and most comprehensive approach to reality which defines for him both his self-image and his world view; for in no other way will we be able to correct the derangement of our modern Western culture, overcome our ontological and social alienation, and salvage the world as a place that will support and nurture the human spirit.

We can here only sketch what such an approach would be like. The humanistic perspective is constituted by man's total experiential encounter and active engagement with reality. It is from within this orientation that one becomes aware of oneself as a being in the world and becomes a functioning person. One's self, what one is, in a most important sense, cannot be separated from one's self-understanding; and one's self-understanding cannot be divorced from one's understanding of the world.

One's self-awareness is first and foremost an awareness of one's social position. The child does not simply become aware of himself as an active, functioning body, but as a being who is accepted and loved or rejected and despised and as an agent with certain powers who wins the approval or disapproval of others in his activities. In time he encounters himself in his own felt embarrassments, shame and guilt feelings, jealousies, felt insults and injustices, self-satisfaction, pride, and the like. What emerges is not only a self-image but the imaged self, a person, a being constituted by the powers and responsibility, along with correlative rights and privileges, to function as an autonomous rational agent in a social environment. One's very identity or selfhood is thus defined in terms of a social position or office. To know oneself is to know one's social position, one's office, one's role, the one that is inherent in and constitutive of one's very being. To be troubled about one's self, to have self-doubt, is to be uncertain about one's identity, one's position, and thus impaired in one's ability to relate meaningfully to others and to function effectively as a person. To suffer from anomie or alienation is to feel that one does not have a social position or office and thus that one does not have an identity or selfhood. It is to experience the nothingness of one's being, the meaninglessness of one's existence, which is to experience one's own loss of identity and disintegration.

To be a self, to be a person, then, involves not only being but understanding oneself as a being who is constituted by categorial structures of fact, value, and meaning. Furthermore, to be a person involves being aware of oneself as, and indeed being, a social being in a social world. A person can no more be devoid of social relationships than a physical thing can lack physical relationships. A person exists in social space. Social reality consists of structures of fact, value, and meaning, with the primary social units being persons; but there are such social entities as families, communities, nations, and the like which have their own identity and life.

The moralist, the legislator, the jurist, the statesman, and everyman seek to discover and to formulate into moral judgment, policy, law, and institution those normative patterns of life that make for personal and social well-being. The biographer, the journalist, and the historian tell of and seek to render intelligible personal and social particulars. The poet, the dramatist, the painter, the artist in whatever form, expresses and gives interpretation to various occurrences, aspects, and dimensions of life and the human condition with special emphasis on their meaning and significance or lack of such. But there is need for a systematic effort to understand man and his world from within humanistic categories, for lacking this the humanities are without intellectual leadership and direction; but, most importantly, it is only through grasping and understanding self and world through humanistic categories that modern man can overcome his alienation and accept himself and relate emotionally to his world in a self-integrating and self-fulfilling way.

A systematic humanistic approach confronts the world with the personal and the social dimensions in the foreground. This is the primary reality encountered and the primary reality to be rendered intelligible in our search for understanding. As a rational being who relates to and tries to cope with himself and his world through his semantic appropriation of reality, man is disturbed and threatened by the fragmentary and the isolated. He has a vital need to understand the realities he encounters, to integrate them into the world he knows, for unless they fit into the world as he understands it, they are a threat to his view of the world and to his way of relating to and coping with reality. So from within the humanistic approach, man develops an intellectual frame of interpretation, consisting of categories of fact, value, and meaning derived from the full spectrum of human experience, for rendering the world intelligible. The development of this approach toward a full world view and a comprehensive theoretical understanding of all that we encounter and the assimilation of it fully into the culture and consciousness of the people would be a monumental task, one that would take generations. But if our assessment of the epistemic powers of the human mind is correct, it is possible.

This approach is not new. In fact, it is the oldest known to man, for it is the human approach to the world. When man was young, even when he was in the process of becoming man, what we are calling the humanistic approach generated folk practices, institutions, symbols, legends, and myths which bound people and their experiences together in a web of meaning and created historical communities. The cultural web of meaning was expanded and enriched by the development of various practical and fine arts. Critical, reflective responsiveness to inconsistencies within the developing culture, especially when it came under impact from and mixed with a foreign culture, generated intellectual pursuits such as history, theology, philosophy, and the sciences, with theology being the dominant unifying first-order intellectual discipline and philosophy its second-order handmaiden. This provided a unified intellectual grasp of the world from within humanistic categories that integrated and supported the whole culture, the social structure, and the life of the people.

This cultural unity was shattered when the sciences under the influence of new cultural priorities went independent and developed their own indigenous categories, and in time something like a unified science became the dominant first-order intellectual discipline and naturalism became the philosophy of our culture. It now seems clear, although not yet widely recognized in our dominant intellectual circles, that our culture cannot be integrated under such an intellectual vision, and that the attempt is destructive of the culture, of the social order, and of man himself.

We cannot at this point in our cultural development simply revert to an earlier humanistic phase of our civilization. We can only move forward from where we are. All that we can hope for is a change in the direction of our cultural development by virtue of some internal shifts within the culture. The shifts I am urging are twofold but closely related. First, a shift to a primary concern for personhood and the ways and means of meaningful and fulfilling life; and second, a corollary of the first, a new emphasis on the humanities and their categories. What is essential, I think, is for the humanities to break free from the reigning intellectual dogmas of naturalism and to have a fresh look at their own subject matter in their own way and to achieve intellectual leadership in the culture. This would require first-order humanistic intellectual disciplines which would seek to understand man and his world in distinctly humanistic categories. Philosophy has a most significant role to play in the study and development of such a categorial framework and its validation in the semantic and epistemic powers of the human mind and the categorial structure of the world. But it is not the task of philosophy to come to grips with and to render intelligible the logically contingent features of reality as experientially available from within our categorial framework, whether humanistic or naturalistic. That is the task of what I am calling first-order disciplines, those that develop and use a conceptual system in getting at experientially determinable truth about the world. But philosophy may be able to play a role in generating humanistic first-order intellectual pursuits just as it did in generating first-order naturalistic disciplines.

It might be helpful to contrast the scientific and the humanistic approaches to a particular social problem. I shall take a paper by Kingsley Davis entitled "Theory of Change and Response in Modern Demographic History"[1] as an example of the scientific approach. Davis's task is to study those societies in which there has been a change in reproductive behavior in response to the modern reduction of the mortality rate and to develop a comprehensive theory of why fertility was reduced, how it was reduced, and why it was reduced in those particular ways in those societies.

Davis seeks to refute what he considers oversimplified theories of population such as the view "that population is simply a matter of two capacities—a 'reproductive urge' on the one hand and 'means of subsistence' on the other—or . . . that demographic behavior is a function of a 'traditional culture' or 'value system.'"[2] The first is rejected on the basis of the fact that the decline in the fertility rate in Japan and in Western industrialized nations has coincided with increasing prosperity and the fact that there has not been a decline in fertility in response to reduced mortality in the less prosperous nations. His argument against the view that demographic behavior is a function of the value system in the culture is that the response to decreased mortality by reduced fertility has been much the same in such diverse cultures as Japan, Northwestern Europe, Eastern Europe, and the United States. He concludes, for example, that abortion as a way of reducing fertility in Japan "is not an outgrowth of ancient tradition . . . ; not an outgrowth of the absence of Christian ideology," for it is not at all peculiar to Japan. "It is," he says, "a response to social and economic conditions arising in country after country at a particular time in the process of modernization."[3]

Davis concludes from his studies that whenever and wherever there has been industrializiation with increasing prosperity there has been reduced fertility and by virtually every known method in response to lowered mortality. This he is prepared to accept as a law of demographic behavior. His explanation of the law is that whenever there is industrialization with rising prosperity there is competition for status based on the extent one shares in the new prosperity, and that whenever such competition exists, the people feel that a large family is a handicap both to parents and to their children in the competition. And they employ all known methods of reducing fertility with the result that fertility declines.*

Davis, in his attempt to give a scientific theory of change in demographic behavior, speaks of "stimulus" and "response." He asks why there is the particular response to a given stimulus, or, in other words, why the cause gives rise to the particular effect that it does. In commenting on his approach and method, he says: "An explanation in terms of 'tradition' has no value in social science, because 'tradition' is merely a name for absence of change. A type of social behavior is like the momentum of a moving body: it will not change unless something forces it to change. If the absence of a contrary force is itself not explained, we have no real theory of the persistence but merely another name for it. As for the so-called values, they should be recognized as being a part, or aspect, of the behavior itself and, accordingly, as requiring to be explained rather than being used as the explanation. . . . The question of change or persistence is therefore a question of what did or did not act upon the total action (motive-plus-conduct)."[4]

It is clear, both from what Davis does and from his theory of what he is doing, that he regards human behavior as events among other events to be described and explained scientifically. Values are identified with value attitudes or motives and thus treated as part of the behavioral complex to be described and explained. He takes it for granted that whenever reproduction has been reduced in response to lowered mortality the people involved looked with favor upon and wanted the reduction. The causal explanation that he seeks applies equally to the favorable attitude toward and the desire for lower fertility and the conduct that results in it.

This kind of approach in the study of demographic behavior, I suggest, miscategorizes the subject matter, perverts our understanding of what is involved, and misleads us in action programs.

---

*It should be pointed out that the above statement of Davis's position involves a slight modification of his own statement in order to place the beliefs of people being studied scientifically on the same basis as their value attitudes and wants. He says, for example: "people *found* (italics added) that their accustomed demographic behavior was handicapping them." A strict scientific method would allow him to report on the basis of observation only "the people *felt* (or *believed*) that. . . ." Such facts are as much in need of scientific explanation as the valuations of the people involved. Indeed a belief that something is a *handicap* is itself a value judgment. But even if it were a factual belief, the scientist as such could deal with it only in terms of its occurrence and its causal conditions, not as an epistemic act and in terms of its correctness, which the word "found" involves.

First of all, consider the beliefs of people. Some psychologists and social scientists who insist upon being strictly scientific regard the beliefs of their subjects as dispositions to act in certain observable ways under specifiable conditions. Furthermore, they regard such dispositions and changes in them as subject to causal explanation. Thus, if one should wish to alter the beliefs of a people, the only action program open to him, according to this theory, would be to manipulate the causal conditions of the beliefs in such a way as to produce the desired changes. Yet it should be obvious that this way of thinking about beliefs is categorially inappropriate and misleading.

"Belief" is not a scientific concept; that is, it is not an empirical concept grounded in scientifically refined sensory observation. It is grounded in self-knowledge and the understanding of other persons in a communicative, intersubjective relationship. Thus, it is a concept that transcends the methodology of the natural sciences. Insofar as the social sciences, in search of intellectual respectability in a scientific age, adopt the methodology of the natural sciences and reduce our ordinary mental and behavioral concepts to their "scientific" shadows, to parallel legitimate concepts within "scientific" methodology, they seal themselves off epistemically from an important and even essential dimension of behavior. The result is not simply a partial account, for even a partial account could be correct so far as it goes. The "scientific" account of behavior miscategorizes its subject matter and thus sets us to thinking about it in terms of a team of concepts inappropriate to it.

A belief, by its very nature, involves meaning. It has a semantic dimension. It is about something. It can be given linguistic expression or articulation. It is in propositional form. The sentence that expresses it is declarative. A report of the belief would be in the form, "I (or he) believe(s) that . . .," where the blank would be filled in by a clause that would, if by itself, *express* the belief. A belief stands in logical relationships to other beliefs, statements, perceptions, etc. It may logically entail others, contradict some, and be logically supported or corroborated by still others. To ask why one believes something is to ask for his reasons, his evidence, his grounds for so believing. A belief may be appraised as rational or irrational, as logical or illogical, as justified or unjustified, as true or false, and the like. Thus, a belief is not simply an event among other events, nor even a disposition among other dispositions, to be simply described and explained scientifically. It is not something to be described in terms of concepts grounded in the sensory discriminations of a scientific observer, but in terms of the concepts that constitute the belief itself. It is not something to be explained in terms of scientifically discovered causal conditions, but in terms of its logical place in the semantic field that constitutes the mind of the person whose belief it is. To understand and to explain a belief one must know the mind of the person whose belief it is in an extra-scientific way; not in an observational way, but in a communicative, intersubjective way in which there is a sharing of concepts, thoughts, semantic contents in various logical forms. This is the humanistic way of knowing as distinct from the scientific approach.

If we approach the beliefs of a person or a people in a humanistic way, any attempt to alter them would not be through the manipulation and control of their scientifically discovered causal conditions, for that would be to understand and to treat people under the categories of *things* rather than those of *people* and therefore would be, by the very nature of the approach, dehumanizing. A humanistic approach would require that the people be approached as people, as rational agents, who are capable of reflective, critical assessment of their beliefs in light of evidence and logical considerations. Thus, any proper attempt to alter their beliefs would use instructional and educational methods rather than causal, manipulatory techniques.

It is interesting to note, as remarked in a footnote above, that Davis speaks of the beliefs of people in a humanistic way even while insisting that their value attitudes and actions be described and explained scientifically. It is not obvious how a social scientist can justify the distinction. Those concerned with being strictly scientific in social studies insist on bringing all behavior and social phenomena under scientific categories. Yet we can understand why the distinction is made. There are more obvious objections to a naturalistic view of beliefs than to a naturalistic account of value attitudes, for even the scientist must talk constantly about his own and his colleagues' scientific beliefs in rational appraisal language. This makes it more difficult to subsume them under the categories of scientific description and explanation. Furthermore, the modern empirical scientific method, as we have previously observed, is premised upon the assumption that value experiences and value attitudes are not epistemic in character, but rather subjective reactions to the realities discerned by sensory observation and scientific thought grounded therein. With such a view of value experiences and value attitudes, one is not as likely to have intellectual cramps in subsuming them under the categories of scientific description and explanation as in the case of beliefs.

But, as we have argued in this work, all subjectivity, including experience, thought, and a dimension of action, is a structure of meaning, and value experiences and attitudes are knowledge-yielding and are of and about an objective value structure. Thus behavior, which embraces semantic, logical, and value structures as well as factual ones cannot be accounted for from within a strictly scientific approach. At best a science of personal and social phenomena is incomplete and limited in restricting itself to sensory data and factual thought. At worst, its one-dimensional perspective distorts even its account of the purely factual aspect of behavior, especially with regard to why the facts are the way they are.

If my account of value experiences and attitudes is correct, then there is a category mistake in Davis's claim that value attitudes are simply part of the behavioral complex to be explained in terms of scientifically discovered causal conditions. He is right, of course, in saying that the attitude and the action go together. To ask why one did something and why he wanted to do it is to ask only one question. My concern is with the meaning of "why?" when asked of either. What would constitute an answer? Not, I submit, a scientifically discovered causal condition, but the agent's reason, which is at once a justifying and an explanatory reason for the action. The agent's reason is some fact which he feels normatively requires the act in question. It supports the claim that the act would be a good thing to do. To accept this claim is to form a value attitude that could be expressed by the sentence, "The act in question would be a good thing to do." The attitude is corrigible. It embodies a claim that is either correct or incorrect. The fact which is felt to be a reason for the act may not normatively require the act at all or it may be an insufficient reason. Both the attitude and the act may be invalid, unfounded, irrational, stupid, etc.; or they may be valid, well-founded, rational, justified, intelligent, etc. Thus, it is not only the attitude but the action also that is subject to rational appraisal.

Human actions, like beliefs and value attitudes, are subject to being described not in terms of concepts grounded in the sensory discriminations of scientific observations of behavior but in terms of the concepts that internally structure the actions themselves, i.e., in terms of the intention of the agent. And human actions are to be explained in terms of the reasons the agents have for doing what they do. Describing and explaining actions is much like describing and explaining beliefs and value attitudes. The strictly scientific approach, in contrast with the humanistic method, denies us epistemic access to the essential structure of all three.

Throughout this discussion I have spoken of the scientific method as restricted to sensory observation for data gathering and semantic ties between language and items in the world. The humanistic method operates from a broader experiential base, drawing upon not only sensory observation but all forms of affective-conative experience, self-knowledge, and communicative inter-subjective encounters. It is, I urge, only from within the humanistic approach that human behavior can be described and explained in categories appropriate to the subject matter. The saving grace of the social sciences is that they seldom, if ever, live up to their scientific pretensions. In spite of themselves, they remain somewhat humanistic. Nevertheless, their scientific bias has its perverting influence.

Contrary to Davis, the traditional beliefs, value attitudes, and practices of a people are very important in understanding their demographic behavior. A humanistic approach would seek to discover, to understand, and to assess critically the relevant beliefs, value attitudes, and actions of the people. An action program aimed at altering their reproductive behavior would be first and foremost educational. It would seek to inform the people about relevant facts and values and to help them to assess critically their relevant prevailing beliefs, value attitudes, and practices for the purpose of getting them to reject the false, the invalid, and the unjustified among them and to accept the true, the valid, and the justified. In addition to the straightforward educational program, the society might be encouraged to provide an incentive program for lower fertility that would mediate and at the same time educationally point to the more remote values for the society and the world at large in such a way that they would be more vividly felt and understood by individual couples and thus become active considerations that would affect their reproductive behavior.

We may interpret Davis's theory of demographic change to mean, not that the value system of a society is irrelevant for explaining its demographic behavior, but that so far only in a materialistic, bourgeois value system have people valued small families enough to control and to limit their reproduction. But perhaps all this proves is that if people feel and understand that small families are better than larger ones, then they will find ways of limiting their size. An educational and an incentive program might succeed in convincing people of the value of a low fertility rate in societies that do not fully share the materialistic, bourgeois value system based on industrializiation, for there are objective reasons for a low fertility rate in other kinds of societies as well. But such a program in any society must take into account and be integrated into the total value system of the society and the beliefs on which it is supervenient.

Returning to the matter of a unified first-order humanistic discipline, historically theology served this role. It took its departure from the folk religious symbols and myths of the culture.

The religious dimension of consciousness consists of our basic emotional and attitudinal response to ourselves as human-beings-in-the-world. Only those beings with sufficient semantic powers to comprehend themselves as beings-in-the-world are capable of religious consciousness. And those with such powers cannot escape it. Religious consciousness is either positive, a sense of man's being at home in the world, having a social place (a position as a person) in a congenial and supporting world, what has been called religious faith; or doubt that this is so, an anxiety about man's position in the world; or a negative attitude, a feeling of alienation, a feeling that man is not at home in the world, that there is no such place or position as that of a person for him, that he is an absurdity, that his existence is meaningless, that he does not fit into the world, or indeed that he is not really a person after all. Only a positive religious consciousness is life-supporting. Both religious anxiety and a negative religious conscious- ness are spirit-shrinking and life-destructive. So it is not surprising that all folk religious symbols and myths are expressions of and promote a positive religious consciousness. The process of natural selection among cultural forms would be sufficient to assure this even if there were no inherent truth embodied in them.

Theology appears on the scene when the folk religious symbols and myths which structure the religious consciousness of a cultural community and unify and support the social institutions and life of the people are somehow disturbed and brought into question. It is an intellectual effort to sort out, to develop, and to defend the truth embodied in the popular religious symbols and myths which sprang without individual authorship from the communal life and consciousness of the people. The work of the theologian has never been easy. It has often been dangerous. The people are very jealous and protective of their vital communal religious symbols and myths, for their very identity, spiritual power, and well-being are tied up with them. And so the theologian who dares to tamper with them in an effort to reveal and to develop in an acceptable intellectual form the truth embodied in them often puts himself in jeopardy. This and the fact that it operates from within the religious symbols and myths of a particular people have always been severe restraints on theology as an intellectual discipline.

Traditional theology is no longer available to modern man. The religious symbols and myths from which it departs and in terms of which it speaks no longer form and structure our consciousness. The inner dynamics of the modern mind has long since broken their grip upon us. It is doubtful if they could be implanted again. Authentic symbols and myths have to grow out of the experience and consciousness of a people. Nevertheless theology at its best develops a comprehensive conceptual system, one consisting of categories of fact, value, and meaning funded by and responsive to the full spectrum of experience from within the humanistic perspective, for making sense out of man, his experience, and his world. Something like this, but divorced from the parochial symbols and myths of a particular people, is what I am urging. We have no adequate term for such an intellectual discipline or set of disciplines. The term "theology" would be misleading and crippling in our present cultural atmosphere. "Humanistic science" sounds self-contradictory. Perhaps "systematic humanities" will do.

What I am suggesting, then, is that the humanities be developed and expanded in terms of their own indigenous categories so that we would have not only a transformation in our present humanistic disciplines of history, literature, art, and religion as they were liberated from foreign domination by naturalistic categories, but also the development of normative ethics, normative social and political thought, humanistic psychology, humanistic social studies, and a unified systematic humanistic study of man and his world as respectable intellectual pursuits. Such a development in systematic humanities would provide leadership and direction in the more conventional humanities and arts and in our total intellectual life.

Under the dominance of naturalism and the sciences, the humanities have been problematic both philosophically and practically. While philosophers have spent a great deal of their energy trying to achieve an acceptable interpretation or explanation of the languages of value and meaning and their sectors of culture from within the naturalistic perspective, the humanities have both progressively lost intellectual respectability and influence and have become increasingly perverted in search of the same. So the question inevitably arises: if the humanities should rise again to a position of dominance and reassert themselves in their own categories, what would be the impact of such a development on the sciences? How would they be philosophically interpreted? How could the sciences be assimilated in such a culture? And how would they be transformed in the process of assimilation?

Here I would like to caution against a possible misreading of this work. It is not antiscience; only antinaturalism. Science is one of the great achievements of the human mind, one that has been highly fruitful in so many constructive ways. What I have argued against is the overextension and dominance of science in our intellectual life and the naturalistic philosophy which it has generated. Science and its positive fruits must be preserved and furthered. The problem is how to assure this while putting science in its rightful place in our intellectual life and culture so that all sectors of the culture and the culture as a whole can flourish in a healthy manner.

To accomplish this we need a new philosophy of science, one which is congruent with and indeed integrated into a comprehensive philosophy of culture based on an epistemology that recognizes and does justice to the full range of our semantic and epistemic powers. In light of the epistemology and philosophy of culture we have developed in this work, we have to conclude that modern science, as it has been developed with its restriction to sensory perception for data gathering and for funding its language with meaning, is limited by its approach to the categorial dimension of factuality. This is, as we observed earlier, the kind of knowledge that is needed for making things and for manipulating and controlling things through physical action, for in this way we can only take hold of and alter the factual structure of the world. We should, then, regard science as a special way of knowing which provides the appropriate kind of knowledge for guiding the making and changing of things through physical action. But science, in its modern form, should not be taken as providing us with our intellectual vision of reality. This should be derived from our total culture and the full spectrum of human experience.

Science in such a cultural and intellectual climate would itself no doubt undergo changes. For one thing, there would not be the same concern with keeping the language of science, especially in its categorial dimension, restricted to what could be funded through sensory observation under scientific refinement. It could operate with categories derived from other dimensions of experience and sectors of culture insofar as they were recognized as intellectually respectable. Indeed liberalization of science in this respect might be a healthy development within science itself, for there are reasons for believing that the excessive puritanism of scientific naturalism has not only deranged the culture as a whole but has had a perverting influence even on science, especially in those areas where the nonfactual structures are most prominent as in biology, psychology, and the so-called social sciences.

It may very well be that the intellectual vision of the world that would emerge from within the cultural perspective I have urged would not generate as neatly arranged and vigorously regimented a body of knowledge as the naturalistic perspective. But I think we have seen some of the consequences of the intellectual puritanism of the modern mind. Indeed its strictures are so great that they not only stifle life but do not even give the scientific intellect logical room to operate. This is the explanation, as I think we have amply shown, for our spiritual depression and the peculiar philosophical perplexities of the modern age.

The humanistic cultural mind we envisage, although perhaps more profligate but still thoroughly under the controls of our liberalized cannons of rationality, would, I think, be true of the constitutional principles of the human mind, free us from the vexing and intractable philosophical perplexities of the modern age which drive us relentlessly toward subjectivism and nihilism, and thus enable us to close the gap between our culture and reality on one hand and the gap between our culture and social structures on the other, and thereby make it possible for us to overcome our ontological and social alienation and spiritual depression.

The humanistic image of man-in-the-world which would emerge once again with full cultural support would be, as we have argued throughout this work, based upon people's self-knowledge of themselves and their intersubjective and perceptual understanding of others in the world as delineated and known in their total experiential encounter and active engagement with reality. The world would be delineated for such beings by their somatic sensations, sensory perceptions, personal and inter-personal self-knowledge, perceptual understanding of others (what they experience, feel, believe, say and do), enjoyments and sufferings, feelings and attitudes, passionate and active engagements, logical insights, and the like. Self-knowledge and knowledge of the world from within this total perspective would be given expression in rituals, institutionalized ways of doing things, various art forms, and ordinary, technical, and theoretical languages. The categories would be those of persons and things; meaning and existence; the factual and the normative; the physical, the organic, the mental, and the social; physical space, logical space, social space; time and eternity; the necessary and the contingent; and the like, all interwoven into a multidimensional conceptual fabric that would be taken to cut reality at the joints. Such an intellectual vision would be grounded in, elicit responses from, and engage all the powers of the human mind; and support and structure all the dimensions of our culture and social order so that life-morale and spiritual zest would again be possible.

Religious experience, the breaking in of ultimate reality upon one's own identity and structured life, the impact of seeing one's own existence and identity in the total scheme of things as one understands the world, would no longer be, as it tends to be for modern man, a crushing, shattering experience like that of Gregor in Kafka's "Metamorphosis." Such an awareness could once again be ennobling, empowering, invigo-rating, reinforcing, and sustaining. Instead of having to live under the crippling existential angst, it would be possible once more for one to live with an affirmative religious consciousness, a high life-morale, grounded in a sense of the meaningfulness of his existence in a world that makes possible, produces, and supports his identity as a person—a world that imposes normative requirements and restraints upon him as well as factual possibilities and limitations and thus defines a way of life for him and gives him a place, direction, and purpose. In time such a culture would generate its own authentic symbols, myths, and institutions to express and to structure and to develop the new communal, perhaps global, conscious-ness. The postmodern era would then be a reality. This would not be the millennium. Sufficient unto every age is the evil thereof. But under the humanistic cultural mind of the new age, man should be better able to know and to cope with reality and to live successfully.

Notes

Chapter 1
1. Max Gerard, *Dali*, trans. Eleanor Moore (New York: Harry N. Abrams, 1968), p. 1.

Chapter 2
1. Daniel P. Moynihan, "Emerging Consensus?" *Newsweek*, 10 July 1972, p. 23.
2. Paul Jacobs and Saul Landau, *The New Radicals* (New York: Random House, Vintage Books, 1966), p. 5.
3. Richard Goodwin, "The Era of Bad Feelings," *Newsweek*, 10 July 1972, p. 26.
4. Rollo May, "Love and Will," *Psychology Today* 3, no. 2 (August 1969): 20.
5. Ibid., p. 21.
6. Rollo May, *Love and Will* (New York: W. W. Norton & Company, 1969), p. 20.
7. Ibid., p. 17.
8. Leslie Farber, *The Ways of the Will* (New York: Basic Books, 1965).
9. Rollo May, *Love and Will*, p. 27.
10. Ibid., p. 14.
11. Erich Fromm, *The Sane Society* (Greenwich, Conn.: Fawcett Publications, 1968).
12. Ibid., p. 312.
13. Ibid., p. 313.
14. Aline B. Saarinen, "'New Images of Man'—Are They?" *New York Times Magazine*, 27 September 1959, p. 18.
15. Irving Howe, "The Idea of the Modern," in *Literary Modernism*, ed. Irving Howe (Greenwich, Conn.: Fawcett Publications, 1967), pp. 37-38.
16. Nathan A. Scott, Jr., *Craters of the Spirit* (Washington, D.C. and Cleveland, Ohio: Corpus Books, 1968).
17. Pearl K. Bell, "Review of Richard B. Wright's *The Weekend Man*," *New Leader* 54, no. 12 (14 June 1971): 19.
18. Nathan A. Scott, Jr., *Craters of the Spirit*, p. 106.
19. Paul Henle, "The Problem of Meaning," *Proceedings and Addresses of the American Philosophical Association* 27 (1953-54): 24.
20. Maurice Natanson, "Existential Categories in Contemporary Literature," *Carolina Quarterly* 10, no. 2 (Spring 1958): 23.
21. See Richard Schacht, *Alienation* (Garden City, N.Y.: Doubleday & Company, 1970).
22. See Walter Kaufmann, "The Inevitability of Alienation," in Richard Schacht, *Alienation*, pp. xiii-lvi.
23. I am indebted to my former student, Harry K. Jones, for this point.
24. Plato *Phaedo* 96-97, in *The Dialogues of Plato*, trans. B. Jowett (New York: Random House, 1937), 1:480-82.
25. W. M. Urban, *The Intelligible World* (New York: Macmillan Co., 1929), p. 3.
26. Friedrich Wilhelm Nietzsche, *The Gay Science*, trans. Walter Kaufmann (New York: Random House, Vintage Books, 1974), p. 181.

27. Ibid., p. 182.

28. Jean-Paul Sartre, "Existentialism and Humanism," trans. Philip Mairet (London: Methuen, 1950); in *Existentialism from Dostoevsky to Sartre*, ed. Walter Kaufmann (Cleveland and New York: World Publishing Co., Meridian Books, 1956), pp. 294-95.

29. Marc Libarle and Tom Seligson, eds., *The High School Revolutionaries* (New York: Random House, 1970), p. 104.

30. Ibid., p. 148.

31. Seymour L. Halleck, "Therapy Is the Handmaiden of the Status Quo," *Psychology Today* 4, no. 11 (April 1971):32.

32. Walter Lippmann, *The Public Philosophy* (Boston: Little, Brown, & Company, 1955), p. 114.

33. Paul Goodman, "The New Reformation," *New York Times Magazine*, 14 September 1969, pp. 33, 142-47, 150, 154-55.

34. Jean-Paul Sartre, "Existentialism and Humanism," p. 295.

35. Lionel Trilling, "On the Modern Element in Modern Literature," in *Literary Modernism*, ed. Irving Howe, p. 82.

36. Charles A. Reich, *The Greening of America* (New York: Bantam Books, 1971).

37. Ibid., p. 241.

38. Ibid., p. 242.

39. Ibid.

40. Ibid., p. 243.

41. Ibid., p. 235.

42. Marjorie Greene, *Dreadful Freedom* (Chicago: University of Chicago Press, 1948).

43. Michael Polanyi, *Personal Knowledge* (Chicago: University of Chicago Press, 1958), p. 134.

44. Irving Howe, "The Idea of the Modern," pp. 14-15.

45. Paul Goodman, "The New Reformation," p. 147.

46. B. F. Skinner, *Beyond Freedom and Dignity* (New York: Alfred A. Knopf, 1971).

47. Ibid., p. 14.

48. Floyd Matson, *The Broken Image* (Garden City, N.Y.: Doubleday & Company, Anchor Books, 1966), p. vi.

49. Rollo May, *Psychology and the Human Dilemma* (Princeton: D. Van Nostrand Co., 1967), p. 2.

50. Hobart Mowrer, "Psychiatry and Religion," *Atlantic* 217, no. 1 (July 1961):8.

51. Conrad Aiken, *Time in the Rock* (New York: Charles Scribner's Sons, 1936), p. 2.

52. Lionel Trilling, "On the Modern Element in Modern Literature," pp. 78-79.

53. Preserved Smith, *Origins of Modern Culture* (New York: Macmillan Co., Collier Books, 1962), p. 388.

54. H. G. Schenk, *The Mind of European Romantics* (New York: Doubleday & Company, Anchor Books, 1969), p. 7.

Chapter 3

1. "What (If Anything) to Expect from Today's Philosophers," *Time*, 7 January 1966, pp. 24-25.

2. William O'Neill, "Philosophical Analysis: A Philosophical Analysis," *Personalist* 47, no. 2 (April 1966): p. 185.

3. Lewis S. Feuer, "Is American Philosophy Dead?" *New York Times Magazine*, 24 April 1966, p. 31.

4. Roderick M. Chisolm et al., *Philosophy* (Englewood Cliffs, N.J.: Prentice-Hall, 1964), p. x.

5. Henry W. Johnstone, Jr., *Philosophy and Argument* (University Park, Penn.: Pennsylvania State University Press, 1959).

Chapter 4
1. David Hume, *A Treatise of Human Nature* (New York: E. P. Dutton & Co., Everyman's Library, 1911), 1:176-78.
2. David W. Falk, "Goading and Guiding," *Mind* 62, no. 246 (April 1953):145-71.
3. John Searle, "How to Derive 'Ought' from 'Is'," *Philosophical Review* 73, no. 1 (January 1964):43-58.
4. Raymond Polin, "Values and Truths," trans. Joseph U. Kockelmans, in *Contemporary European Ethics*, ed. Joseph J. Kockelmans (Garden City, N.Y.: Doubleday & Company, Anchor Books, 1972), pp. 214-17.
5. Ibid., pp. 208-10.

Chapter 5
1. John Rawls, *A Theory of Justice* (Cambridge: Harvard University Press, 1971).
2. R. M. Hare, *Freedom and Reason* (New York: Oxford University Press, 1963).
3. S. W. Blackburn, "Moral Realism," in *Morality and Moral Reasoning*, ed. John Casey (London: Methuen, 1971), pp. 101-24.
4. Ibid., p. 107.
5. Ibid., p. 106.
6. Ibid., p. 110.
7. Ibid., p. 111.
8. Ibid., p. 110.
9. Henry D. Aiken, "The Problem of Evaluative Objectivity," *Southern Journal of Philosophy* 4, no. 3 (Fall 1966): 149-61.
10. B. J. Diggs, "Review of *Ethical Naturalism and the Modern World-View* by E. M. Adams," *Philosophical Review* 71, no. 1 (January 1962):106.

Chapter 6
1. Peter F. Strawson, *Introduction to Logical Theory* (New York: John Wiley & Sons, 1952), pp. 9-10.
2. Ibid., p. 11.
3. David Hume, *A Treatise of Human Nature* (New York: E. P. Dutton & Co., Everyman's Library, 1911), 2:127.
4. B. F. Skinner, "Behaviorism at Fifty," in *Behaviorism and Phenomenology*, ed. T. W. Wann (Chicago: University of Chicago Press, 1964), p. 79.
5. George Mandler and William Kessen, *The Language of Psychology* (New York: John Wiley & Sons, 1959), p. 37.
6. B. F. Skinner, "Behaviorism at Fifty," pp. 90-91.
7. Ibid., p. 91.
8. Ibid.
9. B. F. Skinner, *Verbal Behavior* (New York: Appleton-Century-Crofts, 1957), p. 18.
10. Gilbert Ryle, *Dilemmas* (Cambridge: At the University Press, 1956), p. 11.
11. Ibid., p. 5.
12. Friedrich Waismann, "The Relevance of Psychology to Logic," in *Readings in Philosophical Analysis*, ed. Herbert Feigl and Wilfrid Sellars (New York: Appleton-Century-Crofts, 1949), p. 220.
13. Ibid.
14. Ibid.
15. Stuart Hampshire, *Freedom of the Individual* (New York: Harper & Row Publishers, 1965), p. 110.

Chapter 7
1. H. P. Grice, "Meaning," *Philosophical Review* 66, no. 3 (July 1957):377-88; "Utterer's Meaning, Sentence-Meaning, and Word-Meaning," *Foundations of Language* 4 (1968):1-18; and "Utterer's Meaning and Intentions," *Philosophical Review* 78, no. 2 (April 1969):147-77.
2. Paul Ziff, "On Grice's Account of Meaning," *Analysis* 28, no. 1 (October 1967):1-8.

3. Everett W. Hall, *Our Knowledge of Fact and Value* (Chapel Hill: University of North Carolina Press, 1961), pp. 17-18.

4. Roderick M. Chisholm, *Perceiving* (Ithaca: Cornell University Press, 1957), p. 170.

5. Ibid., p. 171.

6. G. E. M. Anscombe, "The Intentionality of Sensation," in *Analytical Philosophy: Second Series*, ed. R. J. Butler (New York: Barnes and Noble, 1965), p. 161.

7. Everett W. Hall, *Our Knowledge of Fact and Value*, p. 13.

8. Anthony Kenny, *Action, Emotion, and Will* (London: Routledge and Kegan Paul; New York: Humanities Press, 1963), p. 196.

9. Everett W. Hall, *Our Knowledge of Fact and Value*, pp. 14-15.

10. W. V. O. Quine, *Word and Object* (Cambridge, Mass.: M.I.T. Press, 1960), pp. 176 ff.

11. Wilfrid Sellars, "Intentionality and the Mental," in *Concepts, Theories, and the Mind-Body Problem*, ed. Herbert Feigl, Michael Scriven, and Grover Maxwell, Minnesota Studies in the Philosophy of Science, vol. 2 (Minneapolis: University of Minnesota Press, 1958), p. 507.

12. Roderick M. Chisholm, "On Some Psychological Concepts and the 'Logic' of Intentionality," in *Intentionality, Minds, and Perception*, ed. Hector-Neri Castañeda (Detroit: Wayne State University Press, 1967), pp. 11-35, 46-57.

13. Roderick M. Chisholm, *Perceiving*.

14. Wilfrid Sellars, *Science, Perception, and Reality* (New York: Humanities Press, 1965); *Science and Metaphysics* (New York: Humanities Press, 1968); and other writings.

15. Herbert Feigl, "The 'Mental' and 'Physical'," in *Concepts, Theories, and the Mind-Body Problem*, ed. Herbert Feigl, Michael Scriven, and Grover Maxwell, pp. 370 ff.

16. James Cornman, *Materialism and Sensation* (New Haven: Yale University Press, 1971).

17. Wilfrid Sellars, "The Identity Approach to the Mind-Body Problem," *Review of Metaphysics* 18, no. 3 (March 1965):438.

18. See Herbert Feigl, "The 'Mental' and the 'Physical' "; J. J. C. Smart, "Sensations and Brain Processes," *Philosophical Review* 68, no. 2 (April 1959):141-56, and *Philosophy and Scientific Realism* (New York: Humanities Press, 1964); U. T. Place, "Is Consciousness a Brain Process?" *British Journal of Psychology* 47, no. 1 (February 1956):44-50, and "Materialism as a Scientific Hypothesis," *Philosophical Review* 69, no. 1 (January 1960):101-4; James W. Cornman, *Materialism and Sensation*.

19. Romane Clark, "The Sensuous Content of Perception," in *Action, Knowledge, and Reality*, ed. Hector-Neri Castañeda (Indianapolis: Bobbs-Merrill Co., 1975), pp. 109-27.

20. C. G. Hempel, "The Logical Analysis of Psychology," in *Readings in Philosophical Analysis*, ed. Herbert Feigl and Wilfrid Sellars (New York: Appleton-Century-Crofts, 1949), p. 375.

21. Ibid.

22. Rudolf Carnap, "Psychology in Physical Language," trans. George Schick, in *Logical Positivism*, ed. A. J. Ayer (Glencoe, Ill.: Free Press, 1959), pp. 165-98.

23. C. W. Morris, *Signs, Language, and Behavior* (New York: Prentice-Hall, 1946).

24. Rudolf Carnap, "Psychology in Physical Language," p. 167.

25. Ibid., p. 165.

26. W. V. O. Quine, *Word and Object*, p. 221.

27. Ibid., p. 219.

28. Ibid., p. 221.

29. W. V. O. Quine, *Ontological Relativity and Other Essays* (New York: Columbia University Press, 1969), p. 146.

30. Ibid., p. 138.

31. See especially Wilfrid Sellars, "Philosophy and the Scientific Image of Man," in his *Science, Perception, and Reality*, pp. 1-40.

32. Ibid., p. 4.
33. Ibid., p. 19.
34. Ibid., p. 5.
35. Ibid., p. 15.
36. Ibid., p. 18.
37. See note 18 (this chapter) for some of the basic literature advocating this position.
38. See especially Norman Malcolm, "Scientific Materialism and the Identity Theory," *Dialogue* 3, no. 2 (March 1964):115-25, and *Problems of Mind* (New York: Harper & Row Publishers, Torchbooks, 1971), pp. 68-79; Thomas Nagel, "Physicalism," *Philosophical Review* 74, no. 3 (July 1965):339-56. Malcolm argues that there are and Nagel that there are not a priori reasons that rule out the contingent identity thesis.
39. D. C. Dennett, *Content and Consciousness* (New York: Humanities Press, 1969).
40. Ibid., p. 39.
41. Ibid., p. 78.
42. Ibid.
43. Ibid.
44. Ibid., p. 79.
45. Wilfrid Sellars, *Science, Perception, and Reality*, p. 59.
46. Ibid., p. 33.
47. Ibid., p. 34.
48. Ibid., p. 32.
49. Ibid., p. 59.
50. See Wilfrid Sellars, *Science and Metaphysics*, pp. 75-77.
51. Jay F. Rosenberg, *Linguistic Representation* (Dordrecht, Holland/Boston, U.S.A.: D. Reidel Publishing Co., 1974), p. 40.
52. Ibid., p. 47.

Chapter 8
1. Ernest Nagel, "Naturalism Reconsidered," *Proceedings and Addresses of the American Philosophical Association* 28 (1954-55):8.

Chapter 9
1. Kingsley Davis, "Theory of Change and Response in Modern Demographic History," *Population Index* 29, no. 4 (October 1963):345-66.
2. Ibid., p. 345.
3. Ibid., p. 346.
4. Ibid., p. 354.

Index